Marxism After Modernity

Also by Ross Abbinnett

TRUTH AND SOCIAL SCIENCE: From Hegel to Deconstruction
CULTURE AND IDENTITY: Critical Theories

Marxism After Modernity

Politics, Technology and
Social Transformation

Ross Abbinnett
University of Birmingham

First published in 2006 by
PALGRAVE MACMILLAN
Houndmills, Basingstoke, Hampshire RG21 6XS and
175 Fifth Avenue, New York, N.Y. 10010
Companies and representatives throughout the world.

PALGRAVE MACMILLAN is the global academic imprint of the Palgrave Macmillan division of St. Martin's Press, LLC and of Palgrave Macmillan Ltd. Macmillan® is a registered trademark in the United States, United Kingdom and other countries. Palgrave is a registered trademark in the European Union and other countries.

ISBN-13: 978–1–4039–4124–4
ISBN-10: 1–4039–4124–6

This book is printed on paper suitable for recycling and made from fully managed and sustained forest sources.

A catalogue record for this book is available from the British Library.

Library of Congress Cataloging-in-Publication Data

Abbinnett, Ross.
  Marxism after modernity : politics, technology, and social transformation / Ross Abbinnett.
    p. cm.
  Includes bibliographical references and index.
  ISBN 1–4039–4124–6 (cloth)
    1. Communism and society. 2. Postmodernism. 3. Marx, Karl, 1818–1883.
  I. Title.

HX542.A23 2006
335.4—dc22   2006049419

10 9 8 7 6 5 4 3 2 1
15 14 13 12 11 10 09 08 07 06

Printed and bound in Great Britain by
Antony Rowe Ltd, Chippenham and Eastbourne

I will always wonder if the idea of Marxism – the self-identity of Marxist discourse or system or even science of philosophy – is not incompatible with the event-Marx.

Jacques Derrida, 1993

Contents

Introduction   1

Part I   Ideology, Aesthetics and Mass Culture

1   Materialism and Ideology   9
2   The Reification of Culture   18
3   The Rise of Ludic Aestheticism   29
4   Capitalism and the Hyperreal   40
5   Ideology and Difference   51

Part II   Capitalism and Technology

6   Machines and Socialized Production   63
7   The Origins of Technocracy: Heidegger and Marcuse   74
8   Civilized Capitalist Machines: Deleuze and Negri   82
9   The Ethics of Technological Effects: Derrida and Stiegler   101

Part III   Globalization and the New International

10   Colonialism and Imperialism   117
11   World Markets and Global Transformations   126
12   Biopolitical Production and the 'New Science
     of Democracy'   133
13   Transeconomic Capitalism   144
14   The Politics of Hospitality   152

Part IV   Marxism, Postmodernism and the Political

15   Marx and the Powers of Capital   169
16   A Post-Ontological Marxism?   177
17   The Protocols of Class Politics   195
18   Conclusion   204

Notes   208
Bibliography   219
Index   224

Introduction

There is a close relationship between Marx's thought and the onset of modernity; indeed the very idea of Marxism is inconceivable outside of the historical conjunction of Enlightenment philosophy, economic rationalization, techno-scientific innovation and social detradtionalization which emerged in Europe after the Middle Ages. Marx's intellectual project is marked by an increasingly acute sense of the economic and technological mechanisms through which the old feudal order was being displaced by a new regime based on the realization of profit through the sale of commodities. The dynamics of this process are, of course, very complex; the old regime did not simply cede its place to the new, and entered into a period of violent conflict with the emergent forms of mercantile and manufacturing capital. However, the tendency towards the rationalization of production that was initiated by the commodity form is, for Marx, the seed of the future; for in the end, the feudal economy, with its reliance on absolutist authority and archaic agrarianism, could not compete with the new forms of trade and manufacture which had established themselves in the cities. Thus, by the early nineteenth century a proto-capitalist economy had emerged in Europe; an economy which, despite the continued predominance of agricultural production, had begun to establish the exchange of commodities for money as the dominant form of economic activity, to determine the legal conditions of free citizenship, and to extend the cooperative regime of manufacture into a plurality of different kinds of craft production.

Marx's critique of Hegel is focused on the point at which his philosophy makes contact with the violent and contradictory reality of civil society. According to Marx, the *Philosophy of Right* sought to mediate this contact through the categories of absolute spirit, that is, the transcendental forms of unity, particularity and difference whose dialectical movement Hegel mapped out in the *Science of Logic* and *Phenomenology of Mind* (Marx, 1977c: 27). Thus the account of civil society which is present in the *Philosophy of Right* begins with the assumption that the self-interested individuals who make up the sphere of commercial activity, constitute a web of instrumental connections which, in the end, finds its completion in the substantive public morality of the state (Hegel, 1967b: 154–5). For Marx, however, Hegel's assumption of a transcendental unity which precedes the material dynamics of capital, leads his political thought into a kind of archaism; for although he was one of the first philosophers to consider the impact of economic individualism on the organic ties of ethical life (*Sittlichkeit*), his philosophy returns to the corporate structures of the feudal regime as a solution to the moral dislocation of civil society (*Ibid.*: 152–5). The materialist dialectic which Marx proposes, therefore, is more than a simple 'inversion' of Hegel's idealism; rather it establishes the conditions of a critique of (capitalist) modernity in which economic and technological transformations in the mode of production are understood as constantly altering the political and ideological integration of the social bond. For Hegel, the inequalities that are reproduced by the expansion of civil society retain a moral significance which derives from the fact that ethical life ought to reflect the autonomous differentiation of spirit into its implicit/objective and explicit/subjective categories. Marx, on the other hand, conceives such inequalities as intrinsic to the production of commodities; for the acquisitiveness of individual capitalist entrepreneurs constantly intensifies the drive to extend the working day, force down wages, increase expenditure on machine technology and intensify the overall rate of exploitation. It is this logic, this general economy of expropriation, which will occupy the rest of the book.

The *Communist Manifesto* makes it clear that, for Marx, capitalist modernity is simultaneously archaic and progressive, barbarous and civilized. On the one hand it brings about unprecedented growth in the productive potential of humanity, stimulates scientific and technological innovation, and establishes an international market in every conceivable commodity. On the other hand however, the money–commodity–money (M–C–M) relation is still founded upon private ownership; and so the mode of production continues to deprive the majority of workers of their fair share of the social product, alienates them from their essential self-creativity, and produces a class of universally impoverished human beings (Marx, 1998: 3–16). What lies at the core of Marx's analysis therefore is the idea that the evolution of large-scale industrial capitalism pushes the logic of the commodity form (i.e. the constant drive to force up the rate of relative surplus value in order to overcome the decline in profit caused by the application of machine technologies to the productive process) to the point where the economy becomes utterly crisis ridden, and the impoverishment of organic labour gives rise to the means of revolutionary transformation (the international proletariat). This bequeaths us two momentous questions. First, given the history of capitalism since the end of the nineteenth century, is it still credible to maintain that its general evolutionary tendency is determined by the archaism of the M–C–M relation, that is, by the deepening crises of under-consumption, over-production, unemployment and inflation which arise from the ever more intensive exploitation of labour? And second, how has the media-techno-scientific restructuring of capitalism impacted upon the revolutionary dialectics of class struggle?

The history of twentieth-century Marxism has been the history of these two questions; from the Second International onwards Marx's expositors have tried to carry on in the spirit of his critique of capital while modifying the terms of his materialist dialectics. As the title of the book suggests, I am interested in examining the relationship between what David Harvey has called the 'postmodern restructuring' of capitalism and the 'postmodernist theory' through which this restructuring has been conceptualized (Harvey, 1999: 344). Harvey's argument is a familiar one, and deploys a logic which is common to a number of neo-Marxist critics (Perry Anderson, Fredric Jameson, Terry Eagleton, Alex Callinicos). The contention is that, in general, the concepts that are presented in the work of a highly suspect group of French intellectuals, namely Jean Baudrillard, Gilles Deleuze, Jacques Derrida and Jean-Francoise Lyotard, is a disguised form of neo-liberalism: the perpetual pursuit of 'difference' is conceived as the apotheosis of bourgeois individualism, the critique of 'totalizing discourse' is presented as an abandonment of universal principles of justice and the insistence upon the transformative power of the aesthetic is narrated as a retreat from the politics of everyday life into the self-serving intellectualism of the avant garde. In essence, therefore, postmodernist theory could not be further from the spirit of Marxism; for the methodological canon which Marx developed demands that a critical theory of capital should, at the very least, retain a sense of the political complicities of pure 'difference', of the universal principles which ought to govern a properly democratic society, and of the ideological power of the aesthetic in the constitution of mass conformity. Like all generalizations, however, this one is iniquitous; for its staging of the encounter between 'Marxism' and 'post-modernism' relies upon an almost wilful determination to ignore what Baudrillard, Deleuze, Derrida and Lyotard actually say about Marx and their relationship to his work. It should be remembered, after all, that all of them were part of the intellectual debates about the future of Marxism which took place both inside and outside of the academy in the 1960s and 1970s. Of course it may be that a closer examination of this relationship will lead those who distrust the intellectual gestures of postmodernist thought to sharpen their critique. Yet I think it remains intellectually valid to specify as precisely as possible the terms of the postmodernist engagement with Marxism and to evaluate the political implications of this engagement.

Before I set out the expository structure of the book however I want to specify the way in which I have used the terms 'postmodernist', 'post-modernism' and 'postmodernity'. These terms have passed into every-day usage and, as a result, acquired a quite specific set of meanings: to be 'postmodern' in one's lifestyle is to adopt a studied irony towards one's pleasures and satisfactions, to regard one's identity as infinitely mutable and to remain constantly open to the new forms of difference which cir-culate through the global economy. Clearly these meanings are impor-tant, as they have become part of the universe of cultural significance which has arisen from the hegemony of multinational capitalism. It would be wrong, however, to argue that they capture the essence of the postmodernist theory, for they are filtered through processes of ideolog-ical mediation which tend to screen out their ethical and political provocations. Thus in the discussion which follows I have used the terms 'postmodernism' and 'postmodernist' simply as a collective desig-nation of the writings of Baudrillard, Deleuze, Derrida and Lyotard; they are used, in other words, for the sake of convenience and are not intended to impute a collective intention to have done with 'all that is boring and constraining' about modernity (Jameson, 1998: 111). If there is a sense of my having privileged postmodernist ideas, this is perhaps for-givable on the grounds that my project is concerned with the way in which they have configured both the techno-scientific restructuring of capitalism and the revolutionary promise of Marxism.

I have deliberately chosen not to set my exposition of postmodernist thought in relation to a comprehensive history of Marxist theory and politics, for scholars such as Perry Anderson[1] and Martin Jay[2] have already done this with great intellectual cogency and rigour. What I have done is to take the Frankfurt School as my point of departure, for it is in their work that the themes I will pursue (the rise of media, information and prosthetic technologies, the simulation of the real, the constitution of the global economy, the loss of aesthetic imagination) first emerged as issues for the Marxist canon. So, in Part I I will examine the relationship between aesthetics and mass culture in terms of Horkheimer and Adorno's transformation of Marx's ideology thesis. Of particular importance here is the way in which *Dialectic of Enlightenment* shifts the ideological function of the image away from a simple misrepresentation of capitalist relations of production, towards a more general economy in which the real is refracted through the representations of the culture industry. It is this shift to what Baudrillard has called 'third order' simulacra which opens the postmodern problematic of representation; for if it is the case that the technologically reproducible image has attained a self-referential freedom which exceeds the logic of simple dissemblance, it becomes necessary to rethink the basic concepts of reality, ontology and political composition which inform Marxist critique. In Part II I have focused on the question of techno-scientific innovation and its impact on the commodity form. The starting point here is the Heideggarian theory of technological control which Herbert Marcuse presents in *One Dimensional Man*, and which extends Marx's account of industrial production beyond the opposition between fixed and organic capital, 'the technological' and 'the human'. Marcuse's work, in other words, registers an immanent tendency towards the prosthetic integration of human labour into the regime of technological capitalism, a tendency whose most extreme implications are explored by Deleuze, Negri, Baudrillard and Stiegler. Parts III and IV are concerned with the antagonism between the political gestures that arise from postmodernist theories of global-technological capitalism and the more orthodox configurations of class politics espoused by Anderson, Callinicos, Ahmad and Eagleton. Part III deals with the possibility of transforming Marx's idea of the Worker's International through postmodernist conceptions of hospitality, nomadism and multitude, and Part IV with the antagonisms which continue (must continue) to sustain the Marxism-postmodernism debate.

The book therefore is not intended as a farewell to Marx or to Marxism, and I have taken care to situate the postmodernist theories I will examine in relation to Marx's writings on capitalism, ideology, technology and revolution. The starting point of my reading of Marx, as I have said, is his critique of idealist philosophy and his attempt to think through effects of economic rationalization, moral individualism and the fetishization of commodities. This critique, of course, entails a thoroughgoing rejection of Hegel's attempt to imbue the moral, legal and political relations of civil society with an immanently ethical significance;

for according to Marx the commodity form has unleashed an incremental logic of expropriation which is intensified by the ideological forms of its enactment. There are those who disagree with this line of argument. Richard Dien Winfield, for example, maintains that Hegel's analysis reveals that capital 'is but a component of rather than the unifying structure of commodity relations', and that consequently the elements of civil society (abstract difference, exchange, individuation and moral responsibility) make up an organic whole which expresses the universal substance of a just economy (Dien Winfield, 1988: 131).[3] My account of the relationship between Marxism and postmodernism theory however presupposes the force of Marx's critique of Hegelian idealism; for if there is a guiding thread which runs through postmodernist theories of capitalism, it is a determination to think through the logics of complexity, disaggregation and technological prosthesis through which the commodity form has intensified the production of surplus value. As we will see, this theorization has led to a radical questioning of Marx's conception of class politics; a questioning which has concentrated on the labour theory of value and the logics of political composition which are rearticulated in contemporary Marxist thought. My intention, therefore, is to map the contours of a postmodern Marxism which, in its various theoretical strands, has attempted to trace the techno-scientific transformations of capital, to register their effects upon the organic composition of 'the human' and to theorize the political consequences of these effects. For it is, I will argue, through such investigations that we come closest to the 'event' of Marx's intrusion into the dialectics of bourgeois ethical life.

Part I

Ideology, Aesthetics and Mass Culture

This section is concerned primarily with the question of ideology, or, more specifically, with the question of capitalism's power to re-present the fundamental inequalities through which it operates as the essential conditions of liberty, justice and freedom. I will begin by looking at the account of 'ruling class ideas' which Marx set out in *The German Ideology*, for it is here that he offers his first systematic account of the role of art, literature, philosophy, ethics and theology as graphical and discursive forms which legitimize the domination of one class over another. Chapter 2 is concerned with the Frankfurt School's engagement with Marx's ideology thesis, particularly Walter Benjamin, Max Horkheimer and Theodor Adorno's attempts to theorize the relationship between the technological reproduction of the image and the massification of the public sphere. Chapter 3 is a critical examination of the claim that the 'postmodernist' art, theory and culture which has accompanied the technological liberation of image, is no more than an ideological distraction from the political antagonisms of the global economy. Chapter 4 develops the claim that Jean Baudrillard's work on simulation presents both the worst possible outcome of the culture industry thesis and a crucial provocation to rethink the relationship between capital, technology and representation. Finally, Chapter 5 examines Jacque Derrida's attempt to reconfigure the 'messianic' demand of Marxism within the virtual space of media-technological capitalism.

Part I

Ideology, Architecture and Mass Culture

1
Materialism and Ideology

I want to begin this section by examining Marx's relationship to Hegelian philosophy. For Marx the essence of ideology lies in its re-presentation of the material conflicts of capitalism as necessary, legitimate and part of the general progress of humanity towards the realization of its essential freedom. The ideological forms which Marx implicates in this process are well known; ethics, jurisprudence, literature, philosophy, historiography, aesthetics – indeed all of the 'humanities' – are cited in the list of spectres which haunt the capitalist mode of production. Thus the critique of Hegel which Marx develops in his early writings (chiefly *The Critique of Hegel's Philosophy of Right, The Economic and Philosophical Manuscripts, The Holy Family* and *The German Ideology*) is important because it is simultaneously a critique of the method of idealist philosophy and of the processes of 'self-externalization and self-alienation' that are characteristic of all ideological production (Marx, 1977c: 26–7). We need, therefore, to look at the detail of Marx's argument.

The concept of ethical life which Hegel sets out in the *Philosophy of Right* presupposes the historical development of self-consciousness which is presented in the *Phenomenology of Mind*. Constraints of space mean that I cannot give a proper account of this development; however there are a couple of points which need to be made concerning the genesis of Hegel's idea of civil society.[1] The account of the moral will which Hegel presents in the *Phenomenology* describes the historical forms through which self-consciousness attempts to determine its independence from feudal domination: 'conscience', 'virtue', 'duty' and the language of 'Christian forgiveness' all presuppose the lawlessness of the feudal order and the absence of universal recognition in the substance of ethical life. These internalizations of the moral law are originally spiritual forms, for they proceed from consciousness's determination to assert its essential selfhood, independence and purposiveness. Thus, even though Hegel expounds moral consciousness through the antagonisms it produces within the unity of *Sittlichkeit*, its formation and re-formation of the idea of autonomy must be recognized as an immanently ethical demand (Hegel, 1967a: 644–63). The account of morality which is given in the *Philosophy of Right* makes it clear that although the conscientious individual is implicated in the emergence of acquisitiveness and self-interest as the dominant modes of social interaction, the sphere of 'moral reflection' (civil society) remains essential to the idea of a just society. Thus, by positing the concept of freedom as the opposite of undisciplined inclination, the moral consciousness of the individual becomes the determining principle of modern productive activity, political mediation and legal recognition (Hegel, 1967b: 75–104).

The emergence of civil society, in other words, is not simply the emergence of an anarchic state of nature within the substance of ethical life; rather, Hegel argues that each individual is only able to attain satisfaction of his or her particular wants by means of others, and that as such, he or she is part of a system of connections which bind the happiness, livelihood and substance of each person to the totality of the economic sphere (*Ibid.*: 122). These legal and commercial connections, however, remain external to the concept of ethical life; for while it is true that the apprehension of universality to which they give rise among moral citizens gestures towards higher forms of recognition, it is also the case that a certain violence clings to the egoism of civil society – a violence which is proper to and disruptive of the concept of *Sittlichkeit* (*Ibid.*: 126). Thus the formal administration of justice which is necessitated by the possession of property, and the corporate associations (*Stände*) which arise from the recognition of common interests among artisans, are conceived by Hegel as forms of substantive universality which are implicit in the violent, self-seeking egoism of civil society (*Ibid.*: 154).

The problem which Marx identifies in Hegel's philosophy is that of transcendence, or more precisely, the problem of his 'inversion' of the relationship between the material conditions of life and the categories through which human consciousness represents its own activity. Hegel begins the *Phenomenology* with an account of how consciousness's experience of its objects is impossible to articulate simply in terms of sense certainty, and how this leads to the necessity of articulating more sophisticated conceptions of what an object actually is. This process refers the object to the activity of mind – both in its subjective manifestations as judgement, reflection and will, and in the categories through which objectivity exceeds its simple postulation as being (causality, relation, substance, etc.). Thus for Hegel the most basic constituents of experience resolve themselves into a dialectical exchange between subject and object in which the movement of the concept towards absolute knowledge is already in play. According to Marx, however, the very thing which makes the object what is, the natural, sensuous 'thingness' through which it appears to our faculties of apprehension, is conjured away by Hegel's insistence on the secondary status of 'appearances'. For while it is certainly true that objects are governed by causal laws, such laws refer to irreducibly physical things whose being resists their inclusion in the transcendental unity of the concept. Hegel, in other words, transforms real things which conform to their own particular laws, into mere predicates of the absolute idea (Marx, 1977c: 101).

Marx's initial engagement with Hegel, as we have seen, maintains that the spheres of family and civil society which he identifies as essential moments of ethical life 'owe their existence to another spirit than their own' (Marx, 1977c: 26–7). What this means is that instead of beginning with the empirical existence of the family as a mode of private enslavement, and of civil society as the sphere in which private property has come to dominate the productive activity of human beings, Hegel performs a phenomenological transformation of such 'appearances' into necessary elements of *Sittlichkeit*. Hegel's idealism, in other words, is essentially theological; for it begins by treating the finite, empirical and historical relationships through which human consciousness unfolds, as elements of a timeless, self-differentiating idea. According to Marx, however, the emergence of language and the cooperative production of the means of subsistence are conceptually and anthropologically inseparable; and so the practical activities which emerge in the most primitive societies (hunting, foraging, cooking, etc.), initiate a historical development in which the productivity of nature increases, the division of labour becomes more sophisticated and self-consciousness becomes increasingly independent (Marx, 1977b: 51). As this process unfolds the division of labour established in human society exceeds the 'natural' determination with which it began and there emerges a split between material and mental labour. From this moment onwards, Marx claims, 'consciousness is in a position to emancipate itself from the world and to proceed to the formation of "pure" theory, theology, philosophy, ethics etc' (*Ibid.*: 52). The material conflicts between citizens and slaves, lords and surfs, bourgeois and proletarians which have characterized the development of the mode of production, in other words, are represented as elements in the history of ethical substance.

Marx's critique of Hegel begins with his rejection of the power of absolute knowledge to reconcile the ethical substance of the state with the egoistic and self-serving activity of civil society. This rejection marks the beginning of his materialist theory of history; for by maintaining that the social and economic relationships that are constituted in civil society cannot be reduced to mere appearances of the higher forms of *Sittlichkeit*, he shifts the emphasis of theory towards historical analyses of the conflicts that arise from the organization of production around private property relations. According to Marx, civil society 'is the social organization arising directly out of production and commerce, which in all ages forms the basis of the State and the rest of the idealistic superstructure' (Marx, 1977b: 57). Thus civil society is the material basis of all human association; for the way in which productive activity is carried out constitutes a fundamental organization of life which is reflected in the ideological production of any given culture. This reflection however is not a true one; for the ethical, political, religious and aesthetic representations which arise from material relationships which are based upon the dominance of a particular property owning class will always represent that dominance as necessary and legitimate. Hegel's account of feudal bondage, for example, expounds the legitimizing relationship between the medieval church and the productive relationships constituted under the regime of landed property. He argues that the life of the bondsman belongs to the feudal lord, and that consequently the bondsman must serve his master by preparing commodities which are reserved exclusively for his consumption. The lord and the bondsman exist in an economy which can admit of no universal rights, laws or institutions; and so the frustrated development of self-consciousness which is embodied in the work of the bondsman is given illusory solace in the teachings of a church which has been corrupted by the dispensations of the landed aristocracy (Hegel, 1967a: 228–40). In Hegel's thought, this 'perverse' organization of religion and political power is ultimately redeemed by the movement of spirit into the forms of moral individualism; for Marx, however, it reflects the alienation of humanity which will occur for as long as the state functions as the administrator of private property rights.

We need then to examine Marx's account of 'ruling class ideas' and to determine the nature of their relationship to the material processes which constitute civil society. Marx begins his exposition by claiming that ruling ideas never come into material conflict with the interests of the ruling class. His argument is that although the concepts deployed by bourgeois jurists, philosophers, aesthetes and economists *do* attain a certain autonomy from the state, and although they may *seem* to come into conflict with conventional forms of hegemony, this conflict is no more than a 'semblance' which dissolves in the reassertion of class interests (Marx, 1977b: 65). Each generation of the ruling class is forced to modify the ideological forms which it inherits; for as the division of labour and the conditions of exploitation become more complex, so the categories through which the collective good is represented increasingly 'take on the form of universality' (*Ibid.*). Thus the shift from the ideas of poverty, chastity and obedience which were dominant under the feudal regime to those of equality and individual rights which are essential to bourgeois civil society does mark a certain progress in the realization of human freedom. For Marx, however, the increase in self-consciousness which is brought about by the refinement of bourgeois economic and political theory is only significant insofar as it sharpens the contradiction between the ideological forms in which subjective freedom is represented and the material deprivations under which the mass of humanity must live (*Ibid.*: 66). The granting of formal equality before the law and the right to sell one's labour on the open market is not a transcendental differentiation of ethical life; its true significance lies in the fact that it produces a class of workers whose 'free' productive activity is characterized by the experience of loss and physical compulsion.

The background to the account of ruling ideas which Marx presents in the *German Ideology* is the progressive socialization of production that occurs with the rise of capitalism. Under the old feudal regime, the division of labour was tied to a subsistence economy which remained the dominant mode of production from the collapse of the Roman Empire to the beginning of the nineteenth century. According to Marx's schema, political power under feudalism was identical with economic power; for the lord exercised his authority over the working population of surfs through his ability to protect his estate from the incursions of other feudal princes. This state of affairs could only give rise to very limited forms of industry – those which are 'naturally' related to the agricultural labour through which the means of subsistence are produced (Marx, 1977b: 68). It is the emergence of mercantile capital which, for Marx, establishes the antagonism between town and country that eventually leads to the collapse of the old regime of feudal patronage. For as international trade begins to develop and more commodities enter the open market, so a new class of merchants emerges whose capital allows them independence from the power of landed property.

This capital is the foundation of a city economy which is based on trade and the free disposal of labour power; and so it is here that the natural division of labour which is sustained under feudalism is displaced by a vigorous individualism which demands that everyone 'strain their energy to the utmost' (*Ibid*.: 78). It is in the cities, therefore, that the preconditions of industrial capitalism are established: a class of independent 'burghers' who use their capital to employ both skilled and unskilled labour, a class of unskilled 'journeymen' who sell their labour for wages and the development of the commercial and labour markets through which capital is able to expand its productive regime.

For Marx the transition from feudalism to capitalism is by no means a smooth one – in the more detailed analyses which he presents in *Capital* Volume One, he makes it clear that the *ancien régime* does not go quietly and is prepared violently to exploit the labouring population of surfs in order to compete with mercantile capital and the new class of private entrepreneurs (Marx, 1990: 452–4). In the end, however, the increasing productivity of urban capital and the mass migration of surfs into the cities, leads to the collapse of feudal power and the emergence of the moral, economic and political relations of bourgeois civil society. It is at this point that capitalism begins to determine its essential characteristics; for once the ideological conditions for the exploitation of wage labour are put into place, the process of production is able rapidly to expand through the deployment of scientific and technological knowledge. Thus, as the technological organization of production and exchange of commodities becomes increasingly sophisticated, so the means of production converge upon the point at which it would be possible to eliminate scarcity and allow the autonomous development of the human species. As long as they remain the private property of the bourgeoisie, however, their immanently social trajectory is frustrated; the labour power of the worker is bought for subsistence wages and the productivity of individual firms is wasted in the manufacture of commodities whose exchange value constantly diminishes. According to Marx, it is at this point that the ideological relationships of civil society come into conflict with the social trajectory of production: for the exercise of 'free' citizenship is originally bound up with the private appropriation of surplus value, the fetishization of commodities (by both producers and consumers), the objectification of the means of labour as a means of exploitation and the alienation of the worker from the process of production (Marx, 1977a: 89).

In Marx's schema the large-scale industrial stage of capitalism is the point at which the historical conditions for the overthrow of private property come into being. He maintains that what makes capitalism so uniquely unstable is the fact that its violent transformation of the mode of production means that it has constantly to transform the ideas of freedom, legality and justice through which it determines the content of ethical life. Consequently, the class of wage-labourers which comes into existence under capitalism is made subject to two opposing forces: on the one hand their experience of the means of labour becomes increasingly abstract and alienating, while on the other the ideological forms through which they recognize themselves as citizens, workers and individuals produce an acute sense of the deprivations which result from the enforced sale of their labour power. The proletarian revolution as Marx envisaged it, therefore, is both constructive and destructive: it destroys the institutions of class domination and private property (state, civil society, money, exchange value) and transforms the mode of production into a self-consciously communal organization which is designed to meet the needs of all (Marx, 1977b: 94–5). Such a revolution marks the end of ideology; for once private ownership is abolished organic labour ceases to alienate itself into the categories of bourgeois ethical life (morality, taste, religiosity).

From the preceding discussion it should be clear that a certain priority is given in Marx's thought to the ideological powers of philosophy and religion. Marx maintains that as soon as human society moves beyond the simplest forms of productive activity, the religious impulse is transformed from the simple veneration of nature into a theological discourse of transcendental powers, willing obedience and dutiful obligation. Religion and the theological concepts which emerge from it, in other words, are the original forms through which the history of class conflict is transfigured into the history of obedience and redemption. As the division of labour develops, so the ideas through which religion represents the world assume new configurations in the realm of philosophy; and so the concepts of man, freedom, beauty and morality assume a *relative* independence from the transcendental power of God. For Marx Hegel's system represented the definitive expression of this kind of theological philosophy; for by postulating a transcendental idea as the cause of human history (i.e. the differentiation of self-consciousness into particular forms of ethical life) Hegel separated the profane existence of the masses from the evolution of 'spirit' (*Geist*) towards absolute knowledge. Thus the redemption of humanity is to come through a process of what Marx calls 'absolute criticism' in which the violence of empirical history is stripped away and we are left with the struggles of pure thought with its own exterior forms. The evolution of the political freedoms, moral duties and aesthetic sensibilities which is described in the various phases of Hegel's philosophy, in other words, presents the discrete logics of self-alienation through which bourgeois society reproduces itself as *Sittlichkeit* (Marx, 1977c: 141).

The point of Marx's critique of Hegel is to exorcise the ideological ghosts through which man's alienated activity appears as both necessary and desirable. For Marx the negative totality which is constituted under capitalism is possible only on the basis of those forms of moral individualism (free will, citizenship, rational self-interest) that emerge with the abstract relations of civil society. Thus, in order to move beyond the negative totality of work, satisfaction and desire philosophy has to move beyond the limits of transcendental idealism, and to undertake a critique of the social and economic conditions of its own production. We should, however, bear in mind that Marx's concept of negative totality is coupled with a speculative account of the social relations which are implicit in the development of industrial capitalism (Marx, 1977b: 94). Marx tended towards reticence on the subject of what this expressive totality would look like, yet it is possible to discern some fundamental characteristics in *The German Ideology* and the *Economic and Philosophical Manuscripts*. First, the cooperative intercourse, scientific knowledge and technological innovation which have emerged under capitalism are to form the basis of a planned distribution of the means of consumption which will satisfy the needs of all. Second, the technological satisfaction of material needs will increase free time, remove the compulsion from productive activity and allow each individual the freedom to develop his/her creative essence. Third, the concept of social need is transparent to each individual producer, and so she/he is able to recognize his/her responsibility to the collective good. Fourth, 'philosophy', in the sense of transcendental speculation, is replaced by practical thinking about the organization of resources, the utilization of technology, the preservation of nature and all of the material questions which belong to the idea of socialized production.

This concept of expressive totality raises some important questions about the nature and historical development of ideological production. In Marx's writing priority is given to the discursive forms of law, morality, conscience, free will and democracy through which the conflicts of civil society are mediated. This model of ideological production attributes a certain historical agency to the class of individuals who are subject to the constraints of capitalist production; for it is their experience of contradiction between the abstract freedoms of civil society and the concrete processes of alienation which ultimately brings about the emergence of revolutionary consciousness. Thus artistic creativity and its transfigurations of everyday experience occupy a marginal position in Marx's hierarchy of ideological forms: the short section on art in the *German Ideology* is concerned to situate 'artistic genius' within specific relationships of economic and political patronage and says nothing about the power of the aesthetic to manage the conflicts inherent in the mode of production (Marx, 1977b: 108–9). The emergence of media and communications technologies towards the end of the nineteenth century, however, marked the formation of a new sphere in which the power inscription (the experience of rights, duties and obligations as real forms of symbolic exchange) is transformed by the capacity of the image to stage and to transfigure reality. This process of virtualization, I will argue, is important because it has always been a function of technological capitalism: the transition from still photography to moving images, from silent films to talking pictures, from cinema to terrestrial television and from terrestrial television to the satellite networks which dominate broadcasting and communications at the beginning of the twenty-first century, is the result of a complementary process in which the image becomes commodified and the masses are reproduced as ever more distracted consumers. So, if it is the case that the technological reproducibility of the image has displaced Marx's economy of ideological inscription, then what are the consequences of this displacement for the political project of Marxism? The following chapters will consider this question in detail.

2
The Reification of Culture

It is something of a platitude, although none the less true, to say that the post-war writings of the Frankfurt School sought to shift the emphasis of the critique of capitalism away from the economic base and towards the sphere of culture. With the publication of Walter Benjamin's account of the work of art in the age of technological reproducibility, the Institute of Social Research became increasingly concerned with the relationship between mass culture and the evolution of capitalism into a system of totalitarian control.[1] According to Benjamin the emergence of film marked the point at which the Western tradition of art – the 'auratic' tradition which maintained that the genius of the artist lay in his ability to configure the transcendence of the object which he had depicted – was overtaken by the technological media through which the image is produced and disseminated. Art, in other words, loses its place within relatively stable traditions of authority, obedience and obligation and is transformed into a commodity which is designed for consumption by the masses (Benjamin, 1992: 220). For Benjamin the loss of aura in the technological processes of mass representation brought with it certain transformative possibilities; he argued that film, as a sensory-kinaesthetic register of the new forms of proletarian experience within the technological body of capitalism, offered a new resource to the political imagination of the masses. For both Max Horkheimer and Theodor Adorno, however, the loss of aura which began with the emergence of film at the beginning of the twentieth century marks the point at which art and culture lose their independence from the reproduction of capital. Culture, in other words, becomes nothing more than the reproduction of mass conformity.

What is perhaps the Frankfurt School's definitive statement of the relationship between capitalism, mass culture and instrumental reason is set out in Horkheimer and Adorno's collaborative work *Dialectic of Enlightenment*.[2] In the first section of the book, 'The Concept of Enlightenment', Horkheimer and Adorno attempt to set out the connection between the instrumental forms of reason which have come to dominate Western thought and the social, economic, political and aesthetic relationships which have become characteristic of modern capitalism. As we saw in the previous section, one of Marx's primary concerns in the *German Ideology* was the 'forms of intercourse' through which capitalism develops; for as the material forces of production become more sophisticated, so the practical rationality of communication has to evolve in order to realize the productive potential which is inherent in those forces (Marx, 1977b: 86–9). Thus it is capital, conceived as a distinctive form of acquisitive activity, that gives rise to the legal, economic and political structures of domination through which bourgeois society is constituted. For Horkheimer and Adorno, however, the superstructural relationships through which capitalism is sustained are the historically specific expression of a rationality which has its roots in the European Enlightenment. The M–C–M relationship whose economic and political consequences Marx expounded in *Capital*, in other words, presupposes the hegemony of instrumental principles which predate the establishment of capitalism as the dominant mode of economic activity. We need then to look at what these instrumental principles are and how they are related to the emergence and development of the commodity form.

At the beginning of *Dialectic of Enlightenment* Horkheimer and Adorno describe the aim of the Enlightenment project as: 'the liberation of men from fear and the establishing of their sovereignty ... ; the dissolution of myth and the substitution of knowledge for fancy' (Horkheimer and Adorno, 1986: 3). The spirit of the Enlightenment project therefore arises out of the rebellion of the human will against the blind forces of fate and natural necessity to which it has always been subject. Under the conditions of primitive society this will to control the forces of nature was given expression in mimetic ceremonies which, through their attribution of spiritual powers to animate and inanimate objects, attempted to exert a magical influence over the natural world (*Ibid.*: 8–10). As human society developed these animistic mythologies gave fway to more complex theological conceptions of creation: in the Christian and Judaic religions, for example, man is understood as having been made in God's image and as having rightful dominion over all the diverse forms of nature. This religious conception of the world is, as Marx pointed out, complicit with certain distinctive forms of productive activity: the redemptive theology of Catholicism, for example, provides a perfectly rational justification for accepting the rule of the feudal aristocracy and its moribund agrarian economy. For Horkheimer and Adorno this kind of theological 'enchantment' is precisely what the Enlightenment project set out to overcome; for its conception of nature as a realm of particulate transactions which is open to mathematical analysis and technological control, leads to a world view in which 'man' and 'society' are viewed as machines which function all the better for being freed from the mythologies of spirit and religion (*Ibid*.: 28).

According to Horkheimer and Adorno, the common themes which run through the Enlightenment project are the disenchantment of the world, the assertion of man's free will and the constitution of nature as a controllable resource. And so if we were to look at the philosophical, mathematical and natural scientific writings of the seventeenth and eighteen centuries (and particularly those emanating from Britain, France and Germany), it would be possible to discern a paradigm shift in man's relationship to his natural and social environments. Following René Descartes' account of the division of the world into 'thinking' and 'extended' substances, Enlightenment philosophy proceeded to develop this dualism into an absolute break between rational humanity and de-spiritualized nature: thus in Kant's critical idealism the exercise of freedom is determined through the purification of the will of all its animal inclinations; in Hume's skeptical empiricism any move beyond particular events towards the metaphysical necessity of God is denied on the basis of their presentation of radical singularity; and in Newton's physics the world is transformed into a mechanism whose transactions are explicable in entirely mechanistic terms (even though he tried to make room for God in the interstices of the system). For Horkheimer and Adorno the necessary counterpart of this world view is a radical transformation of human society; for as the concept of nature is reduced to a resource which is increasingly susceptible to manipulation and control, so the instrument of reason is increasingly brought to bear on the traditional patterns of culture which have bound human beings to their particular communities. Thus the Enlightenment paradigm transforms reason into 'a pure organ of ends' through which the demands of rational freedom, productive utility and rational-bureaucratic control are made to function in unison (Horkheimer and Adorno, 1986: 30).

This colonization of the lifeworld sets in motion a historical trajectory which both precedes and exceeds Marx's analysis of capital. As we have seen, their account of the Enlightenment concentrates on the development of an instrumental form of reason which begins by asserting the free will of human beings against the blind forces of fate and natural necessity. The initial gesture of independence however is transformed into a disordered will to power; for as the concepts of rationality, functionality and self-determination become elements of an organic unity, so the power of instrumental reason over everything it encounters (nature, tradition, beauty, imagination, love, sexuality, the aboriginal) becomes increasing totalitarian. The instrument which sought to free humanity from its enslavement to irrational mythologies, in other words, determines its own mythology of a pure technological control which finally resolves the ethical, political and philosophical dilemmas of civilization (Horkheimer and Adorno, 1986: 27). This self-engendering system of rationality is, for Horkheimer and Adorno, the implicit condition of the shift from the feudal to the capitalist mode of production; for without the colonization of the lifeworld by the principles of instrumental reason which emerged from the Enlightenment, the development of the productive technologies which enabled the M–C–M relation to become the dominant form of both social and economic exchange would have been impossible. There is nothing in this conception of instrumental reason which is inconsistent with Marx's understanding of the relationship between capital and technology; his account of relative surplus value in *Capital* Volume One makes it clear that science and technology constitute forces of production that are essential to the development of industrial capitalism. What Horkheimer and Adorno's theory of Enlightenment introduces into the Marxist analysis of capital however is the idea of an instrumental rationality which is not necessarily bound to the class dynamics of bourgeois society and which is able constantly to transform the mechanisms of control through which the M–C–M relation is maintained.

At the end of *Capital* Volume One[3] Marx argues that the mercantile capitalists, whose money undermined the old feudal regime, had to bring about a concentration of productive forces which would allow them to maximize the turnover of their capital (Marx, 1990: 928). This process of concentration belongs to the very concept of the M–C–M relation; for it is only through the development of its technological basis that capital can continue to pass through the phases of investment, production and profit. This gathering of the means of production into the cooperative systems characteristic of large-scale industry however reveals the determining contradiction of capitalist accumulation. On the one hand the deployment of technologically integrated systems brings about an increase in productivity which could fulfil all of the basic needs of humanity (*Ibid.*: 929). Conceived in terms of the dynamics of capitalism however, this tendency towards the intensification of labour represents a progressive overburdening of the M–C–M relation with the costs of fixed capital. According to Marx, the resolution of this contradiction is a matter of historical necessity: once the profitability of large-scale industry comes to depend on the speed at which commodities are reproduced, the private appropriation of surplus value constantly channels organic labour into the overproduction of exchange values which can never be redeemed on the open market. According to Marx's analysis, therefore, the overcoming of this crisis-ridden state is implicit in the processes through which capitalism expands; for as the technological basis of production brings 'the mass of the people' into cooperative association, so they are formed into the revolutionary force which will eventually seize the means of production from private ownership (*Ibid*.: 930).

For Horkheimer and Adorno Marx's account of revolution underplays the adaptive potential which is implicit in capitalism's appropriation of scientific and technological knowledge. This is not to say that 'socialist' revolutions are impossible (clearly the Russian and Chinese Revolutions were inspired by Marxist principles of justice and equality), but rather that their occurrence has to be understood in terms of the relative under-development of the technological means through which specific economies have been able to organize production, consumption and political domination. In the most advanced economies, and here we should bear in mind that Horkheimer and Adorno were concerned with the general tendency of capitalist development which emerged in America during the late 1930s and early 1940s, the technological integration of the masses developed as a concomitant of the increased efficiency of industrialized production. Thus the dangerous instability of bourgeois capitalism is neutralized by media technologies which simultaneously reduce 'culture' to schematic representations of conformity and individual consciousness to the atomistic desire to consume.[4] The cultural forms with which the American public had become fixated (movie stars, jazz, sports personalities, detective stories, horoscopes), in other words, served to mediate their experience of the antagonisms of industrial capitalism, and to transform them into docile consumers incapable of thinking beyond the satisfactions already presented to them by the culture industry.

The culture industry thesis has, of course, attracted a great deal of criticism; for the claim that mass culture has corrupted working class consciousness in its deepest social and psychological recesses, and that as a consequence the historical tendency of capitalism has been co-opted by the total administration of work, satisfaction and desire, clearly runs counter to the fundamental principles of orthodox Marxism. Thus in order to evaluate the claim that Horkheimer and Adorno's account of mass culture is no more than a pronounced form of cultural snobbism (and that their unwillingness to grant *any* spontaneity to the cultural practice of the masses is no more than a reflection of their contempt for the organic labour of the working class), we need to look more closely at the development of their concept of the culture industry.

The origin of Horkheimer and Adorno's idea of mass culture can be traced to Georg Lukács's *History and Class Consciousness*. In the section on 'Reification and the Consciousness of the Proletariat' he remarked that:

> The commodity can only be understood in its undistorted essence when it becomes the universal category of society as a whole ... Only then does the commodity become crucial for the subjugation of men's consciousness to the forms in which this reification finds expression and for their attempts to comprehend the process or to rebel against its disastrous effects and liberate themselves from the servitude to the 'second nature' so created. (Lukács, 1971: 86)

This needs a little unpacking. First it must be recognized that Lukács's understanding of reified culture is an elaboration of Marx's account of the fetishism of commodities in *Capital* Volume One. Marx maintained that once the M–C–M relation had become the dominant mode of economic intercourse, the relationship between human beings and the objects they produce is inverted: for once everything is conceived in terms of its current exchange value the behaviour of both producers and consumers is determined by the 'objective' relationships which obtain among commodities at any given time (Marx, 1990: 165). The free will of human beings, in other words, is subsumed under the reified relationships which emerge from the dominance of exchange over use value, and which are experienced as a kind of 'second nature'. Thus if the mode of production is to be transformed there must be radical critique of the cultural relationships through which commodities maintain their objective power over human volition. According to Lukács the possibility of such a critique remains tied to the historical standpoint of the proletariat; for it is through their experience of the antagonisms which spring from the production of commodities (more productivity leads to more social need, more individual freedom leads to more compulsion, more culture leads to more reification) that they become the 'identical subject-object of history whose praxis will change reality' (Lukács, 1971: 197). For Horkheimer and Adorno however Lukács account of revolutionary transformation is too Hegelian; for insofar as he insists upon the conjunction of subjective agency and objective knowledge in the historical consciousness of the proletariat, he fails to recognize the emergent power of the culture industry to reproduce the standardized forms of individualism upon which the commodity form depends.

In an essay which Adorno wrote a few years after the publication of *Dialectic of Enlightenment* – 'The Culture Industry Reconsidered' – he remarked that culture in its true sense 'always raised a protest against the petrified relations in which [human beings] lived, thereby honouring them' (Adorno, 1991: 100). The philosophical, artistic and literary con-figurations which arose before the dominance of the commodity form, in other words, sought to register a protest against the conflicts which resulted from the progressive rationalization of human relations: that is, conflicts between nature and society, love and duty, instinct and reason, the individual and the universal. Such protests were never pure; Adorno's aesthetic theory makes it clear that every style of artistic representation is at least partially complicit with the form of social and political domina-tion from which it springs. The defining characteristic of the great artist however is the fact that he or she gestures beyond the limitations of style: by forcing a particular genre to express the sufferings of those who inhabit the ossified relationships of their time, he or she gives a glimpse of the 'negative truth' which is concealed by more formalistic examples of the genre (Horkheimer and Adorno, 1986: 130). With the increasing domination of the commodity form the relationship between truth and artistic production begins to break down; for as the realm of culture loses its independence from the circulation of capital, so the artistic impulse is absorbed into the rationality of production, exchange and consumption. The collapse of 'high' art into the triviality of the culture industry really begins with what Adorno calls the 'bourgeois demand for materialism'; the censorious attitude of the mercantile classes towards art which registers the contradictions within the established relations of ethical life, marks the point at which cultural production takes on the values of conformity and utility as its own. From then on popular art 'ceases to tol-erate the tension between the individual and the universal', and simply perpetuates the happy conformity of production and consumption, desire and satisfaction, beauty and morality (Adorno, 1991: 66).

There is a sense in which Horkheimer and Adorno's idea of the culture industry presents the total complicity of the aesthetic with the material contradictions through which it is brought into existence. This fulfilment, however, is only possible through the development of appropriate technological means, that is, the mass communications technologies of film and radio which came to dominate the public sphere in the 1930s and 1940s. The essential point to remember is that for Horkheimer and Adorno these technologies are, from the very beginning, an appendage of monopoly capitalism: their reproduction of sound and visual images is organized through technological imperatives that are formulaic rather than auratic, and so the plots, characters and narratives which are typical of the culture industry reveal nothing of the antagonisms inherent in commodity producing societies (Horkheimer and Adorno, 1986: 162–3). The emergence of sound films in the 1930s is perhaps the most significant development in the technological organization of mass culture; for once the complexities of style, plot and character which are present in great literature are compulsively reduced to the strict lineal narratives of the film, the entire sphere of 'culture' is reduced to the reproduction of conformity (Adorno, 1991: 72). The 'film of the book', in other words, is always an exercise in over-simplification; for it turns characters into stereotypes, transforms the plot into a relentless progress towards a happy ending and requires a cognitive ability no higher than that of an 11-year old. In the end it is pointless to judge the productions of the culture industry in terms of their aesthetic merit – for the schema they impose upon the world are simply the 'sheen' of romance which is required for the mass consumption of commodities (*Ibid.*: 61).

The corporate managers of the culture industry therefore both create the masses and despise them: they create the consumers who are addicted to the constant transformations of fashion and despise them for their manipulability; they provoke the desire to be utterly contemporary and snatch away the possibility of its fulfilment; they know the hopelessness of pursuing satisfaction in the object and yet continue to present the commodity as the only legitimate form of satisfaction. This constantly renewed cycle of desire-consumption-desire transforms the individual into an abstract identity with no substantive relationships to other human beings; all that remains of the self is the free floating subject to whom the culture industry addresses its demands for work, conformity and consumption. Thus the advocates of the culture industry who maintain that its schemas are the most benign way of managing the problem of social integration fundamentally miss the point. The order which is imposed by mass culture operates through the reduction of the individual to a standardized part of the commodity producing machine; and so the culture industry must be understood not as a harmless diversion from the obligations of the lifeworld, but rather as destroying the very relationships which bind the self to the substantive concerns of human culture (Adorno, 1991: 105). The pressure exerted by this reified culture ultimately leads to the collapse of the self into mimetic relationships with the stereotypes produced by the culture industry: the masses, in other words, strive to look, dance, dress and make love in ways which, although they seem to be the product of individual choice, always 'reveal a fear of disobedience' (*Ibid.*: 95).

According to Louis Althusser the fundamental difference between Marxist and Hegelian dialectics is the fact that, for Marx, the different ideological limbs of society do not express the immanent unity of human self-consciousness at a given stage of its historical development, but rather have a relative freedom which is ultimately determined by the overarching demand of capital accumulation (Althusser, 1986: 101–2). The realm of 'culture' therefore is implicated in a politics of structural contradiction; for the inherently crisis-ridden development of the economy determines political antagonisms which are mediated through the different ideological limbs of the superstructure. The relative autonomy of the law, popular culture and democratic freedoms, in other words, (usually) function to displace the antagonisms of commodity producing societies. Adorno's reading of Hegel in *Negative Dialectics* presents a similar argument. His claim is that Hegelian dialectics is driven by an 'allergy' to non-identity – and that the general concepts (being, essence, appearance, spirit) through which it approaches the empirical differentiation of the world, are incapable of moving outside of the 'magic circle' of their own immanent identity (Adorno, 1990: 136). Thus by starting from the identity of the concept (and not from the difference of the object from the categories of subjective thought), Hegel made the substantive relationships of ethical life into timeless essences which conceal the antagonisms of commodity production (*Ibid.*: 156). Now the difference between Althusser and Adorno's approaches to the reification of culture derives from their respective accounts of the fate of identity thinking under the conditions of monopoly capitalism. For Althusser the Hegelian concept becomes thoroughly functionalized; its different elements are subsumed under a structural totality which mediates the conflicts that arise from the economic base. For Adorno, on the other hand, the reproduction of the economic base is itself dependent upon the reproduction of cultural and philosophical forms[5] which pre-empt the structural dynamics of displacement, condensation and overdetermination which lie at the heart of Althusser's account of ideology.

In Althusser's reading of Marx the question of revolutionary transcendence is resolved through the concept of overdetermination: the structural conflicts that arise from the economic base, and which are usually displaced through the ideological institutions of the superstructure, occasionally become critical; and it is then that the contradictions of the commodity form threaten to exert their determining effect upon the mode of production, pushing it beyond the inequalities of private ownership. Thus while it true that Althusser's account of the primacy of the economic base seems always to postpone the moment of its historical effectiveness. (Althusser, 1986a: 113), he is still able to maintain a practical linkage between the theory of structural causality, the collective action of the masses, and the transformation of the mode of production. The relationship between theory and political praxis which arises from *Dialectic of Enlightenment* is rather more difficult to specify. As we have seen, Horkheimer and Adorno maintain that the processes of class homogenization which Marx described cannot take place under the conditions of late-capitalism because they are constantly pre-empted by the repetitions of the culture industry. Thus it appears as if critical theory can be no more than a descriptive instrument which registers the transformations of capital and its generation of new cultural forms to re-enchant the circulation of commodities. The theme which runs throughout *Negative Dialectics* however is the transformative potential which is implicit in every forced imposition of identity; for in so far as 'culture' has become a homogenous extension of monopoly capital, it contains within it the sufferings of all those who have undergone its synthetic operations. Adorno's negative dialectics, in other words, takes the form of an immanent critique which seeks constantly to undermine the 'objectivity' of capital, and to respond to the suffering which is perpetuated in its most 'natural' representations of unity (Adorno, 1990: 182).

Two important questions have emerged here. The first concerns Adorno's relationship to Marxism, or, more specifically, to the general concerns which Marxism has with the dynamics of class, power and resistance. Gillian Rose, in *The Melancholy Science*, maintains that insofar as he dispenses with the concept of class and reduces individual subjects to fetishistic dupes of the culture industry, Adorno is unable to determine a concrete alternative to the cycle of reification. Having rejected the actual conditions which make social transformation possible, in other words, she argues that Adorno's concept of negative dialectics ends up prioritizing the pure voluntarism of the individual in relation to the totality of reified culture (Rose, 1978: 141). This, however, seems to

prejudge the issue somewhat; for if it is the case that Adorno is attempting to show that the concrete forms of inequality (class, state, relations
of production) which were characteristic of bourgeois capitalism have
changed fundamentally, then it seems that we ought to judge his
account of reified culture and the demise of class politics on the basis of
its applicability to the contemporary organization of capitalism. If, in
other words, the dominance of the image over the self-consciousness of
the masses has actually been *intensified* by the emergence of new media
technologies (the internet, satellite television, etc.), then might it not be
the case that to assume the continuing primacy of class inequalities and
state domination is to underplay the very effects of false individualism,
fetishistic consumption and loss of identity which Horkheimer and
Adorno present in *Dialectic of Enlightenment*?

The second question concerns the possibility of extending Horkheimer
and Adorno's critique of reification to the cultural forms that have
emerged within the media saturated space of late capitalism. As I have
tried to show, the importance of the culture industry thesis lies in its
account of the relationship between capital and new image technologies: the flow of commodities is no longer conceived as a 'material' fact
to which superstructural forms are simply reducible; rather the
economic base and its structural cognates (class, state and civil society)
are understood as dependent upon the representational powers of image
technologies and the patterns of obedience, conformity and consumption which they sustain. Adorno's attempt to determine the fate of the
masses under the conditions of universal reification therefore marks a
definitive abandonment of the concept of class consciousness: for if, as
he maintains, the administration of culture and consumption has
reached the point where capital is able to forestall the destabilizing
effects of economic crises, then Marxist critique cannot expect to find its
living counterpart in reified consciousness of the masses. Yet for Adorno
the negative cannot be completely expunged from the experience of
reification, and so there is always the possibility that negative critique
will give rise to particular forms of resistance to the dominant strategies
of identity/control (Adorno, 1990: 405–8). In the following section,
therefore, I want to look at the way in which Adorno's critical theory has
been developed by neo-Marxist thought, and particularly at the way in
which Fredric Jameson has used negative dialectics to analyse the
relationship between capitalism, media technologies and postmodern
culture.

3
The Rise of Ludic Aestheticism

There is a sense in which Adorno's account of the culture industry prefigures the encounter between Marxist and postmodernist social theory. *Dialectic of Enlightenment* describes a progressive reification culture in which normative traditions have been ruptured by the interjection of image technologies, truth has become a function of aesthetic representation, and the self has been reduced to a paranoid desire to be contemporary. The continued expansion of capital, in other words, is sustained by the reproduction of passive consumers who are incapable of seeing beyond the desires and satisfactions which are already provided for them by the great corporate monopolies. For Horkheimer and Adorno this cycle of mutual reproduction is virtually hermetic; for once the culture industry has taken hold of the masses, their perception is shifted away from the concrete forms of inequality which they inhabit towards the world of commodities from which they constantly seek satisfaction. The process of rationalization which capitalism undergoes in the twentieth century, therefore, is one which destroys the material foundations of class politics: for once the welfare state, technological production and the culture industry have combined to smooth out their experience of injustice and dissatisfaction, the masses are consigned to the comfortable repetition of their privatized desires. This account of the massification of desire, as I have indicated above, marks a fundamental departure from orthodox Marxism; for by insisting on the power of technologically produced culture to disarm the collective experience of social antagonisms, Horkheimer and Adorno effectively break the link between the self-consciousness of the masses and their material conditions of existence (inequality, injustice, patriarchal domination, racism, etc.). Despite this, however, their analysis does retain a certain commitment to Marx's account of the causative relationship of the economy to cultural production – a relationship which, according to most contemporary Marxists, is completely erased from postmodernist theory.

I have argued elsewhere that Jameson's later work belongs to a particular tradition of neo-Marxist thought which conceives 'postmodernism' as a kind of cultural aesthetic which is, at best, a distraction from the true concerns of late-capitalism (the degradation of the natural environment, the perpetuation of Third World debt, the persistence of genocide), or, at worst, the origin of a pernicious individualism which gives absolute priority to subjective desire over the demands of political reason (Abbinnett, 2003: 5–12). From this perspective the proliferation of postmodernist art, culture and theory which has occurred since the end of the 1960s, constitutes a generic totality in which self-seeking individualism is given the moral status of 'respect for difference' and 'the right to choose'. Thus the determination of the postmodern artist or thinker to question every dialectical structure of conflict or consensus, is seen as the counterpart of a synthetic culture which has transformed the 'passive consumer' into the 'schizophrenic ego' which is essential to capitalism's accelerated cycle of innovation. Postmodern culture, in other words, is a culture of ludic aestheticism; for as new media technologies have penetrated every recess of the lifeworld, so we have been transformed into the desperately playful souls who want everything from the latest ring-tone to total gender re-assignment. The theoretical style that arises from this colonization of the lifeworld is, according to the Jameson, opposed to anything more substantive than the abstract desire of the individual ego; and so even the attempts which Lyotard and Derrida make to determine an ethics of difference end up repeating the aporias abstract volition which lie at the heart of postmodern culture. In the end the generic totality of postmodernist theory and culture is merely the reflex of technological capitalism; an ideological configuration of the present as pure aesthetic immediacy with no past or future beyond the instant of commodified desire.[1] I will look at the detail of Jameson's analysis of postmodern culture shortly. For the moment however I want to say a little more about the neo-Marxist tradition to which his writing belongs.

In *The Condition of Postmodernity* David Harvey claims that postmodernism must be understood in terms of its relationship to the compression of space and time that becomes acute during periods of over-accumulation in capitalist economies (Harvey, 1999: vi). What Harvey is referring to here is the rationalization of public, private and geographical space which, drawing its inspiration from the Enlightenment project, has accompanied the rise of modern capitalism. The necessary involvement of capitalism with the metrical systems through which space and time are quantified, has meant that the periodic crises of the global economy are experienced as the intrusion of pure economic necessity upon the lifeworld: the basic affiliations of class, home and nation, in other words, are made subject to demands whose urgency threatens the normative structures of everyday existence. In the absence of this spatial and temporal stability the relationship between science (rational anthropology, functionalism, utilitarianism) and morality becomes increasingly dislocated, and the turn to aesthetics becomes ever more pronounced (*Ibid.*: 327). Thus if we are to understand postmodernism properly, that is, in terms the 'historical geography of capitalism', we must recognize that as a cultural and intellectual movement it is primarily an attempt to aestheticize the experience of dislocation which has come to afflict the lifeworld of every nation state (*Ibid.*: 328).

For Harvey this postmodernist celebration of the aesthetic, and of the autonomy of cultural practice, should be condemned on the grounds of its neglect of the historical conflicts and resolutions which have produced modern culture. In the end the postmodernist cultural production is much too close to the 'sheer profit-seeking' of late-capitalist enterprise to be considered revolutionary or socially transformative (Harvey, 1999: 328). According to Harvey's analysis however we cannot be satisfied with simply unmasking the complicity of postmodernism, in all it multifarious forms, with the mechanisms of capital accumulation. Rather the flexibility of postmodern varieties of production, communication and subjectivity should be understood as having arisen out of the old Fordist regime as an opposing tendency. For in so far as it is the 'internalized rules' of capital that produce both the cultural crises and the economic dynamism of the mode of production, we must recognize that postmodern flexibility represents one pole of an adaptive process whose variations emerge from the impossibility of resolving the contradictions of global capitalism (*Ibid.*: 343). Fordist modernity offers stable markets, a 'fixed configuration' of economic influence and political power, a well-established process of theoretical legitimation, and a secure grounding in techno-scientific rationality. Postmodern flexibility, on the contrary, is characterized by its virtualization of economic relations: 'fictitious capital, images, ephemerality, chance and flexibility in production techniques, labour markets and consumption niches' (*Ibid.*: 339). Harvey's argument is that this opposition between modernist and postmodernist accounts of the relationship between politics, economics and normative legitimacy should be understood in terms of their relative advantages at any given time. In the end there is little point in pursuing debates about whether or not there has been a transition from modernity to postmodernity. For a historically grounded (i.e. critical Marxist) account of the relationship between cultural and economic production, demands that we recognize that the extent to which a particular economy has adopted the ideology of 'Fordism' or 'flexible postmodernism' will 'vary from time to time ... depending on which configuration is profitable and which is not' (*Ibid.*: 344). The 'aesthetic turn' of the postmodernists, in other words, remains an adaptive strategy of capital: it is a cultural form whose transformation of the established structures of economic and political conformity leads back to the aporias of fetishized desire and abstract individualism.

Alex Callinicos, in *Against Postmodernism*, shifts the emphasis away from the functional utility of postmodern culture for the late capitalist economy, towards a class-based analysis which treats the satisfactions of ludic aestheticism as a distorted expression of the actual human needs which are frustrated by the persistence of the commodity form. His argument is that postmodernist theory is related genealogically to the surrealist and constructivist movements which emerged at the beginning of the twentieth century, and which expressed a kind of 'aesthetic withdraw' from revolutionary struggles taking place in Tsarist Russia. The failure of the 1905 revolution, in other words, produced a burst of radical aestheticism which presented itself as the beginning of a new historical epoch – an epoch in which the constraints of both bourgeois and socialist morality would be cast aside and the brave new world of sublime possibility would emerge (Callinicos, 1989: 49). This, according to Callinicos, is the precursor of the postmodernist art which proclaimed the end of modernism in the 1980s and 1990s; for it is only in so far as it took its lead from the most radical gestures of Joyce, Dali, Mies and Picasso, that it was able to gather the disparate strands of the post-industrialization thesis into the form of an epoch-making shift in the mode of production. Postmodernist art, culture and theory therefore is presented by Callinicos as a 'symptom' of the increasing power of capital to alienate and deform and the most fundamental needs of human individuals, and to present that deformation as the emergence of a new epoch of choice and liberty (*Ibid.*: 7). From this perspective Jameson and Harvey's attempts to explicate the relationship between late capitalism and postmodern culture conceive postmodernist ideologies of choice, flexibility and individualism as part of a process of cultural administration which is immanent in the mode of production, rather than as a result of the disillusionment which followed the radicalism of the 1960s. The turn to the 'overconsumptionist' lifestyle of the Reagan–Thatcher era, in other words, should be understood not simply as the most functional way of integrating the technological operations upon which the turnover of capital has come to depend, but as the result of the willingness of disaffected radicals to buy into the satisfactions of the new 'postmodern' capitalism (*Ibid*.). I will return to this argument in a moment.

The culture critique which Jameson develops in his later writing, and most notably in *Postmodernism, or, The Cultural Logic of Late Capitalism*, takes its inspiration from Adorno's account of negative dialectics. For Adorno 'thinking' is that which registers the violence of objectified totality, that is, the processes through which social, economic and political identities are imposed upon the being of each individual (Adorno, 1990: 174–6). And so his critique of the reified forms of desire, aesthetic sensibility and psychological satisfaction which constitute the modern subject, is configured by a sense of how much more efficient the regimes of rational capitalism are when their violent perfection of the 'standard' personality remains below the level of critical analysis. For Jameson the social, economic and cultural relations through which Adorno presented the dynamics of late capitalism have been superseded: the heavy industrial production which required stable domestic economies has been undermined by the ebbs and flows of multinational capital, global communications networks have facilitated the shift towards a knowledge-based economy, and the proliferation of new image technologies has produced an entirely new range of moral, cultural and political effects. Despite this radical transformation of the operational logic capitalism however, Jameson insists upon the value of negative critique. He argues that postmodernist forms of theory and culture should be the subject of historical analyses which conceive them 'not [as] the determinants of a whole new social order, but only as the reflex and concomitant of yet another systemic modification of capitalism itself' (Jameson, 1995: xii). Ultimately therefore negative critique, or what Jameson calls 'symptomal philosophizing', continues to respond to the violent mutability of capital; it is that which traces the implicitude of autonomous individuality through technological transformations of space, time, habitus and community.

The argument presented in *Postmodernism* is that the new technologies which have exponentially increased the flow of images and information around the world market, function to produce a cultural economy which is based upon the virtual simultaneity of production (of images), consumption (by the masses), and distraction (from the violent deterritorializing power of capital) (Jameson, 1995: xiv–xv). What is important here, and what marks a crucial shift away from the more orthodox Marxisms we have examined, is Jameson's insistence that the practice of negative critique is responsible to the infinitely complex, technologically intensified processes through which capital continues to transform its expropriative regime. Remaining faithful to the Marxist inheritance, in other words, means sustaining a 'polemic stance' which is focused on the mutability of capitalism (its power rapidly to transform the experience of identity, community, love, desire, sexuality), and which eschews materialist logics of revolutionary composition and historical necessity. Thus the postmodernist engagement with the virtualizing powers of technological capitalism finds a certain resonance in Jameson's writing: for his concern with the possibility of representing the heterogeneous forms of subalternity which are distributed across the global economy, has led him at different times to assert the value of Baudrillard's hyperreality thesis and Derrida's notion of the spectre in mapping the cultural dynamics of late capitalism (Jameson, 1995: 203; Jameson in Sprinker, 1999: 47).

Yet Jameson's enthusiasm for the concepts of spectralization and hyperreality is tempered by a certain reserve. In *Late Marxism* he remarks that:

> both [Adorno and Derrida] need something outside the system in order to criticize it, but in Adorno's case this something would remain an idea, while in Derrida's it ought ideally to be a linguistic possibility: the similarity comes from the fact that in neither case can this urgent need be met, except by an elaborate formal subterfuge. (Jameson, 2000: 235)

This distinction between Adornian 'thinking' and deconstructive 'reading' turns upon the idea that the independence of the latter is pre-inscribed in an economy of deferral whose 'formal subterfuge' (trace, supplementarity, *différance*) is rather less engaged with the objective reality of the concept than Adorno's negative critique. This applies with even greater force to Baudrillard's concept of the hyperreal; for insofar as he maintains that the powers of simulation through which capital expands its capacity for symbolic exchange have no internal limit, he eliminates the last traces of the negative from the play of appearances. It is Jameson's suspicion, in other words, that postmodernist figurations of the symbolic economy of exchange tend to exclude a historically grounded, dialectical understanding of the relationships between capitalism, mass culture and the transformation of global space. For the techniques through which they approach the ideological inscription of being remain dangerously close – although perhaps not wholly complicit with – the aestheticism of postmodern culture.

The detail of Jameson's account of the relationship between late capitalism and postmodern culture can be briefly summarized. Under the conditions of what Lenin called the imperialist phase of capitalism economic activity becomes properly international: nation states enter a period of violent competition for new territories and resources which transforms the geopolitical organization of the world economy. It is at this point that the contradiction between the lived experience of the locality and the operational logic of capitalism becomes acute; for as particular lifeworlds are brought into contact with the exoticism of other cultures and the exigencies of international trade and conflict, the bonds of ethical life (*Sittlichkeit*) begin to lose their objective necessity. For Jameson the normative effects of this crisis are configured in the allegorical forms of modernist art: the motifs of subjectivity, transcendence and autonomy are set in relation to an object ('monopoly capital') whose powers of dispersal and integration constantly rupture the internal bonds of particular localities (Jameson, 1995: 412). The insurmountable difficulty of representing *all* of the conditions which have produced this normative crisis, in other words, is manifested in aesthetic forms which give a sense of the totalizing power of the object, while testifying at the same time to their own contingency and inadequacy.

The impossible necessity of representing the operational powers of capital *in toto* becomes even more acute under the conditions of 'late', or 'multinational', capitalism. In this phase capital is no longer anchored in particular nation states: highly mobile technologies and flexible production processes mean that it can flow into and out of particular locations the moment profitability begins to decline. This complete openness of the locality is the outcome of an increasingly close relationship between capital and technology; for it is only in so far as media and communications networks have transformed each particular lifeworld into a node of informatic exchange that it has been possible for capital to mutate into a deterritorialized regime of hyper-accumulation. For Jameson the collective experience of the subjects who inhabit this global network takes on an evanescent and unpredictable character – a character which is configured in the postmodernist art and theory which celebrates heterogeneity as an absolute value (Jameson, 1995: 413). Thus the necessity of a Marxist critique which encourages new practices of 'transcoding' the hegemony of postmodern culture arises from the increasingly violent forms of expropriation which are justified in the name of respect for difference and the virtues of flexibility and lack of attachment.

The distinction which Jameson makes between the 'transcoding' activity of critical Marxism and what he sees as the obsessive 'decoding' practised by postmodernist theory is important here. Decoding, according to Jameson, is one of the generic characteristics of postmodernist theory: Derrida, Baudrillard and Lyotard all practice forms of critique which, in their attempts to undermine the hegemonic categories of ideology, fall back into a ceaseless relativization of narratives which never questions the purpose of its own activity (Jameson, 1995: 395). Transcoding, on the other hand, begins with the determining force of the object: it conceives the multiple discourses which emerge under late capitalism as 'worldviews' (*Weltanshauungen*) which mediate and transform the accumulative powers of the global economy. The cultural dominance of postmodernism for example should be theorized as the reflex of a totality which reproduces itself as total separation: for it is only in so far as the textual, libidinal and aesthetic economies of the postmodernists are conceived as part of the operational logic of abstract difference, that it is possible to understand their complicity with the decentred, distracted forms of individualism which sustain the dominance of consumer capitalism. The concept of transcoding therefore is an attempt to think the idea of totality beyond the regulative structures of the political; an attempt which seeks to generate 'new ambivalent abstractions' from the clash of liberal, Marxist and postmodernist orthodoxies (*Ibid.*: 396).

So where does this leave Jameson's Marxism in relation to the dialectics of class politics? For it would seem as if Jameson's technique of transcoding, of sustaining a linguistic critique which looks to destabilize both left and right-wing orthodoxies, cannot remain attached to the idea of an economically structured antagonism which would exceed (and precede) every form of cultural and ideological mediation. This is true – but only to an extent. In 'Marx's purloined letter' Jameson makes it clear that he has a good deal of sympathy for Derrida's rejection of class as the foundational category of Marxist politics: he remarks upon the power of deconstructive readings to rupture the 'utopian fantasies' through which class is constantly recalled to the political arena (Jameson in Sprinker, 1999: 47). He also maintains that Baudrillard's account of the logic of symbolic exchange through which capital transcends its own internal limits, demands that we treat class solidarity as an infinitely more contingent possibility than is allowed by conventional Marxist theory (Jameson, 1995: 395). There is however a certain reserve in Jameson's welcoming of Baudrillard and Derrida's interventions into the debate over class – a reserve which harks back to his conception of the relationship between postmodernist theory and postmodernist culture.

As we have seen Jameson traces the dominance of postmodern culture to the antagonism between global capital and the concrete forms of life sustained in particular localities. The emergence of cultural, aesthetic and theoretical forms which valorize pure particularity is part of a general shift in the operational logic of capitalism: it is a response to the loss of nature, tradition and history which is brought about by the condensation of geopolitical space into the temporal economy of media and informatic exchange. For Jameson this means that while Marxist politics certainly must avoid utopian fantasies of the revolution, its political activity should remain faithful to the contingent possibilities of resistance that arise from the operational powers of capital. The persistence of class, in other words, lies in what we might call its allegorical impurity; that is, in fact that it is always configured in the multiple forms of identity which haunt the fractured existence of particular lifeworlds (Jameson in Sprinker, 1999: 49). The question which arises here, of course, is that of cosmopolitan hospitality. For if it is the case that the allegorical figures which gather collective identities at a local level cannot be mapped directly onto the global dynamics of impoverishment and exploitation, then the work of Marxist theory must be to configure the strategic ('class') solidarities of particular lifeworlds in discourses which challenge the global hegemony of postmodern capitalism. Jameson admits that such figurations are bound to fail – for they proceed from the impossibility of representing the contradiction between global and local spaces. Yet it is through the necessity of this failure that class politics will always make its return; for even if it is the case that such allegorical figurations run the risk of collapsing into postmodernist simulacra, they still retain a certain purchase on the dialectics of the global and the local, essence and appearance, the human and the inhuman (Jameson, 1995: 415).

The possibility of socialism therefore depends upon the processes of cognitive and aesthetic mapping which politicize the locality; for the allegorical forms through which class relationships are configured open up a plurality of different lifeworlds to the global logic of exploitation which is obscured by the distractions of postmodern culture. Thus if there is to be an international Marxist politics its effectiveness depends upon the aesthetic imagination which is provoked by the totalizing powers of the object: for in so far as all localities have been transformed into penetrable spaces it is possible to configure a new dialectics of class struggle which exceeds the global circulation of commodified images. Clearly this is not too far removed from what Derrida has said about the law of cosmopolitan hospitality which is threatened by, yet continues to disturb, the global-media-technological organization of the capitalism. Yet the difference is significant. Derrida has argued that the possibility of being hospitable to the other depends upon the event of his or her arrival; it is the moment of pure unpredictability which demands that we put our legal-contractual forms of responsibility into suspension (Derrida, 2000: 79). As we have seen Jameson's account of class struggle narrates a double mediation of alterity: it gathers the disparate forms of resistance that arise in particular lifeworlds into new forms of solidarity which are open to the arrival of the destitute and the powerless of the world economy (Jameson, 1995: 417). It is this recursive structure, this attempt to mediate the local and the global significance of class through the cognitive-aesthetic imagination, which marks the difference between Derrida and Jameson's Marxism. For Jameson the dialectics of class disclose the historical thread of a politics of recognition, solidarity and practical agency, while for Derrida this possibility is sustained through the infinite horizon of the other: the unforeseeable futurity which precedes and exceeds every preparation for his or her arrival (Derrida, 2000: 25–6).

In the end the question that arises from Jameson's Marxism concerns the possibility of finding a way back to 'the object' (totality) once it has been acknowledged that the global-technological organization of capital tends to appropriate the negative effects (class solidarity, schizophrenic desire, overproduction, under-consumption) through which the contradictions of commodity production are disclosed. For Callinicos the fact that this question arises with such urgency from Jameson's work attests to the fact that the concept of totality which is deployed in his cultural critique is essentially Hegelian: the vast array of data which is analysed in *Postmodernism's* chapters on culture, ideology, film, video and architecture is treated as if it were expressive of a universal idea ('postmodernism') whose unfolding is 'woven into the texture of history'. Thus the fact that Jameson's thought takes such a tortuous route back from postmodernism to class politics, results from his having started out from a technologically produced culture which appeared to have become independent of the structural organization of ideological apparatuses, class antagonisms and social practices (Callinicos, 1989: 132).

This accusation of idealism however is misguided; for the cultural analyses which Jameson sets out in *Postmodernism* are primarily concerned with the relationship between media-technological capitalism and the cultural aesthetic of difference/evanescence which has come to dominate the lifeworld. Far from assuming a pre-established harmony of the cultural media he examines Jameson continues in the Adornian vein of assessing the impact of mass culture on the conventional structures and institutions of capitalist society (class, state, civil society). This however still leaves open the question of the political significance of Jameson's critique of culture. For if it is the case that the recursive structure of his analyses is fundamentally threatened by his recourse to the concepts of postmodernist theory then might it not be the case that there is no way back to the compositional power of capital (the unrepresentable object)? Might it not be the case, in other words, that remaining faithful to Marxist theory and political praxis means giving up such a recursive structure? I will consider these questions in the final chapters of this section.

4
Capitalism and the Hyperreal

In the introduction to *Postmodernism* Jameson acknowledges a debt to Jean Baudrillard's work – or more precisely to the concepts of simulation and hyperreality which he developed in *Symbolic Exchange and Death* and *Simulation and Simulacra*. As we have seen, the power of Jameson's analyses derives from his appreciation of the complex relationship between capitalism and cultural production: the chapters on ideology, video, film and architecture expound a transition from modernist culture (in which the economy of signs was still relatively confident of its reference to the reality of man, nature and production) to the play of postmodern simulacra in which the sign only ever refers to other signs and 'the real' is transformed into an ungraspable shadow. The relapse of 'culture' into the repetitive forms of the pop video, the B-movie and the porno flick therefore are characteristic of a phase of capitalism which is fundamentally unstable; for as the distribution of capital across international markets becomes more and more chaotic, so the old securities of modernist culture begin to breakdown and are replaced by a play of commodified images which distract the masses from the conflicts of global economic change. This analysis of postmodern culture as the reflex of global capitalism however raises a crucial question: namely, how far is it possible to pursue the idea of culture as technological simulation and still be able to retain the fundamental structures of negative critique, that is, the allegorical forms of organic labour, class solidarity and revolutionary politics which Jameson presents in the conclusion of *Postmodernism*? In what follows I will argue that Baudrillard's account of simulation and the hyperreal is fundamentally opposed not only to Jameson's allegorical configuration of Marxism, but also to the attempts of his 'postmodern' contemporaries – particularly Derrida – to transform the project of historical materialism.

There is a sense in which Baudrillard's work stands as *the* exemplar of everything which neo-Marxism has charged postmodernism with: the reversion to idealism through the autonomy of the sign, the celebration of pure unmediated difference, the validation of the aesthetic as a socially and politically transformative experience, and the privileging of singularity over every manifestation of the universal. There is a measure of truth in this description; Baudrillard does indeed maintain that reality has become 'aestheticized' and that this has led to the emergence of floating, disarticulated subjectivities who value personal choice beyond every appeal to public welfare or the common good. However, it would be wrong to maintain that the description of contemporary social relations which Baudrillard presents in his later writings is an endorsement of the loss of the real and its effects on social and political life. The account of simulation which is presented in *Symbolic Exchange and Death*, for example, is premised upon the idea of simulation as a destructive code which renders every discrete sphere of experience susceptible to death by adulteration. The emergence of the hyperreal, in other words, is the emergence of a universal connectedness in which 'the social' – conceived as the messy, disarticulated conjunction of art, nature, sexuality, love and death – collapses into a play of interchangeable signs, none of which is able to sustain an immunity to any of the others. Thus the choice of every individual is solicited by a technological culture which has ransacked the archive of the beautiful, the moral and the sublime and made it into a procession of predictable images which solicit equally predictable responses. There is then a certain morality in Baudrillard's account simulation, a morality which is configured through the radical 'counter-finality' which death introduces into the spiralling effects of simulation. I will argue however that this account of the transformative power of death is ultimately sacrificed to the logic of simulation which Baudrillard presents in his later writings, and that his understanding of the masses as 'silent majorities' reflects an erroneous belief that simulation is always able to pre-empt the formation of ethical and political questions.

Much of what Baudrillard says about political economy in *Symbolic Exchange and Death* is prefigured in *The Mirror of Production*, and so I want to look briefly at his initial remarks on Marxism and its relationship to the commodity law of value. Let me summarize Baudrillard's argument. Marx begins by insisting that labour power under capitalism is a commodity and that it is this commodity which produces the exchange value of all other commodities. The M–C–M relation therefore presupposes the reduction of concrete labour to abstract 'labour power' and the appearance of commodities as fetishized objects which have an independent existence of their own. Marx's critique of political economy approaches the postulates of bourgeois economics (i.e. the postulation of a 'hidden hand' which equilibrates production and consumption, of a 'natural' limit which regulates human desire, etc.) by insisting on the disruption which the commodity law of value introduces into the mode of production. He insists, in other words, that once exchange value and the fetishism of commodities become predominant, any possibility that an appropriate quantity of use value (or means of subsistence) will find its way to each sector of production is lost. Yet Marx stopped short of the conclusion that use value is actually a product of the play of exchange values; for the concept of socialized production which underlies his critique of political economy is founded on the idea that the *quantitative* diversification of abstract labour presages a *qualitative* shift in the production and distribution use values (Baudrillard, 1975: 25). For Baudrillard the question which arises here concerns the possibility of this transmutation: for if it is the case that the use value of human labour is primary, and if this concrete determination of productive activity is, by definition, incommensurable, then how is it possible for it to have given rise to the commodity law of value? According to Baudrillard's analysis, the only credible answer to this question is that Marx's concept of use value (i.e. the social utility of labour which pre-dates its perversion by the commodity form) already bears the imprint of political economy; for the fact that he envisages the transcendence of capitalism as a return to the rightful distribution of value, immediately implicates the category of abstract labour (and all its 'bourgeois' cog-nates) in the historical necessity of the revolution. Capitalism, in other words, is a kind of detour through the illusions of exchange value which eventually leads back to the proper distribution of social goods (*Ibid.*: 27).

The method of political economy, as Marx pointed out in the *Economic and Philosophical Manuscripts*, proceeds by attributing certain *a priori* characteristics to human beings (industriousness, self-interest, sympathy) and then deducing the fundamental nature of social and economic relationships from those characteristics. Thus, according to Marx, Adam Smith's account of the positive effects of private property rights on the wealth of national economies, is justified by presenting self-interest and productive labour as characteristics which are inscribed in the 'archaic past' of humanity. Smith's analysis, in other words, assumes that the interests of the capitalists are the historically specific form taken by these fundamental characteristics, and that his task is to disclose the optimum conditions for the realization of human labour as social wealth (Marx, 1977a: 66–7). For Baudrillard Marx's concentration on the historical relationship between economic and political domination fails to escape the gravitational pull of political economy: for in so far as his account of the transitions from primitive to feudal to capitalist society is ultimately based upon the law of value (i.e. the transmutation of exchange into use value which is promised by the abstract diversity of the former), his critique lapses into a teleological narration of the different forms of exchange which precede the emergence of capitalism. In the end the immanence of socialized production in Marx's critique obscures the possibility that labour itself might be the cause of human alienation, and that human history is something more than a preparation for the optimized labour of communism (Baudrillard, 1975: 32).

Marx's thought therefore reflects the primacy which is given to production and the accumulation of value under the regime of political economy (Baudrillard, 1975: 33). The concept of labour which he expounds in the *Economic and Philosophical Manuscripts* is presented as the ontological stricture to which human beings are originally subject and through which they are to achieve selfhood by the overcoming of otherness/nature. It is through the hard methodical transformation of his world, in other words, that man achieves his substantive worth; for it is only by his labour that he contributes to the social goods (use values) upon which every mode of production depends. For Baudrillard the question which arises from this ontological designation of labour concerns the fate of those forms of symbolic exchange (the gift, the sacrifice, the sacred, the erotic, the aesthetic) which, in so-called primitive societies, appear to exceed the lineal unfolding of use value as the immanent purpose of human association. For if it is the case that everything is reducible to the primacy of productive labour, then the concepts of spontaneity, excess, transfiguration, beauty and the sublime designate nothing more than the self-consciously programmatic expressions of 'play' through which the real business of production is expanded and intensified (*Ibid.*: 39).[1] Thus the idea of socialized production which founds Marx's critique is complicit with the bourgeois of aesthetics which spring from the law of the commodity; for the 'non-work' that is liberated from the regime of production is no more than an appearance (simulation) of free activity which transfigures and re-enacts the rules value (*Ibid.*: 40).

This brings us to the concept of symbolic exchange. Marx begins by expounding the metaphysics of exchange between man and nature; he identifies productive activity as the essence of the human species and use value as the concrete form in which that labour becomes social, moral and political. Thus for Baudrillard production is locked into a regime of 'rational positive finality'; every generic form of labour has a particular social need which it satisfies and every satisfied social need provides more organic labour for the realization of more use values (Baudrillard, 1975: 42). The very possibility of transcendence is captured within the productive imperative which Marx inherits from bourgeois political economy; and so if there is to be a critique of Marx's critique its first task must be to establish terms of reference to what lies outside the circle of productive recuperation. As Baudrillard puts it:

> There is a choice to be made between value and non-value. Labour is definitely within the sphere of value. This is why Marx's concept of labour ... must be submitted to a radical critique as an *ideological* concept ... this is not the time to generalize it as a *revolutionary* concept. (*Ibid.*: 43)

The 'real rupture' then is not between abstract and concrete labour but between symbolic exchange and the absolute value of work; for in so far as Marx's concept of socialized production remains bewitched by the spell of political economy, he is unable to register the transformative power which death imports into every system of mediated exchange. What Baudrillard is referring to here is an originary relationship between 'life', as the self-conscious pursuit of ends, and 'death', as that which inhabits the ethical, political and normative finalities of every social space. Life, in other words, can be what it is only in its relationship to death, for death is what precipitates the events of religious, erotic and aesthetic transfiguration which Baudrillard calls symbolic exchange. Marxism has tended to subsume this experience of the symbolic under the logic of production; the religious and erotic rites of 'primitive' civilizations are conceived as wasteful discharges of energy which, in more 'developed' societies, would have been put to work in the manufacture of value. For Baudrillard however the complex interrelations of servitude, obligation, mimesis and sacrifice that arise from the experience of death configure a pure exorbitance which cannot be recuperated in the form of value; and so the critique of capital must seek those events in which symbolic exchange outplays the logic of accumulation (*Ibid.*: 48–9).

In *Symbolic Exchange and Death* Baudrillard attempts to expound the relationship between the codification of reality which is implicit in Marx's account of capital (i.e. the reduction of man and nature to elements of the M–C–M relation) and what he calls the 'structural revolution in value'. The structure of his exposition can be briefly summarized. In both primitive and feudal societies symbolic relationships are anchored in a 'natural order' of cruelty; the sacred, religious and erotic dissimulations of power refer directly to the strictures which are imposed upon the body of the slave, the surf, or the warrior (Baudrillard, 2004: 50). The Enlightenment however displaces this assurance; it institutes an economy in which the relationship between the real (signified) and its sign has ceased to be anchored in a shared experience of the immediate and is dispersed into an ever expanding realm of concepts. This process of secularization opens the possibility of the M–C–M relation; the exchangeability of money into commodities and of commodities into money presupposes the reduction of nature and the lifeworld to exchangeable signs which facilitate the production of surplus value (*Ibid.*: 55). Thus for Baudrillard capitalism presupposes an encoding of reality whose effects are technological rather than political; for the fact of expanded commodity production depends upon techniques of mechanical reproducibility which outstrip the crystallization of labour into use value and class solidarity. Rather than determining the crises of failing utility which Marx attributes to the highest stages of capitalism, in other words, industrial capital expands its capacity to produce the signs through which commodities solicit the simulacra of 'lifestyle', 'gender', 'class' and 'ethnicity' (*Ibid.*: 56). This then is the 'current strategic model' through which capital expands: all substantive value is evacuated from the system; everything is reduced to contingent connections which express nothing but the most convenient modulation of nature, or body, or soul into the regime of hyper-accumulation. In the end the generic idea of man is 'wiped from the map' of capital; he is dispersed into simulacra which leave nothing of the transformative power which Marx attributed to productive humanity (*Ibid.*: 60).

This erasure of value from the economy of social signification marks the emergence of what Baudrillard calls the hyperreal. His claim is that once the sign is liberated from any concrete reference to reality, 'the real' becomes a kind of fixed idea which is inscribed in the technological development of the media. The perfection of the virtual, in other words, is paradox; for as the power to simulate the concrete determinations of man, nature and history becomes ever greater, so the perfected copies (simulacra) come to displace the essence of the real. For Baudrillard this process of refraction is inscribed at the very heart of the economic infrastructure; for as soon as anything is produced its 'value' is dispersed into an expanding plurality of connections, none of which designates the finality of purpose and social utility which Marx attributed to the act of labour. Indeed he argues that, under the regime of simulation, productive activity has ceased to be rooted in the regime of ontological suffering which Marx described in the *Economic and Philosophical Manuscripts*; work is now about the 'ritual of signs' through which each of us presents the decency, productivity and individuality of his/her contribution to the social good (Baudrillard, 2004: 10–11). Labour, in other words, is taken up into the spiralling of the hyperreal; it becomes part of an expanding plurality of connections which transform friendship, class, community and politics into parodic enactments of a reality which has long since vanished. Capital therefore expands through the aestheticization of the real; its capacity for growth is engendered by the complete evacuation of value/content from the realm of signification, and by the unlimited play of connections which this introduces into the conventional codes of political economy (*Ibid.*: 75–6).

So there we have it, Baudrillard's postmodernist heresy: the collapse of class struggle, the labour theory of value, modes of production and historical materialism into a play of spectres which offers no hope of redemption. Yet for Baudrillard the very extremity of the transformations which are precipitated by the hyperreal is what revitalizes the primitive configurations of symbolic exchange; for as the system of simulation goes on perfecting its virtual identity, so it becomes increasingly vulnerable to the intrusion of radical acts which arise from its own weightlessness. These acts, according to Baudrillard, spring from the sense of mortality which haunts every system that 'fails to inscribe its own death'; for in so far as the hyperreal refers only to its own signifying economy, the experience of mortality is always co-present with the escalatory play through which the system expands itself (Baudrillard, 2004: 4). This, of course, is close to the account of the death instinct which Freud develops in *Beyond the Pleasure Principle*. His argument is that the death drive (Thanatos) arises out of the very symbolic order which binds the individual to society: for in so far as the world is governed by a reality principle in which reason has assumed command over the primary instincts of the human organism, man's desire for life, peace and security is always haunted by his yearning to destroy both himself and the means of his repression. For Baudrillard however Freud's account of the relationship between social cathexis (Eros) and the death drive (Thanatos) ends up as a 'long detour to death'; for the latter is downgraded to the level of the unconscious motivation which underlies man's striving after peace and productivity. Ultimately Freud's transformation of death into the underlying pulsion of Eros deprives it of the disturbing 'counter-finality' which it introduces into the procession of simulacra (*Ibid.*: 152–4).

So, if the transformative gestures of Marxism and psychoanalysis remain tied to the symbolic economy of value, on what basis is it possible to disrupt the escalatory system of the hyperreal? For Baudrillard the contradictions of the commodity form (tendency of the rate of profit to fall, overproduction, under-consumption, etc.) have determined a fundamental change in the symbolic order of capital; the structural intercourse between producers, consumers and commodities is opened up to an aesthetic play of connections through which capital is able constantly to traverse and transform the lifeworld.[2] What this amounts to is the hyperrealization of identity; for in so far as the system of simulacra functions to eliminate every trace of otherness/resistance from itself, it moves ever closer to the weightlessness of the monad, the I=I. This movement is a fatal one; for its trajectory precipitates the sense of impending collapse which clings to a system which has no immunity to what is not generated from its own resources. The experience of death which is proper to the human individual therefore is not simply the negation of life; rather it is that which issues in the forms of symbolic exchange (the gift, the sacred, the erotic, the aesthetic) which exceed the moribund repetitions into which the system of simulacra has fallen. Thus in his exposition of death as it appears in Bataille's *Eroticism*, Baudrillard remarks that:

> Death as excess, always already there, proves that life is only defective when life has taken it hostage, that life only exists in bursts and in exchanges with death, if it is not condemned to the discontinuity of value and therefore to absolute deficit. (Baudrillard, 2004: 155)

For Bataille, in other words, sex and death exist in a constant prodigal exchange of energies; their relationship is one of absolute, excessive solicitation in which erotic desire snatches the lover/beloved away from the self-engendering unity of the hyperreal. Bataille's conception of death therefore is neither dialectical (Freud) nor productive (Deleuze, Lyotard); it is a 'counter-finality' which erupts from within every apparatus of control, reproduction and repetition (*Ibid.*: 156). So, where does this leave us politically? At the beginning of *Symbolic Exchange* Baudrillard claims that the 'phantom reference' of death is engendered more and more intensely by each higher level of simulation, and that consequently we live in an epoch in which 'theories and practices, themselves floating and indeterminate, can catch up with the hyperreal and strike it dead' (*Ibid.*: 3). What this means is that 'the political' has become a matter of precipitating those forms of symbolic exchange which challenge and exceed the dominance of the hyperreal. Baudrillard's 'utopian' version of the relationships which spring from the primitive experience of death therefore prefigure the fate politics which he outlines in his later writings, particularly *In The Shadow of the Silent Majorities* and *The Transparency of Evil*.

Much of Baudrillard's later work is concerned with registering the unforeseen effects that arise from the expansion of the hyperreal: effects such as the 'hyperconformity' of the masses to the simulacra which are used to solicit their compliance, the rise of terrorism as a strategy of radical disruption aimed against the simulation of the real, and the proliferation of 'extreme phenomena' (AIDS, cancer, drug addiction) which arise from the system's elimination of everything which fails to conform to its operational code. This concern with the relationship between the masses and the molar effects which traverse them under the conditions of third order simulation however is certainly not an attempt to re-designate a Marxist (or even a Deleuzian) politics of resistance. Thus when Baudrillard claims that 'the masses are stronger than the media' his intention is not to present them as a revolutionary subject, but rather as the internal limit that arises from the system of simulation itself (Baudrillard, 1983: 44). This structural designation of the masses is important. We have seen that for Baudrillard the media have reduced the real to a play of refracted appearances and ephemeral connections, and that it is consequently unreasonable to assume that the deliberative powers of 'the public' have survived the drift into the hyperreal. *In the Shadow of the Silent Majorities*, for example, refers to the relationship which has grown up between the masses and public health provision. What emerges from this relationship is not a reflexive aware-ness of the body as an object of care and responsibility, but rather as an insatiable demand for more treatment, more doctors and more drugs. The masses, in other words, respond to their medicalization with a kind of hyperconformity to the operational simulation of health. This, of course, does not reveal the action of a unified deliberative subject, and yet the fact that their resistance to public health programmes and healthy eating campaigns is produced as a 'reversion' of the system means that it cannot be completely erased from the expansion of the hyperreal (*Ibid.*: 46). If there is a political morality which is appropriate to the virtualization of the social therefore it consists in registering the escalatory logic of effects which arise from the system of simulation, and which are played out in the crises of postmodern capitalism. Indeed Baudrillard's discussion of 'The Prophylaxis of Virulence' in *The Transparency of Evil* goes so far as to risk invoking mass phenomena such as AIDS, cancer, computer viruses, and crack addiction as effects which have, for the moment, saved us from the total collapse of the real (Baudrillard, 1995a: 67).

This raises a number of important issues. First there is the question of the fate of symbolic exchange in Baudrillard's later writing; for given that his concept of 'fourth order simulation'[3] assumes total control over the reproduction of the real, it would seem to have foreclosed upon the utopian possibilities of unconditional donation, erotic discharge and sacred devotion which are presented in *Symbolic Exchange*. Thus 'the political', in so far as it is admitted into the realm of the hyperreal at all, is reduced to a play of constantly mutating simulacra which can sustain no universal standards of communication or performativity. For example, in the first chapter of *The Transparency of Evil*, 'After the Orgy', Baudrillard remarks that:

> The orgy in question was the moment when modernity exploded upon us, the moment of liberation in every sphere ... Now everything has been liberated ... all we can do is simulate liberation. We may pretend to carry on in the same direction, accelerating, but we are accelerating in a void, because all the goals of liberation are behind us, and because what haunts and obsesses us is being ahead of all the results – the very availability of all the signs, all the forms, all the desires we had been pursuing. (Baudrillard, 1995a: 3–4)

The sexual, political, economic, aesthetic and psychological liberations which marked the progress of Enlightenment right up to the end of the 1960s, in other words, has been succeeded by a regime of total simulation. Every value which has earned the right to be included in the realm of the political (women's rights, gay rights, racial equality, animal rights, etc.) has been subjected to the logic of reversibility; the value of women's rights, for example, may for a moment appear as the defining characteristic of a progressive and productive society, and the next as entirely subservient to the demands of economic expansion or the rights of men to express their 'natural' masculinity. Nothing, in other words, retains its identity: patriarchy becomes feminized, capitalism becomes socialized, racism becomes humanized and the whole system of simulation goes on circling around the lost values of modernity. In the end therefore all we are left with is the aleatory play of effects which traverse the masses, effects such as the 'viral racism' which clings to the constant displacement of difference into its opposite (*Ibid.*: 130).

This is the irreproachable logic of simulation. For if it is the case that the catastrophic occurrence of fourth order simulation has reduced the social to a play of reversible signs, and if this 'ecstasy of communication' is the form through which capital has been able to circumvent the negative teleology of falling rates of profit and the misappropriation of use value, then it is clear that Baudrillard's recourse to a kind of floating interrogation of the hyperreal is the only alternative (Baudrillard, 1993: 125). The question which arises here, of course, concerns the status of Baudrillard's theory; that is, the degree to which his account of the communicative reduction of the real, the transitivity/reversibility of difference, and the escalatory logic of simulation *is* the logic of postmodern capitalism, and also the degree to which his account of theory as *agent provocateur* has determined its ethical and political limits. Jameson's *Postmodernism*, as we have seen, attempted to marry a Baudrillardian account of culture to Adorno's theory of negative dialectics. His treatment of the effects of new media technologies picks out a relationship between the global organization of capitalism and its need to manage the conflicts which arise from its geopolitical interventions. The air of unintentional parody which Baudrillard takes to be the sign of the hyperreal, in other words, is treated by Jameson as the 'reflex' of global capitalism; it is the ideological form which is appropriate to the geopolitical expansion of the commodity law of value. Yet it strikes me that this attribution of functionality to a culture which has been theorized as an aleatory play of effects and solicitations is untenable, and that Harvey's claim that Jameson's critique of culture becomes 'fused' with Baudrillard's account of simulation is substantively correct (Harvey, 1999: 351–2). What this means, in other words, is that if one wishes to be a critical Marxist in the economistic sense of Harvey's *The Condition of Postmodernity*, one should stay well away from the temptations of the simulacrum; for having made the Faustian bargain with Baudrillard, there is no way back to the dialectical securities of base and superstructure, class and ideology, man and nature. If, on the other hand, one wishes to retain a certain 'spirit' of Marxism which is solicited by the effects of new media technologies *but without being consumed by them*, it may perhaps be necessary to drop the recursive logic of negative dialectics altogether. This is the approach which emerges from Derrida's idea of deconstruction – and so I want to conclude this section by looking at the politics of difference which he formulates in *Spectres of Marx*.

5
Ideology and Difference

There is, as I have said, an irreproachable logic to Baudrillard's thought: for if it is the case that the transition from third to fourth order simulation is marked by the erasure of the ostensive power of the sign, and if it is that loss which opens the regime of capital up to the exorbitant forms of production, consumption and self-identification which characterize the hyperreal, then Baudrillard's later writing provides a comprehensive account of the complicity between capitalism, the media and postmodern culture. Thus, if we are prepared to accompany Baudrillard to the logical conclusion of his thesis, we are left with the endless multiplication of simulacra, none of which have any value beyond their solicitation of particular, contingent effects within the resistive body of the masses. Ultimately the only political response to the loss of the real which is not itself a simulation, consists in registering the 'return of the repressed' which afflicts every system of undifferentiated identity; that is, the registration of the extreme phenomena which reveal the irrecuperable presence of death within the weightlessness of the hyperreal. The question which arises here, of course, is whether the hermetic system which Baudrillard describes has actually succeeded in evacuating 'the real' from the social relationships we inhabit. The answer to this question, I will argue, is not the simple negative which emanates from conventional Marxist and structuralist thought. Rather the problematic which is posed in Baudrillard's later writing is best understood as a kind of limit case; that is, as the most extreme possible statement of the virtualizing effects which have arisen from the media-technological organization of social relations. What I want to look at in this section therefore is Derrida's account of the ethico-political demand which arises from the performance of simulation; for it is in the effects of silencing, erasure and death which play around the multiplication of difference that he seeks to locate the 'spirit' of Marxism (Derrida, 1994: xxii–xx).

I want to begin by specifying the significance of Derrida's distinction between 'restricted' and 'general' economy, for it is this distinction which initiates the possibility of an ethical relationship which exceeds the recuperative dialectics of class solidarity. The encounter between Hegel and Bataille which Derrida examines in his essay 'From Restricted to General Economy: A Hegelianism Without Reserve', is one which seeks to open Hegel's philosophy to the originary condition of its possibility. This origin appears in the *Phenomenology of Spirit* as the life or death struggle through which self-consciousness emerges from its subjugation to nature. In order for this transformation to take place, it is necessary for both combatants to survive; for if one or both are killed, the possibility of 'consciousness' finding the confirmation in the other which marks the transition to 'self-consciousness', is negated. Thus the two distinct forms of being which institute the historical drama of signification – the Master and the Slave – are established through the moment of capitulation in which the latter accepts enslavement in return for his life (Hegel, 1967a: 228–40). Bataille's interest in this moment of instigation is significant because it raises the question of the possibility of recuperating the 'occurrence' of historical events (their heterogeneity, immediacy and uniqueness) through the timeless categories of absolute knowledge. He argues that Hegel's brief encounter with the unthinkable contingency which is put into play by the life or death struggle, immediately discounts the moment of absolute risk which founds the recuperative economy of signification. History as the unfolding of spirit, in other words, is instituted by a gamble; a gamble in which Hegel has bet on the sublation of mortal desire (its excessiveness, its *jouissance*) under the forms of recognition in which the integrity of ethical life, or *Sittlichkeit*, is recuperated (Derrida, 1990: 260). What is important here is Bataille's insistence that what Hegel does in the Master-Slave dialectic is to reveal, and then immediately rescind, the interruptive significance of death for the restricted economy of philosophical discourse. The Hegelian logos, in other words, is haunted in advance by the excessive performativity which it is possible for any mortal being to exercise in relation to its own death (*Ibid.*: 261). The concepts of sovereignty, non-meaning and general economy therefore are placed close together in Derrida's exposition of Bataille's *Hegel, la mort*: for it is through the pure expenditure of the mortal being (in art, poetry, eroticism) that it is sometimes possible to disrupt the 'immense enveloping resources' of the Hegelian system.

In the *Phenomenology of Spirit*, productive negation (*Aufhebung*) works through what Bataille calls the 'logic of servility': the progress of self-consciousness takes place through a teleological movement which rends the historical forms of ethical life, but only in so far as what is destroyed is conserved in higher, more self-consciously universal, expressions of spirit. Everyday consciousness, in other words, is always ready to be taken up in the logic of signification; its experience is always prepared for the conserving destruction of the *Aufhebung* and the recuperation of absolute knowledge. Thus to take on Hegel on his own ground is always to lose; for the power of dialectical sublation (the gathering of the antithesis into the synthetic order of the system) operates in every argument that seeks to reconfigure his dialectics of recognition and ethical life. What Bataille attempts however is to bring the unpredictable excess of mortality into the very centre of the Hegelian logos. Sovereignty, as he conceives it, expends itself 'without reserve'; its events occur as moments of spontaneity which immediately withdraw from the system of recuperable meanings (Derrida, 1990b: 265). The relationship between the general economy of mortal desire and the restricted economy of absolute knowledge therefore is one in which the received meanings of the logos are constantly at risk from the excessiveness which defines 'being towards death'. And so the 'sovereign' forms of writing to which Bataille refers have no meaning beyond their immediate occurrence; their performativity is simply the transmission of unforeseeable effects which disrupt the movement of spirit towards its self-realization (*Ibid.*: 273–5).

What Derrida takes from Bataille's account of the events of mortal excess which make the Hegelian system waver, is the need to subject every form of restricted economy to an analysis of the conditions under which it determines its own necessity. In Bataille's thought the irrecuperable excess which disrupts the order of the logos is the sovereign relationship of mortal beings to their own death. For the performativity through which the recuperation of meaning is made possible (the pure expenditure of the life or death struggle), is also that which imports a non-dialectical contingency (what Derrida names *différance*) into the very heart of the Hegelian system. This reading of Bataille's *Hegel la mort* is, of course, very close to the account of *Eroticism* which is presented in *Symbolic Exchange*: both Derrida and Baudrillard focus on the excessive, 'counter-teleological' power which death imports into the restricted economy of signification. There is however a crucial difference between their respective readings. For Baudrillard the notion of mortality which emerges from Bataille is expressed in forms of symbolic exchange – the gift, the sacred, the erotic, the aesthetic – which both precede and exceed the recuperative powers of meaning. Death, in other words, provokes a kind of utopian primitivism within the signifying body of modernity; a primitivism which, as we have seen, issues in the multiplication of fatal strategies against the disordered unity of the hyperreal. For Derrida, on the other hand, it is the relationship between death and inscription which is the most important aspect of Bataille's thought; the 'minor writing' which is provoked by the experience of morality disseminates accidental effects of poiesis, eroticism, love and donation across the established relationships of objective morality (*Sittlichkeit*), and thereby raises ethical questions about the relationship between difference, authority and the law. Derrida's reading of Bataille, in other words, rejects the idea of death as an experience through which human beings are put into contact with an absolute past which precedes the order of representation; rather he conceives the effects of mortality as an irreducible part of the symbolic/metaphysical order of difference, and of the possibility of remaining open to the unforeseen demands (of the other/others) which arise from within that order. Ultimately therefore the difference between Derrida and Baudrillard is marked by the latter's insistence that death and simulation converge through the progressive erasure of being from the economy of the sign. For Derrida, as we will seen in moment, such an erasure is impossible; for even the most perfect ('fourth order') simulacra are contaminated with the ontological questions of belonging, community and identity which are the very condition of ethics and politics.[1]

Spectres of Marx is above all a critique of Marx's critique of ideology – and yet we should recognize that in subjecting the tortuous passages of *The German Ideology* to the strictures of deconstructive analysis, Derrida is also questioning the whole dialectical apparatus of historical materialism. The focus of his investigation is Marx and Engel's critique of the now almost forgotten figure of Max Stirner, whose book *The Ego and Its Own* had attempted to show that the path to human salvation consisted in rejecting every ideological ghost which threatened the integrity of the sacred ego. Thus, for Stirner, Feurbach's rejection of Hegel's philosophy on the grounds that it transformed human attributes (such as love and productive activity) into attributes of spirit, had not managed to escape the theological implications of absolute idealism.[2] In the end Feurbach's determination to ground the 'spiritual' characteristics of humanity in the material existence of human beings, does no more than re-establish the power of abstract ideas (humanity, community, etc.) over the unique human ego. Ultimately, therefore, Stirner's critique of Feurbach demands a change in the *attitude* of the ego towards the abstractions which had come to dominate it; for once it completes the circle of its own subjective freedom, it has passed beyond the metaphysical damage which is inflicted by the reified authority of spirit(s). All this, of course, is of largely academic interest – for Marx and Engel's savage lampoon of 'Saint Max' certainly destroyed any brief credibility which *The Ego and Its Own* may have enjoyed. Derrida however picks up on something obsessive in their attempts to exorcise the ghost of Stirner; for even though his attempts to reduce the dynamics of history to the struggles of the monadic ego are patently absurd, the fact that they solicited such a voluminous response seems to indicate that the 'ghosting' of the categories of historical materialism (economic base, generic man, organic labour) is something which haunts Marx and Engels's account of ideology from the very beginning (Derrida, 1994: 106).

For Derrida the logic of Marx's critique of ideology is one of exorcism, of summoning the ghosts of the old regime to appear before the tribunal of scientific socialism and to await the final judgement of history. Thus the opening lines of *The Communist Manifesto*, '[a] spectre is haunting Europe – the spectre of communism', designate a universal class whose experience of the antagonisms of capital has become increasingly independent of the powers of ideological representation. Consequently the spectres of the old regime – religious piety, patriotism, monarchism, militarism, racism – are mobilized against the impending transformation of wage labour into the politically self-conscious body of the proletariat (Marx, 1998: 2). What the *Manifesto* demands therefore is an end to the repetitive power of spectres; for the fact that the material world, with all its variegations of suffering, has always been enchanted by ruling ideas, is a testament to the power of ideology to inhabit any exploitative regime. *The Eighteenth Brumaire of Louis Bonaparte* makes this demand even more forcefully; for Marx claims that 'the tradition of all dead generations weighs like a nightmare on the brain of the living', and that the only way to escape this repetition is through the revolutionary transcendence of private property relations (Marx, 1977c: 300). The 'spirit' of the revolution therefore is solicited by the gathering of old reactionary spectres around the dying regime of private appropriation; a gathering which, for Marx, promised the final vanquishing of ghosts from the realm of human society. According to Derrida however the task of distinguishing between the 'spirit' of the revolution and the 'spectres' which belong to the pre-revolutionary past is 'difficult and risky beyond any possible mastery'; for the unquiet ghosts that arise from every 'living present' are necessary to the ethical demand which is proper to the spirit of Marxism. Inheriting the revolutionary promise, in other words, is always an obligation to the dead, who are summoned as nameless ghosts to the violence of the day (Derrida, 1994: 107–8).

This 'hauntological' reading of Marx has some controversial consequences. First, the entire political apparatus of historical materialism is transformed; for if the conflictual gathering of spectres – ultra-nationalism, religious fundamentalism, state socialism, etc. – is taken to be *constitutive* of every living present, then the ethical demand of Marxism cannot be mapped directly onto the evolving contradictions of the mode of production. The economy of signs through which capital maintains itself as a hegemonic system, in other words, operates through what Derrida calls the 'law of anachrony'; for every appeal to the value of religious obedience, the spirit of the nation, or the brotherhood of productive humanity is contaminated by the history of violence in which it is always already embroiled. The revolutionary promise of Marxism therefore is a demand for radical transformation; it inhabits the present as a ghost which arises from the past (the violence inscribed in every assertion of ontological or theological necessity) and which is responsible to the undetermined possibility of the future ('democracy to come'):

> By all logic one ought to recognize it [the spirit of the revolution] by nothing more than the excess of its untimely dis-identification, therefore by nothing that is. By nothing that is present and identifiable. (Derrida, 1994: 115)

Thus the political praxis which is demanded by this revolutionary spirit is infinitely contemporary, for it arises from the media-techno-scientific transformations through which capital has overcome the dialectical limits of its expansion. Now as we have seen, Baudrillard contends that this 'overcoming' is possible only through the erasure of the real from the economy of signification, and that consequently the 'politics' of hyperlogical capitalism has collapsed into an obsessive exchange of simulacra which seek to designate the reality of freedom, truth and equality. For Derrida, however, the informatic/cybernetic transformation of capitalism cannot swallow up the ontological questions to which it gives rise; in fact he argues that the processes of virtualization through which capital continues to expand make these questions increasingly urgent. For example, the reduction of the body to a genetic code, or to a cybernetic appendage, or to bits of forensic information, determines a cluster of exploitative effects which recall the transformative demand of Marxism. The politics of 'real', in other words, always re-emerges through the 'bloodless' violence of simulation.

So, what kind of politics does Derrida's 'spectral' Marxism determine? Well, for most orthodox Marxists his attempt to open up the dialectical apparatus of historical materialism to the questions that arise from the media-techno-scientific organization of capital, is done at the cost of relinquishing the political significance of class, the very thing which makes Marxism what it is. Terry Eagleton,[3] Alex Callinicos,[4] and Aijaz Ahmad,[5] to name only three of a large constituency, argue that the possibility of overthrowing the liberal capitalist hegemony depends on the compositional power of class struggle. And so if the Marxist International is to have any political significance, it must work to focus the disparate struggles of the global working class; it must seek to organize the 'real' commonalities of experience that underlie the racial, religious, cultural and gender differences which fracture its revolutionary potential. The International as Derrida conceives it therefore has no substance; it has degenerated into an ideology of abstract difference which deliberately multiplies the figures (*'différance'*, 'alterity', 'the other', 'the feminine') through which the negative power of capital is dispersed. Indeed both Ahmad and Eagleton complain that Derrida's stripping away of the class content of the International leaves him with nothing more to do than solicit deconstructive critiques of state authority, national cultures, and international law (Ahmad in Sprinker, 1999: 104–5; Eagleton in Sprinker, 1999: 85). Thus Derrida's idea of revolutionary community is seen as having no concrete relationship with the experience of the masses; it exists merely as an ideological phantasm whose demands are withdrawn from the class dynamics of the mode of production (Callinicos, 1996: 40).

These remarks however miss the point of Derrida's reconfiguration of Marxist politics – which explicitly *is not* to defend the dialectical apparatus of class politics. As we have seen his account of the political is closely related to the concepts of *différance* and alterity through which he expounds the condition of 'living in' the symbolic order of the social. So if we begin from the position that the originary act which constitutes that order also determines a 'promise' that gives us over to the question of its legislative power, then the possibility of the political must be referred to a 'faith' (in democracy to come) which cannot be erased from the narrative structures of authority (Derrida, 1989: 129–30). Politics, in other words, begins with the disruptive events which mark the (necessary) presence of the other within the system of symbolic identity; it is that which responds to the traces of difference upon which the prosecution of identity is founded. So, for example, the concept of femininity which accompanies Derrida's exposition of the symbolic order of reason (the logos) is not a dialectical concept which is simply opposed to the masculine/capitalist order of patriarchy. Rather the feminine, as Derrida conceives it, is that which haunts the supposedly neutral order of democracy in advance; for in so far as the rights, duties and obligations which emerge in civil society are always already marked with the imprimatur of the masculine, the feminine is that which arises as a possibility (of disruption, invention, community) which cannot be 'signed up' to the established structures of democratic recognition (Bennington and Derrida, 1993: 218). Sexual difference, in other words, exceeds both the dialectics of a radical feminism which demands the complete separation of 'woman' from the phallocentric order, and of a Marxist feminism which assumes the total complicity of patriarchy and capitalism (*Ibid.*: 225). Thus the feminine should be thought of as an alterity/otherness which haunts the phallocentric order of the logos 'in advance'; it is the unspecifiable 'x' whose provocations (to art, literature, poetry, performance, etc.) constantly trouble the categories of domination/mastery which have informed the deployment of capital, technology and power.[6]

So where does this leave us in respect of the 'spirit' of Marxism which Derrida has invoked? As we have seen the orthodox criticisms of *Spectres of Marx* have concentrated on what they consider to be the indeterminacy of Derrida's idea of the New International: they have maintained that deconstruction provokes an endless multiplication of the 'literatures' of racial, sexual and cultural difference, none of which is capable of communicating politically with any of the others. Thus Derrida's idea of a revolutionary community whose 'praxis' is radically singularized and whose 'being' is 'without status, without title, and without name' (Derrida, 1994: 85), is conceived as a complete abandonment of the principles of Marxism and international socialism. This may be so, but we still need to examine the logic of Derrida's engagement with Marx and to specify the political provocation which he discerns in this 'abandonment'. For Derrida Marx's account of the revolutionary transcendence of capital relies upon a compositional logic which achieves its most determinate expression in the Enlightenment project. Thus Marx's argument that under the conditions of primitive communism a break is made from the 'natural' reproduction of pre-hominids to the 'social' cooperation of human beings, designates the original movement of humanity into the symbolic order of the law. This transition is important because it marks the point at which 'man' (as self-creative labour) is gathered into the reproductive logic of the mode of production; his being and activity are conceived in terms of their participation in the general tendencies which animate each historical epoch. The apparatus of dialectical materialism therefore re-configures the identity between the laws of nature and the laws of history which is pursued by Enlightenment philosophy; for in seeking to restore the immanent unity of primitive communism to the mode of production, Marxism repeats the (Rousseauist) aporia of the origin: the fact that the primitive beginning can never be primitive enough, and that its violence/harmony always reflects a certain defection of the present social order. This then is the logic which provokes Derrida's questioning of Marxist politics; for if it is the case that the concept of socialized production is *enacted* by Marxism from within its own restricted economy, then the rationality of class antagonism will always already have gathered the occurrence of difference, the 'is it happening' of racial and sexual alterities, into the totalizing logic of historical necessity (Derrida, 1994: 30–1).

This brings me back to Walter Benjamin's idea of post-auratic art and the revolutionary potential which it configures. In the essay on surrealism published in *One Way Street* he maintained that the technological body of society, with its new lines of communication, architectural spaces and intensified work practices, demands an art which is able to represent the constant transformation which has become the *modus vivendi* of the urban proletariat. Such an art is not embedded in the auratic tradition; for although the cubist, surrealist and dadaist movements which arose at the beginning of the twentieth century still worked within the static media of painting and sculpture, their strange configurations of the urban landscape sought to reflect the shock and transience which characterized life in the modern city (Benjamin, 1997a: 239). Benjamin, as we have seen, develops this notion of a post-auratic art more fully in 'The Work of Art in the Age of Mechanical Reproduction', and it is here that he examines the power of the moving image to transfigure the everyday experience of domination, servitude, adaptation and autonomy. However he does not assert that film is the eschatological counterpart of a new revolutionary politics: the epilogue to 'The Work of Art' makes it clear that the moving image is just as capable of reactionary configurations of racism and nationalism as it is of revolutionary gestures towards new forms of freedom and democracy (Benjamin, 1992: 234–5). This messianic wavering of the image between ideological complicity and revolutionary imagination is significant because it raises the question how, or indeed whether, technologically reproducible culture is able to reflect upon itself. Adorno's correspondence with Benjamin makes his position clear: the culture industry has effected an all but total reification of culture which excludes the possibility of its reflecting/reproducing anything but mass conformity (Adorno *et al.*, 1977: 110–33). Derrida, however, conceives Benjamin's configuration of the relationship between time, technology and the aesthetic as expressing something of the contingency which haunts every 'living present': for the fact that the image can never complete the conformity it represents gestures towards a politics of the unforeseen in which the inscription of 'class', 'state', 'economy' and 'power' always offers the chance of unexpected transformations (Derrida in Sprinker, 1999: 59–65).[7] I will return to this 'messianic' conception of the political in the concluding section.

To conclude then, the culture industry thesis is fundamentally important to the idea of a post-modern Marxism because it raises the question of how far the technologically reproducible image is capable of determining mass conformity. This question becomes increasingly urgent as new media technologies (virtual reality, the internet, satellite TV) penetrate those spheres of the lifeworld which have traditionally been regarded as off-limits to the public gaze: for if it is the case, as Baudrillard claims, that every facet of the social has collapsed into the simulacra through which it is represented, then what is the future of political agency in the time of the global network society? Before attempting to answer this question however I need to examine its preconditions; that is, the conjunction of mathematical, scientific and technological knowledge through which capitalism progressed from the simple coordination of craft manufacture towards the large-scale industrial phase which Marx analysed in *Capital*. For it is only in so far as the dynamics of technocratic control which are implicit in Marx's analysis of the mode of production have been properly theorized, that it is possible to understand the ways in which capital has become a 'prosthetic' force which is able to integrate the biological constitution of human beings into the complexity of the global economy.

Part II

Capitalism and Technology

This section is concerned with the relationship between capitalism and technology. Chapter six examines Marx's account of the connection between technological innovation and the emergence of what he calls 'large-scale industrial' manufacture. Of particular importance here is the long exposition of the impact of machinery on the turnover of capital which Marx presents in part four of *Capital* Volume One ('The Production of Relative Surplus Value'), and his account of the relationship between over-investment in technological means of production and the general tendency of the rate of profit to fall. For as the reproduction of surplus value comes to depend upon the increased speed of production which is offered by the use of new machinery, so the costs incurred in remaining competitive become too high for more and more commercial enterprises. This analysis, as we will see, presupposes a philosophical anthropology in which the essence of humanity is articulated in its productive relations with the 'inorganic body' of nature; and so the evolution of capitalism is simultaneously determined by the subsumption of human labour under an increasingly repetitive regime of productive activity, and by the fact that the creation of commodities for exchange always leads to crises of under-consumption, overproduction and unemployment. Chapter 7 looks at Martin Heidegger's claim that in order to understand the ethical and philosophical consequences of the technocratic organization of society, it must be recognized that this organization arises from an instrumental orientation towards the world which both precedes and exceeds the dynamics of need and economic utility. This reconfiguration of the 'question concerning technology' is important because it opens up a cluster of issues (about the prosthetic transformation of humanity, the commodification of life, and the utilization of nature) which were taken up by the Frankfurt School, particularly in the theory of technocratic control presented by Herbert Marcuse in *One Dimensional Man*.

Chapter 9 looks at the concept of 'machinic desire' as it is set out by Gilles Deleuze and Felix Guattari in *Capitalism and Schizophrenia* and Michael Hardt and Antonio Negri in *Empire*. The aim of this chapter is to examine the relationship between the prosthetic supplementation of humanity which is brought about by techno-scientific capitalism and the unpredictable flows of desire which arise from this radical transformation of the conditions of life. Both Deleuze and Guattari and Hardt and Negri maintain that it is possible to reconfigure Marxist politics around the fugitive events of 'becoming other' that arise from the technocratic order of capital; however their respective accounts of this reconfiguration lead down radically different paths both of which I will examine. Finally, in Chapter 9, I will look at Jacques Derrida and Bernard Stiegler's remarks on the concept of technological supplementation, or 'technicity'. My specific concern here is to articulate the ethical position which differentiates Derrida's account of technology from the Deleuzian stance taken by Stiegler, and to show how this informs his understanding of the revolutionary demand which is bequeathed in Marx's writing.

6
Machines and Socialized Production

In order to understand Marx's account of the relationship between capitalism and technology we need first to examine what he called 'The General Formula of Capital' (Marx, 1990: 247–57). According to Marx's analysis what is distinctive about capitalism is the fact that commodities are produced not for the purpose of consumption but rather for the purpose of converting them into money. The capitalist, in other words, produces commodities with the sole intention of selling them on the open market for more money than he invested in their manufacture. This mode of distribution, or the money–commodity–money (M–C–M) relation, arises from what Marx refers to as the 'simple circulation of commodities'; for once money has emerged as a universal equivalent capable of securing any of the means of subsistence, it then becomes possible for capital to reproduce itself in the form of profit (*Ibid.*: 247–8). For Marx therefore the M–C–M relation expresses the limitless capacity of capital to expand itself through the 'reflux' of monetary expenditure into profit via the production of exchange value. Implicit in this relation is the demand to decrease the amount of time taken to transform raw materials into commodities which can be sold on the open market. Any given productive enterprise, in other words, is placed under the necessity to make its operations as efficient as possible; for if its manufacture of commodities is slower than the average rate established in its particular branch of the market, it will accrue insufficient surplus value to remain competitive. It is this hard economic necessity which Marx identifies as the driving force behind the introduction of machine technology into the productive process. And so we will need briefly to examine his account of the impact of machines on the dynamics of capital accumulation and on the worker's experience of his productive activity.

The most comprehensive exposition of the relationship between capitalism and technology is given in part four of *Capital* Volume One, 'The Production of Relative Surplus Value'. According to Marx it is the productive power worker, and this alone, which adds value to commodities; and so the expansion of capital which is described in the M–C–M relation can only take place through the employment of 'organic labour' in the process of production. This organic labour however is not an abstract category; it belongs to real human beings whose physical constitution places certain limits on the expansion of production. One cannot, for example, demand that workers labour for more than twelve hours a day without ruining their physical and mental abilities. And so every capitalist is faced with the problem of how to *reduce* the proportion of the working day during which organic labour works for itself (i.e. during which the value created returns to the worker in the form of wages), and thereby *increase* the time available for extraction of surplus value from the workforce. The introduction of machinery into the productive process therefore is implicit in the M–C–M relation; for the integration of organic labour into automated systems radically decreases the time it takes to pay for itself and thereby releases a greater proportion of the day for the creation of surplus value (*Ibid.*: 435). This progressive devaluation of labour power is reinforced by the general cheapening of commodities which results from mechanized production; for as the cost of the means of subsistence is lowered, so the price of maintaining the physical existence of the worker also goes down (*Ibid.*: 437).

The concept of relative surplus value therefore explains how capital is still able to accumulate even as it reduces the exchange value of commodities. The reduction in the value of labour power constantly moves back the point in the working day at which the worker starts to produce surplus value for the capitalist (*Ibid.*: 430). According to Marx, however, this progressive devaluation of labour reveals an essential fact about large-scale industrial capitalism: that the use of automatic systems to increase the rate at which surplus value is created fundamentally changes the conditions under which commodities can be transformed into money. The fact is that machines can only increase the raw number of things created, an increase which drives down the social value of commodities and leaves each individual capitalist with the problem of having to sell more and more products at lower and lower prices. This, as we will see in a moment, determines the crises of over-production, under-consumption and unemployment which Marx describes in the second and third volumes of *Capital*. Before I come to these 'objective tendencies' however I want to look at what Marx conceives as their origin, that is, the progressive increase in the ratio of 'fixed' to 'organic' capital deployed in the production of commodities.

Marx begins his exposition of relative surplus value with an historical account of the transformation of the technological foundation of production. He argues that the power of cooperation is not fully realized until the emergence of industrial capitalism; for the increase in social productivity which is achieved through the concentration of labour and the means of production depends on the development of the competitive necessity which is implicit in M–C–M relation. Thus the handicraft production which is characteristic of feudal-agrarian societies is transformed by the emergence of a mercantile capitalism which is based on the exchange-value of commodities. As a result of this transformation the guild associations which kept the secrets of the various trades are destroyed by the determination to concentrate the means of labour in one place, and to break up the process of production into repetitive tasks performed by wage labourers. This transformation of the division of labour marks the point at which capital becomes the determining factor in the process of production (*Ibid.*: 453). For as the knowledge and skill of the worker is appropriated by the regime of workshop manufacturing, so the 'means of labour' (fixed capital in the form of tools, machines and buildings) comes to determine the exchange-value of commodities, the intensity of competition, and the general rate of profit (*Ibid.*: 490–1).

In the *Grundrisse* Marx argued that the machine is the realization of fixed capital; that it transforms the means of labour from tools which have a specific relation to the autonomous activity of the worker, into an 'objective power' which determines the process and temporality of production (Marx, 1993: 692). It is not until the publication of *Capital* Volume One however that he gives a historical account of how this objective power of fixed capital is constituted. Let me summarize. Manufacture, despite its revolutionary impact on the division of labour, is still based upon the 'folk knowledge' of handicrafts. However the 'organic cooperation' of labour which develops under the regime of workshop production provides the basis for the introduction of machine technology. For as the tasks performed by wage labourers become more and more simplified, so the way is opened for the introduction of machines which replicate their productive actions (Marx, 1990: 495). These machines (the loom, for example) make their first appearance under handicraft production, but it is not until mathematical and scientific principles are applied to the productive regime of the workshop that they emerge as a real productive force. The motive power for this type of production is initially supplied by a mixture of sources: wind, water, draft animals, or the worker himself. These sources however belong to a smaller scale and slower temporality of production than the one which is implicit in the technological basis of manufacture. And so it is through the combined force of economic and technological necessity that they are replaced by the thermodynamic technologies which powered the industrial revolution – namely steam and caloric engines (*Ibid.*: 497).

The motive power of the steam engine is initially supplied to machines which function separately from one another. Eventually however its productive potential is realized in the development of machines which are designed to operate as part of an integrated system (*Ibid.*: 499). This progressive integration of thermodynamic power and productive machinery constitutes the technological basis of industrial capitalism; it is through the establishment of the factory as a 'vast automaton' which functions to increase the speed at which commodities are produced, that the turnover of capital is constantly expanded. The logic of this model is such that once it takes hold in one branch of industry, all of the others are forced to follow. The production of cloth, for example, cannot continue as a cottage industry once the manufacture of clothing has become mechanized. It must transform its productive techniques in order to supply the quantity of material which is required and to sustain a viable level of profitability. This revolution in the technological basis of production extends to the infrastructures which support the turnover of capital: roads, railways and ships have to be able to meet the demands of an economy which functions through the exchange of commodities across an expanding world market (*Ibid.*: 506).

So, how does this revolution in the technological basis of production affect the reproduction of surplus value? In order to answer this question we will need to look at the 'formal distinctions' between fixed and circulating capital which are set out in chapter eight of *Capital* Volume Two. Marx argues that the value of the means of labour (fixed capital in the form of machines, buildings and infrastructure) are determined by the average rate at which they are used up in the process of production. And so a machine which cost the capitalist £10,000 to purchase and which has a productive life of ten years, will repay his initial outlay at a rate of £1000 per annum. Once the value of the machine is realized in the commodities it has produced over ten years, the turnover of this particular fixed capital is complete and the machine can be replaced by a more efficient one (Marx, 1992: 243). Fixed capital therefore has a different 'shape' from the labour power and the ancillary means of production (raw materials, lighting, heating) which Marx refers to as circulating capital. The latter are purchased on the free market (the sphere of 'circulation'), immediately used up in the production of commodities, transformed into money, and then purchased again on the free market. Fixed capital, on the other hand, gives up its value to commodities only very slowly; and so as long as it retains some of its use value it has to remain part of the productive process (*Ibid.*: 246).

According to Marx the technological development of capitalism inevitably increases the amount of fixed capital which is deployed in M–C–M relation. For as the old handicraft industries are squeezed out of existence by the factory system, so expenditure on machinery which is designed to increase relative surplus value expresses a larger and larger proportion of productive capital. As we have seen the value of this fixed capital turns over much more slowly than the organic labour which is employed in any given branch of production. From the standpoint of the capitalist therefore it is essential that the machinery he has purchased remains part of his enterprise until it has produced enough commodities to cover his original outlay (Marx, 1990: 509). Given the competitive organization of the market however the longevity of machines constantly diminishes; for as the maintenance of profit comes to depend upon increasing the number of commodities that can be produced in a given period, so the ability to replace obsolescent machines becomes a determining factor in 'free market' competition. Those firms who are large enough to bear the cost of replacing their machines more often, in other words, will ultimately absorb the smaller ones who are unable to keep reinvesting in new technological means of production.

It is this material necessity which forces individual capitalists to introduce new methods of production; for although it is true that new technological means of labour increase relative surplus value, this increase always incurs the costs that are associated with the deployment of fixed capital (repairs, maintenance, servicing). The immediate advantage that a few entrepreneurs secure by adopting new productive technologies therefore is always short-lived; all those who *can* afford such technologies *will* adopt them, and the average rate of profit will be brought down by the resulting increase in productivity and the general cheapening of commodities. For Marx this intensification of competition is part of what he identifies in *Capital* Volume Three as 'The Law of the Tendential Fall in the Rate of Profit'. What is important here is that the underlying cause of the composition of industrial capital into larger and larger corporations is the increasing efficiency with which machines transform organic labour into commodities (Marx, 1991: 373–4). In the end however the use of technological innovation to prop up declining profitability serves only to intensify the crises which afflict the historical development of capitalism: for as the organic labour of the worker is made increasingly productive, so the general level of wages tends to fall, levels of unemployment to rise and the market to become flooded with commodities which the greater part of society cannot afford to buy (*Ibid.*: 375).[1]

In his account of 'The Historical Tendency of Capitalist Accumulation' Marx argues that mercantile capitalists, whose money undermined the old feudal regime, had to bring about a concentration of productive forces which would allow them to maximize the turnover of their capital (Marx, 1990: 928). This process of concentration, as we have seen, belongs to the very concept of the M–C–M relation; for it is only through the development of its technological basis that capital can continue to pass through the phases of investment, production and profit. This gathering of the means of production into the cooperative systems characteristic of large-scale industry however reveals the determining contradiction of capitalist accumulation. On the one hand the deployment of technologically integrated systems brings about an increase in productivity which could fulfil the basic needs of every human being (*Ibid.*: 929). Conceived in terms of the dynamics of capitalism however, this tendency towards the intensification of labour represents a progressive overburdening of the M–C–M relation with the costs of fixed capital. According to Marx the resolution of this contradiction is a matter of historical necessity. Once the profitability of large-scale industry comes to depend on the speed at which commodities are reproduced, so the private appropriation of surplus value (by capitalists and their stockholders) constantly channels organic labour into the overproduction of exchange-values which can never be redeemed on the open market. According to Marx's analysis therefore the overcoming of this crisis-ridden state is implicit in the processes through which capital develops; for as the technological basis of production brings 'the mass of the people' into cooperative association, so they are formed into the revolutionary force which will expropriate the means of production from private ownership (*Ibid.*: 930).

This brings me to the question of the relationship between capital, technology and the political composition of the working class. So far we have looked at Marx's account of the laws which govern the 'shape' of fixed and organic capital and at the ways in which these laws have determined technology as a force in the development of the mode of production. What Marx's account of the historical tendency of capitalism brings into focus however is an ethico-political demand which constantly returns to supplement the 'scientific' analyses he presents in *Capital*. His call for the 'mass of the people' to expropriate the owners of the means of production, for example, exceeds the register of strict historical necessity and addresses the collective will and desire of the working classes. The nature of this demand is important in the present context for two reasons: first it opens up a series of questions about Marx's concept of alienation (particularly the relationship between man's 'species being' and the technological means of labour); and second it raises issues concerning the revolutionary transcendence of capitalism (especially the social organization of production which is to follow the abolition of private property relations).

Marx's first and most extensive account of alienation is presented in the *Economic and Philosophical Manuscripts of 1844*. He begins by criticizing conventional 'bourgeois' political economy for failing to provide a historical account of the phenomena (money, private property, competition, wages, capital) which it seeks to analyse (Marx, 1977a: 66). Adam Smith, for example, argued in *The Wealth of Nations* that it is only insofar as the market reflects the dynamism of natural competition that the general prosperity of human society can continue to increase (Smith, 1950: 62–71). This way of proceeding however is blind to the historical effects of capitalism; for by insisting that competition among private owners is the natural counterpart of prosperity, bourgeois political economy connives at the 'contemporary fact' of expropriation which arises from private property relations (Marx, 1977a: 67). Marx therefore disregards the naturalistic arguments of the political economists and proceeds to examine the historical conditions under which labour is expropriated from the worker.

The speculative basis of Marx's account of alienation is an ethico-aesthetic idea of human nature, or 'species being', which accompanies his description of the ways in which the worker is estranged from the process, object and fellowship of his labour. According to Marx what differentiates the productive activity of human beings from that of animals is the fact that:

> An animal forms objects only in accordance with the standard and need of the species to which it belongs, whilst man knows how to produce in accordance with the standard of every species, and knows how to apply everywhere the inherent standard of the object. Man therefore also forms objects in accordance with the laws of beauty. (Marx, 1977a: 74)

Animals, in other words, are submerged in nature; even their most complex constructions merely express instinctual behaviour which is inscribed in the genetic code of the species. The productive activity of human beings, on the contrary, is not limited by any such genetic inscription; for while it is true that they are part of nature, the fact that they *self-consciously* reproduce their subsistence, means that their productive activity is promised to a higher goal: the perfectibility of nature. The freedom of humanity therefore is originally bound up with its dialectical relationship to the external world; for it is only in so far as human beings, as self-conscious creators, are able to re-make nature in accordance with the immanent laws of its beauty, that they can fulfil the promise of their species being.[2]

The immediate impact of capitalism however is the expropriation of nature from the mass of productive humanity and the transformation of their work into pure physical compulsion: what should be performed as a 'spontaneous free activity' is bound in servitude to the capitalist who pays just enough wages for the worker to sustain his or her physical existence (Marx, 1977a: 74). The concrete processes through which this expropriation is experienced are presented in the *Economic and Philosophical Manuscripts* as alienation from the object labour, alienation from the process of production, and alienation of 'man from man'. In the first of these Marx concentrates on the way in which the worker's labour serves only to impoverish his creative essence. For the more that is taken from him/her in the form of commodities the more the world of objects is constituted as an alien power opposed to his/her spontaneous creativity (*Ibid*.: 72). This is compounded by the fact that the process of production is reduced to actions which confine the universality of self-consciousness to mutilating repetition. The intellectual energy of the worker, in other words, is deprived of its proper relation to external nature, and so his physical existence is reduced to a bestial pursuit of the necessities of life (*Ibid*.). Finally Marx maintains that the worker's experience of estrangement in the process of production determines a more general condition of social and ethical displacement which he calls the alienation of man from man. For the fact that capital expands by monopolizing the means of production (and by making labour power into a commodity whose value depends upon the competition for jobs), means that social relations are dominated by a pernicious individualism which sets each man against every other (*Ibid*.: 75).

So, how is this ethico-aesthetic idea of the alienation related to Marx's account of the technological development of capitalism? In the *Grundrisse* (particularly the note on the 'Transposition of Powers of

Labour into Powers of Capital') he argues that the machine has transformed the means of labour from instruments which have a specific relation to handicraft production, into an 'objective power' which dictates the temporality of the labour process (Marx, 1993: 692). Marx, as we have seen, conceives this deployment of machinery as essential to the historical evolution of the mode of production; for in so far as it is true that machines can fulfil their potential for increasing relative surplus value only if they are run without cessation (or at least as close to this as constraints of cleaning and servicing will allow), the consequence for those who remain employed is that they are forced to perform ever more repetitive tasks for an ever larger portion of the working day (*Ibid.*: 822). Considered from the standpoint of the worker therefore the tendency to increase expenditure on machinery results in the 'real subsumption' of his creative essence under the objective power of capital (*Ibid.*: 694). Considered from a historical perspective however this tendency is *immanently social*; for even though the accelerated temporality of the labour process arises from the demands of private appropriation, its overall effect is constantly to reduce the time necessary for the production of use values. And so for Marx the evolution of capitalism is determined by a contradiction; on the one hand it increases the efficiency with which organic labour can produce the means of subsistence (and thereby determines the foundation of a social form of production in which labour would be freed from the yoke of physical necessity), while on the other it channels this intensified labour power into the production of superfluous commodities whose exchange value is constantly diminished (Marx, 1993: 824).

Marx expresses the contradictory determination of capital's pursuit of organic labour in two different registers. In the first of these his aim is to set out the different shapes which fixed and organic capital assume under large-scale industry and to map out the crises of over-production and under-consumption which are entailed in the technological intensification of labour power. This 'scientific' register however is interwoven with the ethico-aesthetic demand which we identified in the *Economic and Philosophical Manuscripts*, that is, the demand that the productive desire and intellect of self-conscious humanity should regain its right of access to external nature. The alienation of human beings from their productive essence therefore begins with the M–C–M relation; it is brought into existence through capital's first moment of self-valorization and made increasingly acute by its transformation of the technological means of labour. According to Marx the dialectics of historical necessity and human emancipation are intrinsically related; for while it is true that his theory of ideology discloses a powerful movement of displacement among the forms of religion and citizenship, the practical experience of alienation always haunts the illusory satisfactions of bourgeois society (Marx, 1977c: 48–52). The end of capitalism therefore is determined by its concentration of three contradictory effects: the over-representation of fixed capital in the M–C–M relation, the socialization of labour under automated systems, and the practical composition of the working class as a revolutionary subject (Marx, 1993: 831–3).

At the end of *Capital* Volume One Marx expresses this immanent tendency of capitalist accumulation as follows:

> The capitalist mode of appropriation ... produces capitalist private property. This is the first negation of individual private property as founded on the labour of its proprietor. But capitalist production begets, with the inexorability of a natural process, its own negation ... It does not re-establish private property, but it does indeed establish individual property on the basis of the achievements of the capitalist era: namely the cooperation and possession in common of the land and the means of production produced by labour itself. (Marx, 1990: 926)

The material relations of capitalism, in other words, determine a dialectical logic in which both the objective and subjective conditions of revolutionary transformation are gathered. However the nature of this revolutionary logic is not entirely clear. There are passages in the *Grundrisse* where Marx seems to maintain that the constitution of the proletariat as a revolutionary force depends upon its integration into the technological systems through which capitalism expands. The real subsumption of labour, in other words, gives rise to a fundamental change in the mode of production; for as the turnover of capital becomes increasingly dependent on the 'general intellect' of society, so the workforce becomes increasingly aware of its transformative power *vis-à-vis* the regime of private appropriation (Marx, 1993: 795). In *Capital* however Marx tends to theorize the relationship between revolutionary consciousness and the technological basis of production in terms of the cumulative estrangement of humanity's creative essence. As we have seen his account of relative surplus value in *Capital* Volume One describes the processes of practical alienation, egoistic individualism and material impoverishment which accompany the socialization of productive forces (Marx, 1990: 517–45). The end of capitalism, in other words, can only come about through the power of collective dehumanization which afflicts the whole of the working class.

This apparently minor inflection has turned out to be extremely important in the history of Marxist theories of technology. If we take the second line of argument (that industrial capitalism ruins the hominiz-ing spontaneity through which human beings transform themselves and the conditions of their existence) we can determine a genealogical line which leads to the Frankfurt School. In Marcuse's work, for example, the technological development of capitalism is presented as having subsumed all but the last vestiges of humanity under the functional demands of the industrial production. This of course raises serious questions about the relationship of revolutionary consciousness to the system of false needs and desires through which capital has appropriated the idea of socialized production. For if there is no longer any transcendent sense of alienation then what chance is there for a rad-ically transformative politics? As we saw the argument which Marx sketches in the *Grundrisse* claims that the socializing tendency of capital evolves through its constant transformation of the relationship between the technological means of labour and the general intellect of society. This line of argument is important because it forms the basis of a funda-mental reconceptualization of the relationship between politics, capital and technology. The work of Deleuze and Guattari and Hardt and Negri, for example, is concerned with the biological, psychical and libidinal transformations through which the masses are integrated into networks of global exchange. And so the focus of revolutionary politics is shifted towards the transgressive acts which may arise from this technological integration, acts which disrupt the flow of capital from territory to terri-tory and from network to network. In the chapters which follow I will examine these different attempts to think through the idea of technology and its relationship to the social, economic and political institutions of capital.

7
The Origins of Technocracy: Heidegger and Marcuse

The essence of Marx's account of the relationship between capitalism and technology boils down to the following. The M–C–M relation is able to become the dominant mode of social and economic intercourse only because of capital's capacity to transform itself from commodities into surplus value. Initially this relationship is facilitated by innovations in handicraft manufacturing; the concentration of labour in one place, the increasing complexity of the division of labour and the use of simple machinery to facilitate the production of exchange values and a relatively stable rate of profit. This state of affairs however is disrupted by the bourgeoning competition which capitalism introduces into civil society; each individual capitalist will inevitably try to reduce the amount of labour time it takes for him to cover the cost of the wages he pays to his workforce. In the end the competitiveness of the market means that only those capitalists who can afford to deploy automated systems to increase the rate at which commodities are produced, will survive. Marx therefore conceives the impact of machine technologies in terms of their *intensification of the labour process* – that is, in terms of their reduction of the socially necessary time it takes to produce the means of subsistence.

As we have seen Marx presents this reduction of necessary labour time as an immanent socialization of the means of production; it is only the fact that commodities are still determined as exchange values which blocks the universal satisfaction of human need and the free self-development of every individual. This, however, raises a question: what if the kind of technological development which Marx conceives in terms of the historical abolition of capitalism is part of a more fundamental logic of control which threatens every form of ethical, political and aesthetic transcendence? Or to put it another way, what if the very possibility of technological innovation is founded on the prior subjection of human beings to the demands of instrumental reason? It is to this question, and its implications for the political project of Marxism, that I will now turn.

Martin Heidegger's essay 'The Question Concerning Technology' was written in 1953 and expresses a profound trepidation towards the technocratic society which he saw emerging after the Second World War. This trepidation is not informed by the potentially lethal effects of new technologies, but rather with the impact that the reduction of nature to a manipulable resource has upon the vocation of humanity. The argument is that the essence of technology lies in a particular form of 'revealing' which is characteristic of western metaphysics; one in which nature is made to reveal itself not as the sublime, or the sacred, or the mysterious but simply as a resource, as that which is ready to be put to work. The problem, for Heidegger, is that this utilitarian approach to the world is carried over into the administration of society; relations between human beings are increasingly dominated by the demand that each should perform a useful role in the systemic-technological engendering of nature's productivity. The basic concepts of this argument are closely followed in the theory of technology presented by Herbert Marcuse in *One Dimensional Man*. As we will see in a moment, however, Marcuse's determination to map the *a priori* conditions of technocratic society onto the dynamics of class antagonism is quite distinct from Heidegger's ethico-political agenda, and maintains his earliest intention to ground the phenomenological forms of agency, authenticity and desire in the historical evolution of capitalism (Jay, 1996: 71–4).

Let us return to Heidegger and his attempt to expound the metaphysical conditions of technocratic society. At the beginning of his essay Heidegger claims that 'the essence of technology is ... nothing technological', and that as long as we continue to believe that scientific innovation promotes a steady improvement in the condition of humanity we will remain enslaved to the ethos of technocratic control (Heidegger, 1996: 311–13). The possibility of determining a proper relationship between humanity and the instruments which have come to dominate their lives therefore depends upon correctly understanding the *a priori* conditions on which the technological manipulation of nature is founded. Heidegger's approach to this question focuses on the origin of a particular worldview in Classical Greek philosophy; a worldview which valorises the revelation of nature through the projective imagination of man, and which challenges its being to come forth in the products of his activity (*Ibid.*: 318). In Greek thought this kind of revealing through making (*technē*) stands very close to artistic inspiration (*poiēsis*) and demands a certain poetic sensitivity of the craftsman in his relationship to nature. In this sense the artisan remains faithful to the vocation of humanity, that is, to the responsibility each of us has to the mystery of Being (*Sein*) and to the truth of its revelation (*Ibid.*: 319). However it is in the kind of revealing which is characteristic of *technē* that Heidegger situates the origin of modern technological domination.

In *An Introduction to Metaphysics* Heidegger proposes that language 'can only have arisen from the overpowering, the strange and the terrible, from man's departure into being' (Heidegger, 1987: 171). The tropes and modulations through which language came to be were ultimately poetic expressions of man's confrontation with the overpowering mystery of Being. Living within the demands of this poetic language therefore should be conceived as living within a medium which constantly reopens the question of Being, moving beyond its dissimulation in the categories of the 'governing order' (*Ibid.*: 170). What is important here is Heidegger's claim that language (or rather the metaphysical categories through which it 'cuts into' the world) initiates a clash of true apprehensions of Being and that it is the necessity of this conflict which founds the historical essence of man, his 'being in the truth' (*Ibid.*: 152). Now if we return to the essay on technology we can begin to make out the 'supreme danger' which Heidegger discerns in modern technologies. His argument is that the scientific paradigm upon which the modern technological revolution depends, is a mathematical extension of the utilitarian principles of *technē*, or making. Nature, in other words, is forced to appear in molecular and sub-molecular systems which offer an ever expanding potential for its exploitation as a resource. In Heidegger's terms the world is transformed into a 'standing-reserve' of energy which awaits deployment in man's productive activity (Heidegger, 1996: 322).

The danger inherent in this 'enframing' (*Gestell*) of the world within the limits of techno-scientific reason is that man's responsibility to the question of Being is fundamentally threatened. The reduction of nature to mathematical relationships means that it no longer stands overagainst man as an object which provokes and exceeds his powers of religiosity, veneration and *poiēsis*. Rather it has become a resource which awaits the technological innovations that are implicit in the scientific paradigm; innovations which simultaneously increase the material wealth of humanity and intensify the crises that result from the loss of its spiritual vocation. The danger which arises from the technological organization of society therefore has a dual aspect: first, when the objectivity of the world is reduced to standing-reserve man himself is reduced to an element in the technological exploitation of nature, and second, as a consequence of this reduction man fails to recognize enframing as a mode of revelation which challenges his capacity for truth (*Ibid.*: 332). Yet Heidegger insists that it is the very extremity of this crisis which precipitates the return of humanity to its original vocation. For as soon as the demand for utility assumes the epochal dimensions which he describes in *An Introduction to Metaphysics* and the essay on technology, fundamental questions arise which cannot be subsumed under conventional logics of technological progress – be they Marxist or bourgeois. For Heidegger these questions demand that we attend to the relationship between the existential constitution of the body and the spiritual vocation of man, the relationship between science and the revelation of Being, and the power of *poiēsis* to transform the technocratic organization of man and nature. And so in the end the essence of modern technology is 'in a lofty sense ambiguous' and always refers us back to the relationship between the poetic imagination and the revelation of Being (*Ibid.*: 339).

So where does this leave us? On the one hand the rapprochement of *technē* and *poiēsis*, making and art, whose possibility Heidegger discerns in the crisis of technological modernity, exemplifies a strand of deep metaphysical conservatism which runs throughout his work. The idea of the aesthetic which he presents at the conclusion of his essay is part of a classical tradition in which the revelation of nature as beautiful or sublime symbolizes the ethical responsibility of man. As Walter Benjamin pointed out however the very technological innovations which have transformed the spatial and temporal dimensions of human society, have also transformed the media through which that society represents itself. And so Heidegger's recourse to *poiēsis* fails to acknowledge the fact that the classical tradition of art, with all of the hierarchical divisions it entails, stands opposed to the democratization of the image which is implicit in film and photographic technologies. Hence Benjamin's remarks on the complicity between fascist politics and the use of film to re-present the 'aura' of the people, the *Volk* (Benjamin, 1992: 234–5). Yet in spite of the conservatism which clings to Heidegger's confrontation with modernity, his account of technology opens up a number of important questions to which Marxism must respond. In particular there is the question of how the scientific investigation of nature (whose horizon is the regression of matter into ever more infinitesimal structures) has impacted upon the power of capital to reproduce itself, and upon the fate of humanity within its technological systems. These questions are taken up in Herbert Marcuse's version of critical theory, especially in *One Dimensional Man* and *Eros and Civilization*, and so we need to take a look at his arguments.

At the end of chapter 6 he suggested that it is possible to discern two lines of argument in his account of the revolutionary potential of technology. The first of these, which originates in the *Grundrisse*, is that the deployment of new technologies increases the 'general intellect' of society and that this forms the basis of a self-conscious proletarian movement. The second, which is woven into the text of *Capital*, is that the alienation which results from the technological exploitation of organic labour is what will ultimately determine the event of revolutionary transcendence. What Heidegger's account of technology has done is to suggest that *both* of these logics, the compositional and the apophatic, are disrupted by the transformation of nature into a manipulable resource. For if it is the case that the scientific enframing of the world constantly increases the exploitability of man and nature then Marx's account of the limits within which the technological regime of capital can operate is called into question. Might it not be the case, in other words, that techno-scientific capitalism is able to extend its powers of exploitation indefinitely – both in the realm of nature and in the realm of society? It is this question which lies at the centre of Marcuse's work on the rise of technocratic society.

For Marcuse scientific rationality is not concerned with metaphysical conjectures about the nature of 'what is', but merely with the investigation of causal chains which determine the occurrence of particular events. This instrumental orientation presupposes and intensifies a fundamental change in the subject–object relations which constitute human experience. In Hegelian philosophy, as Marcuse points out in *Reason and Revolution*, the activity of spirit is presented as the constant mediation of mind, nature and history; its self-constitutive movement, in other words, depends upon its differentiation into each of these 'objective' forms (Marcuse, 1968: 62–90). The intervention of theoretical science however 'de-realizes' the objectivity of nature and transforms humanity into the instrument of technological control. Instead of apprehending the immanent unities which arise from the historical evolution of *Sittlichkeit*, man has become a mere 'residue' of the reflective understanding which Hegel referred to as subjective mind (Marcuse, 1964: 152–3). Thus for both Marcuse and Heidegger the expansion of technocratic society presupposes the reduction of man and nature to resources which await their most productive organization.

So how does Marcuse make his way back to the imperatives of a Marxist critique from this Heideggarian analysis of scientific rationality? In *One Dimensional Man* he begins by drawing on the concept of the *Lebenswelt*, or lifeworld, which Edmund Husserl developed in his book

The Crisis of European Sciences and Phenomenology. Husserl argues that in order to understand the processes of mathematical abstraction which characterize the scientific paradigm we must understand that these processes arise from a particular kind of practical orientation which originates in the lifeworld. Galileo's New Science for example was only possible on the basis of man's increasingly calculative relationship to nature as a resource which is open to technological manipulation. Husserl's conception of scientific rationality therefore refers to a set of instrumental practices (measuring, quantifying, schematizing) which evolve within the lifeworld and which come to establish themselves as the foundation of all true knowledge. For Marcuse the importance of this analysis lies in the historical element which Husserl attributes to the concrete practices of the lifeworld. For if it is the case that the shape of modern capitalism presupposes the rationalization of socioeconomic relations, then Marx's analyses of the production of exchange value, the fetishism of commodities, and the intensification of labour power provides an essential description of how science and technology are implicated in the reproduction of political domination (Marcuse, 1964: 166).[1]

In *The Poverty of Philosophy* Marx famously stated that 'the hand-mill gives you society with the feudal lord; the steam-mill society with the industrial capitalist (Marx, 1977c: 202). Technology, in other words, is not a mere instrument which remains external to the purposes of human beings; rather it is a force which shapes the totality of social, economic and ideological relationships which constitute the mode of production. The question which emerges here concerns the compatibility of Marx's revolutionary dialectics with the transformative power of scientific reason which he acknowledges in *The Poverty of Philosophy*. According to Marcuse the kind of science which has arisen from the instrumental orientation of human agency is one whose concepts are based on the projection of knowledge upon the world. The development of this scientific rationality does not take place outside of the social, economic and political relationships which constitute the mode of production; rather it presupposes a lifeworld which is cut up into definite hierarchical relationships. What this means is that the deployment of new technologies depends on a type of scientific reason which begins with the exercise of domination and control. So, if there is 'no such thing as a purely rational scientific order', and if technological rationality is originally implicated in the exercise of political control, then a Marxist analysis of late capitalism must address the ways in which new technologies have taken the very essence of the individual (his/her work, satisfaction and desire) into its administered, functionalized totality (Marcuse, 1964: 168–9).

Marcuse's account of the relationship between scientific rationality and the technocratic organization of capitalism however is not meant to signify the end of Marxism as a revolutionary politics. Rather the idea of 'technics' which he develops in *One Dimensional Man* attempts to salvage the possibility of socialized production, or the 'pacification of existence' as he called it, from the functionalizing powers of capitalism. His argument is that even though the deployment of new technologies has resulted in overproduction and the proliferation of false needs, this does not mean that these technologies will always maintain such a distorted unity of the individual and society. The functionalizing logic which seeks to integrate the whole of humanity's emotional, affective and aesthetic life into the production, consumption and wastage of obsolescent commodities, in other words, does at least gesture towards an expressive totality in which social need would be met by a non-antagonistic organization of technological means (Marcuse, 1964: 236). This account of the socializing possibilities of technics follows on from the analysis of Freud's reality principle which Marcuse presented in *Eros and Civilization*. He argued that Freud's theory of the repressive formation of the ego failed to recognize that the performative necessities constituted through this formation (productivity, functionality, fungibility) are historically specific. The organization of social life through the excessively functional demands of technological capitalism, in other words, has its own historical dialectic; for in so far as the unlimited expansion of productivity is fundamentally unsatisfying to the instinctual life of the genetic individual (what Freud called the 'archaic past' of the human organism), it gives rise to a demand for a more expressive configuration of social relationships (Marcuse, 1962: 144).

In both *One Dimensional Man* and *Eros and Civilization* Marcuse claims that science has opened up a new sphere of social possibilities; for even if it is the case that technological innovation has tended to facilitate the performative determination of the individual ego, it also entails a radical expansion of the ends which it is possible for human beings to achieve (Marcuse, 1664: 234, 1962: 142). Science in the service of sheer accumulation, in other words, is opened up to metaphysical questions of 'finality'; the transformative power of its praxis means that it reencounters concepts of peace, hospitality, love, responsibility and justice which capital's forced division of labour had consigned to the realm of 'abstract' art and philosophy (Marcuse, 1964: 234). In Marcuse's thought these concepts are intrinsically related to the technological transformation of social life; and it is only in so far as this transformation reveals the possibility of a 'free play' of human faculties removed from the total administration of capital, that humanity could achieve its 'optimum' – although always less than sublime – liberation from repression (Marcuse, 1962: 143). This however begs an important question: if it is the case that a more expressive social totality is immanent in the technological organization of production, how is this possibility to be realized if the primary effect of productive technology is to increase the repressive standardization of the ego and the atrophy of imagination and aesthetic sensibility? Marcuse's response to this question is to invoke a certain exilic experience which haunts the boundaries of Western technocratic society; for he suggests that the mobilization of technology by industrial capital has so depoliticized the working classes that the chance of revolution is sustained primarily by the desire of those who are excluded from political and economic integration (Marcuse, 1964: 257).

In the end what differentiates Heidegger and Marcuse's accounts of the instrumental trajectory of human society is the fact that, for Marcuse, the fate which Heidegger conceives in terms of man's loss of his metaphysical vocation, is in fact part of the material deprivation which capitalism reproduces in a particular class – the proletariat. The Marxist reading of Heidegger presented in *One Dimensional Man* therefore is important because it raises fundamental questions about the relationship between capitalism, desire and technology. Heidegger's approach to the question of technocratic society is concerned with the loss and redemption of man's 'being in the truth' which occurs through the infringement of instrumental reason on the objectivity of nature. And so the vocation of *Dasein* – its desire for the truth of its relationship to the functional-instrumental temporality of the machine – returns, in the form of *poiēsis*, at the very extremity of technocratic control. For Marcuse, on the contrary, the expression of man's ethico-aesthetic desire for truth is what the regime of technological capitalism has made all but impossible. The mathematical principles through which nature has been transformed into a resource which is ready for any kind of exploitation, have also produced a system of material and ideological relationships which constantly extend the functionality of the social machine. This, of course, raises the question of repetition; for even though Marcuse gestures towards the possibility of redemption through the archaic pulsions of the body, his account of technological reification suggests that there are few – if any – transformations of desire which do not already have the imprimatur of capital upon them. In the following chapters I will examine the possibility of a politics of technological effects that might outplay this logic of repetition, and which could perhaps inherit the revolutionary promise of Marxism.

8
Civilized Capitalist Machines: Deleuze and Negri

In their most recent collaborations, *Empire* and *Multitude*, Michael Hardt and Antonio Negri argue that the primary effect of informatic, cybernetic and prosthetic technologies is neither the precipitation of absolute chaos (*a la* Baudrillard) nor the fulfilment of absolute repetition (*a la* Jameson) in the mode of production. Rather the growth of the 'immaterial' forms of labour which has arisen from the global distribution of these technologies has revitalized the flow of revolutionary desire. New forms of praxis arise, the general intellect and aesthetic imagination of the masses are recharged, and the global-technological systems of capitalism conspire to produce a new revolutionary subject – 'the multitude' – which will eventually transform the repressive organization of the world economy. Thus for Hardt and Negri it is the symbiotic relationship between capital and the technologies which have precipitated the virtual expansion of debt, exploitation, consumption and productivity which gives rise to the countervailing force/subject which is the inheritor of Marx's revolutionary demand. This account of the transformative power of technological systems depends upon a very specific reading of Deleuze and Guattari's *Capitalism and Schizophrenia*: one in which the 'schizophrenic' flows of desire that are put into play by techno-scientific capitalism are conceived as cumulative and universal rather than nomadic and contingent. In what follows I will set out the conditions of this reading, and what I consider to be the inconsistency between Deleuze and Guattari's account of the technological dispersion of life and Hardt and Negri's insistence on the 'hermeneutic' of labour which is implicit in the biopolitical regime of production.

Capital, Technology and Machinic Desire

In order to understand Deleuze and Guattari's account of the relationship between politics, capital and desire, we need to look at the two volumes of their work on capitalism and schizophrenia: *Anti-Oedipus* and *A Thousand Plateaus*. The notion of desire which Deleuze and Guattari present in *Anti-Oedipus* is embedded in a general idea of the real as a process of machinic differentiation. The core of their idea is that every entity which comes into existence does so as a purposive organization of energy which seeks to engender its own power, and which, in so doing, enters into transformative relationships with other purposive machines (Deleuze and Guattari, 2000: 36). The 'substance' of reality therefore is conceived as the product of these relationships; for it is only in so far as desire belongs to the idea of difference, that we can understand the possibilities of domination, autonomy and symbiosis which arise out of its original designation as will to power. For Deleuze and Guattari, therefore, 'machinic differentiation' is an ontological fact which both precedes and exceeds the historical formation of every kind of desiring activity. For if it is true that the flow of energy through different assemblages of conductivity and resistance is what establishes the substance of the real, then it must also be true that the transcendental categories through which we understand ourselves as agents, citizens and human beings, belong to a continuum of effects which begins with the very first assemblages of inorganic life (Ansell Pearson, 1997: 182–3).[1]

This account of a material desire which simultaneously produces life and death, subject and object, structure and agency has a number of important consequences. First, rather than existing as a metaphysical 'lack' in the human organism, desire constitutes the flows and intensities through which it makes the transition from nature to culture, pre-hominid to hominid. Second, this means that in assessing the transformative possibilities that are opened up by Deleuze and Guattari's account of purposive energy, we must consider how the social field is constituted as a mechanism of capture which blocks, solicits, engages and transforms the flow of desire. Third, this requires us to transform our understanding of the concept of agency. The Enlightenment tradition has tended to theorize autonomy in terms of the power of a rational subject to integrate his/her desires into a coherent frame of action. For Deleuze and Guattari however the subject is always an effect of desire; he or she is constituted (and de-constituted) through the flows and intensities that arise from living in the legislative space of the social machine. This, as we will see in a moment, does not mean that intellect is made into a mere epiphenomenon of desire; rather Deleuze and Guattari's argument follows Spinoza's claim that it is the modifications of the conative body (with its unpredictable powers of composition, affection and resistance) which exercise a transformative power over the intellect (Armstrong in Ansell Pearson, 1997: 49). Finally, this analysis of the relationship between desire and autonomy demands that we change the way in which we think about politics. For if it is the case that machinic desire simply 'wants what it wants' in any given conjunction of forces, then it is no longer possible to revert to the schemas of repression, alienation and anomie which have informed modernist theories of revolution. Thus, we need to ask how Deleuze and Guattari's account of desire might transform the political problematic we identified in relation to the technological development of capitalism.

Part 3 of *Anti-Oedipus* sets out a universal history in which the three fundamental types of social machine are introduced: 'the primitive', 'the despotic' and 'the civilized capitalist'. As we have seen Deleuze and Guattari's theory of desire attempts to shift the focus of theoretical debate away from the metaphysical deficiencies of the human subject and towards an analysis of the particular breaks, flows and alliances which belong to each kind of social machine. What this means is that the inception of history and the inception of machinic desire are simultaneous, and that in order to understand the evolutionary processes through which desire is provoked and controlled within the social field, we must first understand the primitive conditions under which it is originally encoded. In Marx's speculative anthropology the first stages of a genuinely social existence emerge when human beings start self-consciously to organize their means of subsistence. The earliest hunter-gatherer tribes break with their simian ancestry once the 'inorganic body of nature' appears to them as an object which requires the practical application of cooperative strategies, tools, weapons and the most basic laws of sociality. Marx therefore begins by inscribing material desire at the very centre of primitive society, for it is only in so far as the dialectic of natural/animal instinct and human/self conscious desire is resolved in favour of the latter, that it is possible for truly social relationships to emerge (Marx, 1977b: 42–8). For Deleuze and Guattari this description of the material processes which found primitive society remains too anthropocentric; for despite his attempts to break with the abstract self-consciousness which he took to be the motor of Hegelian historiography, Marx still retained a concept of 'species being' whose essence was to be realized in the harmonious desires of socialized production. The analysis of the primitive social machine set out in *Anti-Oedipus* however presents the transition from nature to society not as a dialectical overcoming of the latter, but as a capturing of primitive flows of desire (which are not so very distinct from the simian) within a particular kind of territorial organization. The flows through which social production is sustained – 'flows of women and children, flows of herds and of seed, sperm flows, flows of shit, menstrual flows' – are inscribed on the surface of the earth and on the bodies of the tribe. And so the inorganic body of nature becomes the object of desire and the source of repression; it becomes the 'mega machine' which encodes the animality of the human organism (Deleuze and Guattari, 2000: 140–2).

For Deleuze and Guattari the emergence of the despotic state is not an evolutionary process: its possibility depends upon the departure of a certain asceticism from the primitive machine, its constitution as a spiritual-religious alliance in which the despot becomes the universal focus of desire, and the return of this ascetic desire to the primitive machine as 'a terror without precedent, in comparison with the ancient system of cruelty ... is nothing' (Deleuze and Guattari, 2000: 192). We need to look at the nature of this encounter between the 'primitive' and the 'barbarian' machines. Deleuze and Guattari characterize primitive society as a hierarchical organization of family groups whose powers of inscription, alliance and reproduction are nomadic rather than institutional. Thus the coming of the despot from out of exile strikes like lightning upon the old territorialities; for he arrives as a messiah whose knowledge links him directly to God, to his religious alliance (scribes, disciples, converts, priests) and to the primitive souls he has come to save (*Ibid.*: 194). The barbarian machine therefore exceeds all of the filiations of primitive society; for the paranoiac desire of the despot flows straight from a transcendent God, and as such, announces His dominion over the earth and the 'savages' who populate it. This shift marks the origin of the state; for everything is made to converge upon the sovereign and to participate in a social machine (hierarchical castes, religious doctrine, bureaucratic elites) which puts people to work in the service of the secular/divine lord. The territoriality of the barbarian state however does not mark the death of primitive codes of filiation; rather the colonizing process is shaped by a contingent play of resistances and symbioses which shape the spatial and temporal expansion of the imperial code (*Ibid.*: 195).

The barbarian machine transforms the segmented structures of primitive society into 'working parts' of its internal territory; each extended family group is absolved of its economic and honorific obligations to the Chieftain and thereby takes on an unpayable debt to the despotic lord (Deleuze and Guattari, 2000: 197). It is within this distribution of responsibility that money emerges as the universal equivalent through which 'the people' are able to discharge their obligations to the sovereign. Taxation and not commerce, in other words, is what originally releases the unpredictable effects of monetary exchange (venality, corruption, indulgence, patronage) into the territorial space of the state. According to Deleuze and Guattari it is these 'deterritorializing' effects which reveal something like the essence of the state, that is, the 'dread of mercantile flows' which escape its mechanisms of capture. In the case of the barbarian machine this essential determination reveals itself in the paranoiac desire of the sovereign to appropriate every libidinal flow and intensity as his own property (*Ibid.*: 199). The sovereign becomes the death instinct: the absent presence who constantly reinscribes his demands in the legal, theological and economic organs of the state, and whose desire of desire suppresses the free intensities which spring up in the masses. Thus the despotic machine introduces a transcendental signifier (the despot) into the primitive system of representations: graphic inscription cedes place to a written text which narrates the power of the despot, and which channels the old nomadic flows of desire into a universal fear of/desire for the body of the sovereign. Ultimately the law proscribing incest springs from this appropriation of desire; for it allows the despot to put an end to the filiations of primitive society and to put all of the people to work within the representative order of the state (*Ibid.*: 206–10).

The question which has emerged here is a familiar one, that is, the question of the transition from feudalism to capitalism. According to Deleuze and Guattari the possibility of this shift should be conceived in terms of the flows of mercantile desire which are liberated within the barbarian machine; for it is only in so far as money has emerged as part of the economy of debt instituted by the despot, that unregulated flows of desire emerge which threaten the absolute sovereignty of the state. The internal space of the despotic order, in other words, is traversed by private property relations, classes and status groups which emerge over time and which compromise its original powers of territoriality (Deleuze and Guattari, 2000: 218–19). Feudalism is one of the outcomes of this period of latency in the despotic order; for while it is true that the system of taxation, tribute and rent which grew up around landed property retained much of the coercive power instituted by the despotic machine, it is also the case that it produced flows of desire which transformed the dynamics of production, consumption and political activity. So how does capitalism emerge from this unstable play of mercantile desire and repressive authority? For Deleuze and Guattari it is a misreading of Marx to suggest that historical materialism asserts a necessary simultaneity of the rise of mercantile capital and the dissolution of the feudal regime. Rather they maintain that Marx acknowledged that the decoding effect of private property, large accumulations of money and the growth of world trade produced unpredictable forms of reversion, innovation, prosperity and degradation in the ancient regime. Thus the temporality of the capitalist machine is diachronic; for unlike imperial despotism it develops through a consolidation of contingent effects which arise from its rupturing of the old feudalist codes (*Ibid.*: 224).

At the beginning of section three of *Anti-Oedipus* Deleuze and Guattari remarked that:

> In a sense capitalism has haunted all forms of society, but it haunts them as their terrifying nightmare, it is the dread they feel of a flow that would elude their codes. (Deleuze and Guattari, 2000: 140)

As we have seen their account of the three kinds of social machine does not present a simple diachronic progression from primitive to despotic to civilized capitalist forms of society. Rather the exposition traces a play of immanence (each machine is defined as a predominant territoriality which produces flows and intensities that exceed it) and dispersal (every excess of desire constitutes a trajectory which threatens the existing mechanism of capture) in which 'progress' is always displaced by unpredictable effects of desire. It is in this sense that capitalism has 'haunted all forms of society'. For what is named here is not a historically specific mode of production (in Marx's sense), but rather the very condition of history: the excessive flows of desire which are put into play by every territorial machine and against which every machine reconfigures its strategy of capture. Thus in the transition from feudalism to capitalism the alliance into which the *ancien régime* is forced to enter with mercantile capitalism is not immediately fatal to it, and even produces periods of relative prosperity before it is subordinated to the capitalist machine. What is important here is the originary power which Deleuze and Guattari seek to designate in the concept of capitalism. Clearly what they are referring to is the immanent excess of machinic desire; for even in the primitive territorial machine intensities arise which exceed the dominant system of encoding and anticipate the asceticism which founds the barbarian despotic regime. What the idea of capitalism designates therefore is the immanent power of desire to precipitate unpredictable flows, breaks and intensities within every regime of domination, that is, the 'schizophrenic desire' whose multiple trajectories are able to outplay the state and its mechanisms of capture (Deleuze and Guattari, 2000: 260). Three 'Marxist' questions arise here. First, how can totally decoded desire function to reproduce surplus value and meet social need? Second, how can the state exert control over a mode of production which operates through the constant precipitation of new flows of capital, knowledge and technology? And third, what is the political significance of this 'becoming of desire' which is set in motion by the capitalist machine?

Let me address the first two questions together. At the beginning of their exposition of the capitalist machine Deleuze and Guattari restate Marx's proposition that capitalism only really comes into existence when the M–C–M relation (the transformation of money into commodities and commodities into profit) has ceased to depend on alliances with the feudal regime (Deleuze and Guattari, 2000: 227). This 'filial' capital operates by monopolizing the means of production (fixed capital in the form of machines, factory buildings, transport systems) and transforming the organic labour of the masses into a commodity which is subject to unlimited exploitation. This process is intensified by the emergence of credit as a form of the M–C–M relation; the banks, in other words, lend money to enterprises which are able to expand the technological basis of the labour process, increase their profits and contribute to the overall social product. The effect of this is to transform the state into the universal regulator of debts; it controls the value of currency and guarantees a uniform rate of interest thereby allowing the capitalist machine to expand its exorbitant productivity into every area of society (*Ibid*.: 229). Where Deleuze and Guattari part company with Marx is in their analysis of the internal limit of capitalism. As we have seen Marx maintains that capital's increasing reliance on technology to prop up the rate at which surplus value is produced, results in an ever increasing expenditure on the purchase and maintenance of machinery. The over burdening of production with fixed capital determines three dialectically related effects: the constant diminution in the rate of profit produced by technological innovation, the general depression of wages and the consequent decline of the proletariat into a state of absolute impoverishment. For Deleuze and Guattari, however, the two registers (profit and wages) which Marx brings together in his account of the limits of capitalist accumulation remain heterogeneous. They argue that capital, conceived as the absolute decoding of desire, has no external limits; and that its powers of technological innovation, scientific objectification and graphic representation enable it constantly to exceed the boundaries that are set upon it by dialectical conceptions of nature and productive humanity.

This absence of an internal limit to capitalism's powers of expansion means that there is no necessary relationship between the tendency of the rate of profit to fall and the revolutionary impoverishment of the working class. For the capacity of the capitalist machine to overcome every internal limitation means that it is able constantly to displace the moment of revolutionary composition, that is, to infuse the masses with newly exploitable flows of sexual, economic and aesthetic desire (Deleuze and Guattari, 2000: 230–1). This process of displacement is essentially technological; for as the flows of knowledge and information put into play by capital become more and more decoded, so the technological production of desire becomes an increasingly transformative power within the social machine. What is important here is the position which these techno-systems occupy in relation to the two poles of civilized capitalist society, that is, the 'decoded flux' of schizophrenic desire and 'paranoiac despotic' operations of the state (*Ibid.*: 260). I will argue, in opposition to the claims which Hardt and Negri make in *Empire*, that although Deleuze and Guattari's idea of machinic desire presents a compelling account of the technological supplementation of the masses (and of the unforeseen desires and events to which that supplementation gives rise), their conception of capital entails a reactive movement that is virtually simultaneous with those desires and events (*Ibid.*: 258).

Let me begin by specifying the difference between social machines and technological systems which informs Deleuze and Guattari's universal history of desire. Perhaps the clearest statement of this difference is made in their 'Treatise on the Nomadology' in *A Thousand Plateaus*:

> The principle behind all technology is to demonstrate that a technological element remains abstract, entirely undetermined, as long as one does not relate it to an *assemblage* it presupposes. It is the machine that is primary in relation to the technical element: not the technical machine, itself a collection of elements, but the social collective machine, the machinic assemblage, that determines what is a technical element at a given time. (Deleuze and Guattari, 2004: 439)

This argument has a structure similar to the one Marcuse set out in *One Dimensional Man*, for it maintains that in order to understand the genesis of particular technologies and the way in which they reproduce certain kinds of domination, it is necessary to understand how instrumental reason has come to dominate the lifeworld. According to Marcuse the rise of technocratic capitalism depends on an instrumental organization of social relationships which is implicit in the Western idea of civilization, and which becomes fully explicit in Enlightenment science and philosophy. Ultimately the reproduction of the individuals who work within the homogeneous organization of capitalist society is achieved through a process of reification in which technological systems intensify the objective and subjective conditions of class domination (Marcuse, 1964: 166). For Deleuze and Guattari however this type of argument remains complicit with the one dimensionality of the social, economic and technological relations it seeks to criticize. By maintaining that 'true' desire is inscribed in a Freudian economy of primal drives and instincts, and that civilization progresses by sacrificing that desire to the techno-instrumental organization of society, Marcuse's analysis ends up postulating capital as a universally objectifying power which subsumes every free intensity that it encounters. This is clearly at odds with the account of social machines presented in *Anti-Oedipus* and *A Thousand Plateaus*. Deleuze and Guattari maintain that power is a relationship which emerges from the differentiation of being into conative assemblages which seek to engender their own existence, and that consequently the 'primal' expression of human desire has always already been transformed by the mechanisms of capture, territoriality and inscription with which universal history begins (Deleuze and Guattari, 2004: 440–1).

Thus if we are to understand Deleuze and Guattari's conception of technology we need to return to their account of primitive society. As we have seen, the territoriality of social machines is fissile; each includes a multiplicity of contingent flows which transforms its mechanisms of capture, and which point to a genealogy of effects which traverse the phylum of machinic desire (Deleuze and Guattari, 2004: 450). Deleuze and Guattari argue that the primitive segmental organization of family groups is an essentially mobile territoriality characterized by speed and the fluid deployment of its number across an unbounded space (*Ibid.*: 430). This means that the originary form of the social machine is a nomadic assemblage which conducts desire into a ceaseless 'vortical' movement which deploys itself against the striated space of barbarian empires. The development of weapons is intrinsic to this nomadic war machine; for it is through the speed of nomad territoriality that weapons (the saber and the 'man-animal-weapon' assemblage) emerge as technological projections of desire into the sedentary assemblage of the state (nation, civil society and standing army). The major consequence of this is to provoke a reaction on the part of the imperial powers; and so the tools of the state economy are organized to produce heavier and more sophisticated weapons which are brought to bear on the nomadic machine. Two important points emerge here. The first is that the technological precipitation of desire is present from the very beginning in the organization of social machines (they are simultaneously natural and artificial), and the second is that the technological/ metallurgical precipitation of desire is conceived by Deleuze and Guattari as a deterritorializing movement which threatens the sedentary powers of the state: 'there is always the nomad at the horizon of a given *technological lineage*' (*Ibid.*: 446).

The real question here concerns the virtual simultaneity with which the civilized capitalist machine is able to colonize the desires to which it has given rise. Pre-capitalist societies, we have seen, function through an 'excess of code'; the social machine operates through cultural, legal and political signs which maintain the infinite debt of the subjects to the despot. Capital, on the other hand, introduces a 'social axiomatic' which is opposed to every territorializing code; it breaks all the substantive bonds which are sustained by the inscription of a transcendent sovereign. As an axiomatic which functions to destroy the traditional order, capital has no internal limit and the only constraint under which it operates is the need to discipline the aleatory flows to which its techno-prosthetic-supplementary regime gives rise. Thus the free play of schizophrenic desire is constantly postponed through the absorption of surplus value in the 'politico-military-economic complex', the infinite debt incurred in the form of futural projects, and the expansion of technological production to include every strand of organic and non-organic life (Deleuze and Guattari, 2000: 249–51). What this means is that technological capitalism should not be conceived merely as the substitution of social for technical codes. For while it is true that the capitalist axiomatic has a temporality which originates in the deployment of technological means of production (i.e. their acceleration, virtualization and dissemination of surplus value), it is also true that this entails a potentially infinite multiplication of the 'axioms' through which capital postpones its collapse into schizoid desire (*Ibid.*: 252–3). According to Deleuze and Guattari the capitalist state is the universal form of this movement from schizophrenia to repression; for by subsuming mass desire under the Oedipal forms that are released by the technological production of surplus value, it constantly transforms itself into the transcendental limit of will and imagination. This marks a radical departure from conventional Marxist politics. The oscillation of the capitalist machine between the poles of schizoid desire and Oedipal repression forbids recourse to conventional notions of class identity; for in so far as the reterritorializing movement of the state occurs through 'operations that are not failures of [class] recognition, but perfectly reactionary unconscious investments', we must recognize that the technological development of the mode of production is not in any way incompatible with the 'modern archaisms' (racism, fascism, ultra nationalism, orientalism) which channel mass desire into the state's field of immanence (*Ibid.*: 257–8).

So what is the place of politics in this virtually simultaneous movement of deterritorialization-reterritorialization? In order to answer this question we need to look at the relationship between capitalism, technological systems and the cluster of concepts through which Deleuze and Guattari configure the idea of 'becoming' (war machine, nomad, rhizome, speed, smooth space). From the point of view of Deleuze and Guattari's universal history the conflict between nomadic and barbarian social machines is played out through two divergent technological flows: in the former the weapon evolves as the projection of unpredictable flows of desire into the heart of striated space, in the latter the tool evolves as a productive force which channels desire into the organic body of the state. The originary form of this encounter however is not static; for as the economic power of imperial states increases, so they begin to develop their own war machines and to integrate nomadic 'techniques' and strategies into standing armies. This leads to an increasingly uneven struggle in which nomad desire is driven to the margins of the imperial territories. These nomadic flows however do not perish in the desert or on the steppe. Once the state has appropriated the war machine the supplementary relationship of violence to its assemblage is transformed: the economics of fortification, armament and the maintenance of a military caste creates an instrument of aggression whose object is always the annihilation of the enemy. Thus the classical fascist state operates as a death cult in which civil society is mobilized into a war machine which takes conflict with other states to be its ultimate end and justification. Under the post-fascist state, on the contrary, the war machine has become intrinsically bound up with the smooth flows of commodities, information and money which are characteristic of global capitalism; and so the enemy against which it is ranged becomes 'unspecific' and is constantly recreated by its technical, economic and disciplinary operations:

The very conditions that make the State war machine possible, in other words, constant capital (resources and equipment) and human variable capital, continually recreate unexpected possibilities for counterattack, unforeseen initiatives determining revolutionary, popular, minority, militant machines'. (Deleuze and Guattari, 2004: 465)

This points to a certain nomadic potential of technological systems: for the mobilization of techno-economic forces by the state war machine against unspecified enemies, results in the production of 'minor' war machines (technical assemblages, artistic movements, musical styles) which take up unpredictable positions within the global space of capital.

What is at stake here are the dialectics of fixed and organic capital through which Marx expounded the concept of socialized production. In *Capital* Volume One he maintained that the increasing reliance of capitalist enterprise on technology leads to a disproportionate expenditure on machines (fixed capital) which cannot be realized in the sale of commodities on the open market. And so the tendencies towards overproduction, unemployment and falling rates of profit which afflict the mode of production are determined by an internally necessary relationship between the acquisitive regime of capital and its universal appropriation of the scientific and technological means of labour. Deleuze and Guattari's idea of capitalism as a social machine however maintains a fragile, rhizomatic difference between the economic and technological codes through which surplus value is produced. This difference is the key to understanding the political significance of technology in their thought, and so we need to specify the conditions under which it operates in the mode of production.

It should be recognized that social machines, as they are defined in *Anti-Oedipus* and *A Thousand Plateaus*, cannot be reduced to technocratic codes of control; for it is only in so far as the social machine has established certain fundamental principles of capture (Oedipal desire, infinite debt) that technology is able to intensify the biopolitical organization of the masses. This does not imply that once capitalism reaches its fully developed industrial stage, the overburdening of organic labour with fixed capital will produce a catastrophic fall in the rate of profit and a revolutionary homogenization of the working class. Rather Deleuze and Guattari contend that technological innovation and the schizophrenic desires to which it gives rise, are coeval with the mechanisms of anti-production and Oedipal desire through which the capital postpones the moment of revolutionary transcendence (Deleuze and Guattari, 2000: 263). It would however be wrong to imply that Deleuze and Guattari do no more than confirm the instrumental status which Heidegger and Marcuse attribute to technology; for the systems through which the capitalist machine expands are precisely those which precipitate the effects (of virtualization, prosthesis, supplementation, symbiosis and manipulation) which exceed its sedentary-disciplinary organization of space. For Deleuze and Guattari it is the *difference* between social and technological codes of production which opens the possibility of a politics of minoritized desire; a politics that would constantly precipitate unpredictable events of resistance, symbiosis and conductivity within the edifice of regulated biopolitical production. For Hardt and Negri however this account of the differentiated flows that arise from techno-scientific capitalism, transforms desire from an 'organic' power which is grounded in the material processes of production and exploitation, into ineffectual singularities which have no political significance beyond the moment of their occurrence (Hardt and Negri, 2000a: 28). In the section which follows I will look at their attempts to trace the ontological implications of *Anti-Oedipus* and *A Thousand Plateaus*, and to reconfigure Marx's ideas of class politics, collective agency and revolutionary transcendence through the concept of 'the multitude'.

Biopolitical production and the multitude

The concept of biopolitical production which is sketched at the beginning of *Empire* is concerned with the way in which we should inherit the political demand of Marx's critique of capital. Hardt and Negri claim that in order to understand the truth of this demand we should attend to the point in his analysis where the technological development of capitalism is recognized as a transformative influence on the physical and intellectual constitution of the masses. This point, they argue, comes in the discussion of the 'Transposition of the Powers of Labour into Powers of Capital' which Marx sets out at the end of the *Grundrisse*. His argument is that machinery is the realization of fixed capital, and that as such, it has transformed the means of labour from 'instruments' which have a specific relationship to the autonomous activity of the worker, into an objective power which determines the process and temporality of his work. The consequence of this process is what Marx refers to as the 'real subsumption' of labour, that is, the objectification of all the knowledge, virtuosity and skill of the workforce under the operations of complex automated systems (Marx, 1993: 694). For Hardt and Negri the importance of Marx's idea lies in its admission of a transformative relationship between technological systems and the desiring body of the masses. For even though Marx conceives the real subsumption of labour in terms of the mutual impoverishment of individual creativity and social production (universal alienation), they argue that the very idea of 'subsumption' entails a practical development of the relationship between technological means and the level of physical and intellectual autonomy exercised by the workforce. According to the line of argument pursued in *Empire*, it is the evolution of this relationship which determines the historical development of capitalism from its 'industrial' to its 'biopolitical' phase: for as the technological conditions of production transform the commodity into an immaterial expression of exchange value, so the practical activity of the workforce becomes increasingly engaged with the types of affective and intellectual production that are characteristic of the global information economy (Hardt and Negri, 2000: 24). For Hardt and Negri this shift in the productive regime of capitalism is crucially important because it marks the point at which capital, in order to continue reproducing itself, must constantly reinvest in the practical intellect of the masses; and so the political project of *Empire* is focused on the effects (of composition, affiliation and resistance) produced by this constant provocation of autonomy and desire among the global workforce.

This is not to say that Hardt and Negri assume that the involvement of the masses in the communicative and informatic networks of global capitalism leads to a steady increase in their revolutionary consciousness. Indeed one of the primary objectives of *Empire* is to show how the mechanisms of capture which have evolved under the regime of biopolitical production (international organizations like NATO, the IMF, the World Bank, G8) work to pre-empt the lines of flight which arise from the networking of the masses (Hardt and Negri, 2000: 39–40). However from the very beginning of their account of the new world order Hardt and Negri maintain that the differentiation of desire which is brought about by the total involvement of mind and body in the networks of immaterial labour, has its counterpart in new forms of political praxis which challenge the disciplinary regime of capital. Thus the constitution of the revolutionary subjectivity, or 'multitude', which is the subject of the final section of *Empire*, begins with the shift from industrial to immaterial forms of labour which is set out in the introduction (*Ibid.*: 27–30).

Two important issues have emerged here. First there is the question of Hardt and Negri's transcription of the concept of machinic desire. As we have seen, Deleuze and Guattari present an account of 'the real' in which each assemblage (mind, body, spirit, resistance, inertia) is conceived as a purposive desire which seeks to maintain itself in relation to other desiring machines. The transformative power of this desire acts upon the body of each individual, and so the capacity of desiring machines to transform themselves in relation to others finds its expression in unforeseen associations which become detached from conventional (transcendental and jurisprudential) encodings of authority. Thus for Deleuze and Guattari the re-production of desire through social and technological machines is always a transformation of the real, for it gives rise to 'absolute flows' which exceed the temporal organization of the present and require new axiological forms of integration (Deleuze and Guattari, 2000: 36). This account of desire is crucial to the political manifesto which is presented in *Empire*. For the concepts of agency, gathering and resistance which are developed in Hardt and Negri's account of the development of biopolitical capitalism, only make sense if the latter is conceived as a social machine in Deleuze and Guattari's sense of the term. The second issue we need to address concerns Hardt and Negri's account of the deterritorializing power of capitalism. Deleuze and Guattari understand capital as the absolute antithesis of transcendence; it is a machine which systematically destroys every social code that would limit its power to accumulate. However, they also claim that this constant destruction of traditional codes presupposes the kind of Oedipal subjectivity through which the state retains its original function as the universal object of desire; and so the lines of flight which depart towards the chance of further 'becoming' always arise out of, and offer resistance to, the reactionary innovations of territoriality (*Ibid.*: 267). Hardt and Negri, on the other hand, conceive the deterritorializing power of capital as part of a process through which biopolitical production gathers the multitude into an *ontological* constituency. Their claim is that the flow of capital into and out of the normative economy of nation states establishes a network of socio-technological relationships which are less and less reliant on valorizing ethnic, cultural and religious codes of self-identification. Deterritorialization, in other words, gives rise to an immanent transformation of capitalism's possessive economy: for in so far as the affective and intellectual praxis of immaterial labour arrives on the scene of production before the discipline of the negative (order, legality, appropriation), capital always encounters a resistance which is prior to its constitution as legitimate power (Hardt and Negri, 2000: 25).

For Hardt and Negri the technologies through which capital moves towards the ideal of unlimited accumulation can no longer be regarded as external to the bodily and intellectual constitution of the masses. Within the networks of informatic exchange labour and desire have become virtualized; they are no longer quantifiable in the substantive form of the commodity and have passed over into the 'immaterial' expressions of language, innovation and technique through which biopolitical capital expands (Hardt and Negri, 2000: 366). The being of the multitude therefore is intrinsically bound up with immaterial labour; for the direct engagement of their sensations, desires and practices within the networks of biopolitical capital, means that they have become 'machines of innovation' which resist both the transcendental structures of imperial authority and the reduction of desire to the acquisitiveness imposed by dominant culture industries (*Ibid.*: 355). Thus if there is to be a new proletarian politics, Hardt and Negri argue, it must proceed from this immanent power of self-composition; for the 'immateriality' of new forms of labour (their infinite valencies and lines of autonomous becoming) is exactly what produces the constantly evolving identity of the multitude (*Ibid.*: 358).

This brings us back to the question of revolutionary agency, or, more precisely, to Hardt and Negri's account of the relationship between social labour, the conative desires of the body and the constitution of the general intellect of the multitude (Hardt and Negri, 2000: 364–7). In both *Empire* and *Multitude* they set out the immanent forms of subjectivity which belong to the 'pre-history' of capitalism: the radical Enlightenment of the French Revolution, the different forms of colonial consciousness which arose from Western imperialist rule, the proletarian movements of the Russian and Chinese Revolutions and even the worker's organizations that were found in America during the Depression (*Ibid.*: 364). According to Hardt and Negri, biopolitical production marks the end of this pre-history: new technologies have consolidated the whole of life into networks of global exchange, and so the counter power of the multitude, if such a thing is possible, can emerge only through the forms of language, innovation and technique which are necessary to the continued expansion of capital. The types of technological sabotage, mobile confrontation and aesthetic subversion which are characteristic of anti-capitalist politics therefore arise as heterogeneous (but connected) events of resistance which are already latent in the total mobilization of intellect and desire. These events however are constantly blocked by the repressive activity of empire: at the disciplinary level they are subject to police actions which seek physically to control the expression of dissent, and at the ideological level they are excluded from the register of transcendental ethics, aesthetics and jurisprudence (*Ibid.*: 373–80).

So, how is it possible for the multitude to emerge as the socially transformative, globally inclusive body whose sovereignty is expounded in the concluding chapters of *Empire*? The answer to this question is given in Hardt and Negri's account of the logic of corruption which afflicts the new imperialist regime. Corruption, according to their analysis, becomes the operational principle of capitalism as soon as it has exceeded every measure of exploitation and every norm of common identity (Hardt and Negri, 2000: 390). At this point it mutates into a globally accumulative system which functions to suppress, de-legitimize and castrate the forms of autonomous praxis which it has released, and upon which it depends. The logic of imperial corruption therefore reconfigures Marx's account of the immanence of socialized production; for the total mobilization of practical desire through which the biopolitical regime operates, discloses the fundamentally inhuman nature of those institutions which are designed to preserve the rights of private appropriation. Thus in so far as empire is bound to sustain its 'coercive unifications' of the multitude, it simultaneously undermines its material basis and regenerates the desire of the multitude as a universal counter-power (*Ibid.*: 392).

It should be noted that there is a considerable literature which questions the compatibility of both Deleuze and Guattari and Hardt and Negri's ideas with the fundamental principles of Marxism. Their concentration on flows of desire which exceed the dialectics of class inequality, the privileging of immaterial forms of labour and the concentration on new technological effects has been thoroughly criticized for its supposed complicity with the operations of multinational capitalism.[2] However, if we are prepared to admit that the preceding discussion has raised serious questions about the fate of class politics under the regime of biopolitical production, then we must consider the question of how Deleuze and Negri have attempted to sustain Marx's revolutionary demand within the repressive organization of empire. In the introduction to *Difference and Repetition* Deleuze makes a brief allusion to the difference between Marx and Hegel's conceptions of history. With Hegel, he argues, history unfolds as the history of a universal idea which constantly reproduces its own generality: each particular existent is conceived as a unity which finds its proper fulfilment in the symbolic order of the universal. With Marx on the other hand, the perfect reproducibility of Hegelian forms is always fallen into heterogeneous repetitions in which it is impossible to discern univocal lines of progress (Deleuze, 2004b: 11). What is important here is that, for Deleuze, Marx's break with the Hegelian economy of resemblance opens up a history of production in which the mechanics of flow, territoriality and capture determine contingent forms of economic and political domination (*Ibid.*: 224). As we have seen, historical materialism includes the development of technological systems as part of the immanent tendency of capitalism towards the socialization of production. For Deleuze and Guattari however new technologies determine effects which are radically singular and which exceed the logic of equivalence which Marx tried to establish between class homogenization and the increase in relative surplus value produced by machines. Ultimately, therefore, the exchange between the territoriality of the state and the virtualizing powers of technology takes the form of a multiplication of the rules through which unforeseeable flows of desire are integrated into a present from which they have already departed. For Negri, on the other hand, the biopolitical machine produces forms of revolutionary difference which retain a concrete relationship to the history of class struggle (Negri, 2003: 122–6). And so while it is certainly true that *Empire* proclaims the end of class politics (that is, the end of a dialectical antagonism of 'bourgeois' and 'proletarians'), the deterritorialized flows which Hardt and Negri describe take place within a socio-technological machine whose production of the multitude (as a *real* identity in difference) is perfected within the parasitic order of capital (Hardt and Negri, 2000: 393–413).

The question we are left with therefore concerns the compatibility of Hardt and Negri's account of a prescient Marx who recognized the immanence of concrete desire in the technological development of capitalism with Deleuze and Guattari's account of civilized capitalist machines. For if it is the case that the deterritorialized flows which spring from technological capitalism are radically heterogeneous, and if these flows determine events (of resistance, transgression, symbiosis) which are untotalizable moments of pure possibility, then we must question the logic of composition through which Hardt and Negri expound the being/subjectivity of the multitude. According to Deleuze and Guattari the lines of flight which arise from technological assemblages of capital are 'minor' and 'nomadic'; the becoming of desire which they produce is simultaneously disruptive of the smooth space of accumulation (for its conductivities cannot be calculated), and destined to provoke the reterritorializing powers of the state. Technical systems therefore constantly fold the space of capital outward; they give rise to events for which there is no existing axiom and through which the future approaches the juridical-disciplinary organization of space as an incalculable horizon. This is clearly at odds with the arguments Hardt and Negri present in *Empire*. Their claim is that Deleuze and Guattari's attempt to expound the logic of transgressive praxis neglects the universal transformations of mass desire which arise from biopolitical production, and that they alienate the compositional power of labour to the reproduction of pure, unmediated events of difference/becoming (Hardt and Negri, 2000: 27). In the end however the problem with Hardt and Negri's attempt to reconstruct the organic structure and historical evolution of Marx's proletariat concerns the synthesis of difference. Deleuze and Guattari's account of social machines makes it clear that desire, despite its susceptibility to capture, gives rise to events which run in excess of every *ontological* formation, that is, events which burn themselves up in effects and conductivities which exceed the boundaries of sedentary space. What Hardt and Negri propose however is that it is possible to discern a synthetic movement in the technological connections of biopolitical production, and that consequently the transformative power of the multitude is founded upon the common rights of labour which are constrained and segmented by the global regime of empire. In Part IV I will argue that such a synthesis gives rise to a cluster of issues concerning the cosmopolitical being of the multitude, the ethical recognition of difference and the conflation of sovereignty and ontology. For the moment however, I want to pursue the relationship between Deleuze and Guattari's account of machinic desire and the concepts of technicity which have been developed by Jacques Derrida and Bernard Stiegler.

9
The Ethics of Technological Effects: Derrida and Stiegler

Deconstruction and technics

Put very simply the reading strategy which Derrida pursues in *Spectres of Marx* attempts to expound the internal logic of historical materialism (the primacy of the economic base, use value, organic labour and class identity), and to configure the possibility of revolutionary politics around the spectral transformations by which capital has expanded its performative regime. This strategy has a long history in Derrida's writing, and so I propose to look briefly at what has become its canonical application: the reading of Rousseau's *Essay on the Origin of Languages*[1] in *Of Grammatology*. There is in Rousseau's account of the birth of society a moment at which humanity hangs between the natural and the social; a time before historical time when human beings were both naturally desirous and freely social and when the law proscribing incest was present but not felt as a restraint upon an uncorrupted human nature. The essence of this moment is narrated by Rousseau in his account of the festival (fête); the gathering of freely desirous human beings which has yet to require the law that it has, never the less, founded. Derrida's argument is that this account of the origin of society is contradictory; for it posits the prescription of incest as that which is present in and absent from the founding configuration of language and desire. The law, in other words, has to have been present in order for 'incest' to be named and proscribed, but has to have been absent from the free expression of desire which brings forth the 'golden age' of pre-technological civilization (Derrida, 1976: 242–68). It is this 'fictive point' which grounds Rousseau's account of natural virtue; for it is only in so far as the natural and the social are permitted to operate simultaneously in his account of the festival, that he is able to assert the primacy of 'natural' passions over the corrupted desires of civil society.

This account of Rousseau's narration of an originally benign human nature highlights the logic of supplementarity which accompanies every attempt to ground the law in the absolute necessity of God, Nature or Spirit. The unconditional demand of the law, in other words, always refers back to a narrative which unites contradictory elements in an imaginary synthesis that is beyond realization. According to Derrida's analysis, Rousseau's *Discourse* inevitably leads (via a history of graphical, aesthetic and dramatological simulations) to a substantiation of its 'fictive point' in the general will, or, more precisely, in the collective enunciations through which the universal nature of man is expressed. There are, of course, similarities between Rousseau's conception of human nature and Marx's account of the origins of humanity in the *Economic and Philosophical Manuscripts*. And it is certainly true that the concepts of alienation, estrangement and expropriation which inform Marx's initial engagement with the capital do retain a certain logic of corruption and redemption. In Marx's thought however the inscription of human nature in the corruptive logic of capitalism is subject to processes of simulation and displacement which are much more complex than those presented in Rousseau's critique of civil society. The logic of historical materialism is articulated through modes of production which, in each of their discrete forms, express a complex displacement of domination and servitude into ideological representations of honesty, duty and obedience. What is important here is that, for Marx, the historical development of productive activity expresses an immanent socialization of organic labour, and that this process eventually becomes self-conscious under the conditions of industrial-technological exploitation. For Derrida however the possibility of this inscription of human essence in revolutionary class consciousness is precisely what is excluded by the technological regime of capital. The means of labour, as Marx acknowledged in *Capital* Volume One, have reduced labour power to an abstract commodity which is infinitely susceptible to exploitation, and the emergence of new media and communications systems have opened up a sphere of ideological displacement which is able constantly to transform the experience of expropriation (Derrida, 1994: 79).

This brings us back to Derrida's account of the revolutionary promise of Marxism, or, more precisely, to the question of how 'we' ('our' generation and those that are to follow 'us') are to inherit that promise. In the first chapter of *Spectres* Derrida says of the *Communist Manifesto*: 'I know of few possible texts whose lesson seems more urgent *today*, provided one takes into account what Marx and Engels themselves say about their intrinsically irreducible historicity' (Derrida, 1994: 13). So what is the nature of this 'intrinsically irreducible historicity'? We have seen that Derrida's approach to the law is concerned with the aporetic forms which precede the enunciation of its necessity; and so the aim of deconstructive analysis is to disclose the logics of supplementation through which the force of the law – its power to unify, silence and exclude – is sustained. Derrida's reading of Marx therefore proceeds from the impossibility of inscribing the productive essence of humanity in the technological organization of capitalism; for as the prosthetic, informatic and cybernetic organization of capital expands, so the ontological constitution of 'the human' which is implicit in Marx's account of historical necessity, becomes ever more dispersed. This process of technological dispersal, or 'spectralization' as Derrida calls it, has two important consequences. First, we should acknowledge that the political history of twentieth century Marxism is not simply the betrayal of Marx's thought, and that the totalitarian forms of Maoism and Stalinism are 'specters' which haunted his writing from the very beginning (*Ibid.*: 13). And second, that the revolutionary promise of Marx's work lies not in the concepts through which he sought to substantiate the universal being of the proletariat (alienation, species being, class identity), but rather in the 'specter' of Marxism which is provoked by the transformations of 'the human' that occur within the biopolitical matrix of capitalism.

In the first chapter of *Spectres of Marx* Derrida returns to the question of the law – or rather to the law's inability to determine institutional forms without simultaneously precipitating events of silencing, exclusion and erasure. The time of the historical present therefore is always 'out of joint'; for in so far as it is the law which constitutes the temporality of the present (its currentness, its self-referentiality, its place in the continuum of history), it is also that which determines a certain responsibility for those who are not, and cannot, be recognized in its present institutional structures (Derrida, 1994: 21). According to Derrida, the revolutionary promise of Marxism is directly related to this disjunctive structure of the law. The industrial phase of capitalism, as Marx showed, operates through the multiplication of technological means of production. These technological means determine effects of virtualization, instantaneity, supplementation, speed, commerce, credit and dissemination which exceed the absolute limits which Marx set upon the production of relative surplus value. Effects of this kind are the conditions upon which the global economy depends; for without the instantaneous exchange of information, the vast capacities of digital retrieval systems, and the pervasiveness of the mass media, the flows of capital into and out of particular markets could not have achieved its current global velocity. Capital, in other words, becomes a deterritorial-izing machine whose operations constantly rupture the national and international structures through which justice and the law are adminis-tered (*Ibid.*: 79). And so it is to this point of absolute disjuncture that the ghost of Marx returns to haunt the 'tele-techno-scientific' organization of biopolitical capitalism.

Derrida presents the return of Marx's revolutionary demand through the concept of the spectre, the 'body without flesh' which inhabits the ruins of justice and the law. He remarks that:

> The spectral is *someone other who looks at us*, we feel ourselves being looked at by it, outside of any synchrony, even before any look on our part, according to an absolute anteriority (which may be on the order of generation, of more than one generation) and asymmetry, according to an unmasterable disproportion. Here anachrony makes the law. (Derrida, 1994: 7)

This passage sets out a complex reconfiguration of the political ontology of Marxism and requires some careful unpacking. First there is the question of the spectre, or more precisely, of the *return* of the spectre. As capitalism expands through the technological means we have identi-fied, so human beings have become increasingly subject to effects of dispersal, supplementation and modification. These effects constantly transform the nature of exploitation; for they open up new configura-tions of the relationship between the human and the technological which exceed the transcendental inscription of the law. The 'other who looks at us' in the midst of this infinitely disjointed time is the specter of Marx's revolutionary promise; for every rupturing of the law and its categories of recognition, every loss of autonomous being, recalls a transformative responsibility which precedes and exceeds our historical present. The revolutionary promise which Derrida identifies in Marx's writing therefore has a 'messianic' structure, for its performative demand remains ethical only for as long as it answers *immediately* to the events of silencing, erasure and dispersal which accompany the limitless expansion of technological capitalism. That we cannot designate the ontology of such a promise is, according to Derrida, precisely what opens the constancy of its return (*Ibid.*: 10).

Derrida's reading of Marx turns upon what he calls the 'aporia of time', that is, on the fact that the future is absolutely undeterminable and yet depends upon a generational responsibility to the revolutionary promise. In other words, the fact that we cannot *know* the future places us under the most extreme ethical obligation to the Marxist law of anachrony – the law which exceeds the disordered operations of the capitalist machine and which returns through those 'others' who are denied the possibility of justice and recognition. This brings us back to Heidegger. According to Derrida, the notion of justice which Heidegger presents in the 'Anaximander Fragment' gestures towards an ethical stricture which exceeds every positive designation of the right and the good. The relationship of *Dasein* to the being of the other is conceived as one whose horizon is an obligation to 'let the other be', or rather, to give him the gift of his own particular relationship to Being. For Derrida however, Heidegger's fundamental ontology makes Being into the implicit condition of ethics; for in so far as the fundamental ground of responsibility is determined through *Dasein's* relationship to Being, solicitude for the other is conceived as a moment which occurs in the existential pursuit of authenticity (Derrida, 1994: 27). What is important to the present discussion is the fact that, for Heidegger, the question concerning technology is posed in terms of how technological means impact upon the ontic designation of *Dasein* as care, solicitude and authenticity. Ultimately, therefore, the ethical relationship is subsumed under a fundamental opposition between the human and the technological; an opposition which, according to Derrida, functions to exclude the very questions (about who is to be cloned, who is to be genetically manipulated, who is to be cybernetically enhanced) through which technology is designated as an ethical concern.

The concept through which Derrida seeks to characterize the effects of digital and informatic technologies is spectralization, and so we need briefly to specify the relationship between the global market and the disembodied flows through which capital constantly exceeds the established limits of accumulation. The idea of democracy, in the sense of *res publica*, is fundamentally transformed by the mass media; the powers of judgement, discrimination and reflection which belong to classical conceptions of the agora are increasingly difficult to exercise in a global space which is dominated by the reproduction of the image (Derrida, 1994: 80). This process of ideological distraction is the counterpart of a regime in which virtual flows of knowledge, information and money have become essential to the turnover of capital. The global-technological machine, in other words, constantly increases the speed at which surplus value is produced, and with which the questions that arise from the hyper-exploitation of humanity become part of the logic of ideological simulation (*Ibid.*: 50). For Derrida, however, the constitution of this feedback mechanism cannot overcome the disjuncture of the present; for every technological innovation gives rise to possibilities (of dispersal, connection, supplementation, liberation and domination) that have *not yet been determined* by the accumulative regime of capitalism. Thus the aporetic structure of the present is intensified by the global-technological operations of the market; for the events that arise from the synthetic reproduction/distribution of life designate an ethical responsibility to those who are currently subjected to its worst effects (silencing, exclusion from the purview of the law), and to those who will be subject to its expanding powers of virtualization and erasure.

So what kind of politics is demanded by this ethics of technological effects? If we begin with Derrida's account of technology as a spectralizing force which constantly expands the possibilities of capital accumulation, the question concerning technology becomes one which is essentially bound up with the question of who suffers the worst effects of this expansion. Thus our approach to the technological 'progress' which has been made by neo-liberal capitalism since the war should be informed by a sense of responsibility to the 'others' who have come to haunt the 'New World Order': the people and nations who are drawn into and then expelled from the global market, the 'new working class' for whom technology functions mainly as a means of surveillance and exploitation, the Third World populations who have become 'recipients' of technological aid (genetically modified crops, experimental medicines), and those whose lives are most immediately subject to techno-scientific imperatives (the physically disabled, the chronically and terminally ill, the unborn foetus). The question of technology cannot be disengaged from the responsibilities which are constituted in the techno-scientific supplementation of life, responsibilities which are always concerned with the presence of those who, through their very lack of legal recognition and economic power, constitute an ethical demand *par excellence*. Their approach to the dominant structures of democracy, in other words, is the unsolicited arrival of ghosts (Who is this? What are you? Is this a human?) who destabilize both the New World Order and its conventional Marxist critiques (Derrida, 1994: 63–4).

As I have indicated above, Derrida's reading of Marx is highly controversial, not least because it transforms the idea of international socialism from a class based movement into a disaggregated 'community' of artists, philosophers and activists in whose work:

> [O]ne may still find the ... Marxist 'spirit' to criticize the presumed autonomy of the juridical and to denounce endlessly the *de facto* take-over of international authorities by powerful Nation States, by

concentrations of techno-scientific capital, symbolic capital, and financial capital. (*Ibid.*: 85)

I will return to the cosmopolitical questions which arise from this account of the 'New International' in section three. For the present however I want to look at Derrida's understanding of the relationship between the 'spirit' of Marxism and the fate of the law under the conditions of technological capitalism. Derrida maintains that the law has a dual aspect: it is both the condition upon which collective identity is enacted and the chance that that identity will admit the voice of the other into its autochthonous domain. Under the regime of biopolitical capitalism this economy is radically intensified; for as the alterity of difference is ever more entwined with the technological and ideological powers of capital, the ethical demand of singularity becomes an increasingly 'spectralized' obligation which is constantly menaced by the threat of erasure. So, given this radical disordering of the normative dialectics of class, how is it possible for ethical recognition to be effective within the logic of prosthetic/artificial difference through which biopolitical capitalism expands? Derrida's argument is that this logic is always a solicitation of ghosts; for the constant transformation of the technological conditions of life is simultaneously a constant struggle of the global-hegemonic order to control the effects of marginalization, dispersal and destitution which it creates. Ultimately therefore the 'weak messianic power' of those others who come to the established structures of liberal democracy is the power of specters; the power of the indelible and untimely trace which reopens the question of technological prosthesis and its relationship to the fundamental categories of law and ethical life (*Ibid.*: 54).

Derrida's idea of technics therefore begins by placing the concept of prosthetic humanity in relation to the metaphysical structures of positive legality; for it is only in so far as the juridical inscription of identity has been established as the ground of universal recognition (culture) that we are able to determine the limits and possibilities of an ethics of technology. Such an ethics, as is made clear in both *Spectres of Marx* and *Of Grammatology*, cannot begin by assuming an essential distinction between the human and the technological. Derrida's account of inscription means that even though the process of hominization is marked by a movement into language which is simultaneously the instigation of writing and its metaphysical resources, the concept of humanity is always already technological. The emergence of the first tool-using hominids, in other words, entails a technicized organization of life which is simultaneous with the formation of self-consciousness. Thus in Derrida's conception of technics the Heideggarian opposition between man and technology is replaced by a demand constantly to re-think what humanity is, and how its prosthetic dispersal impacts upon the logos of democracy and law. This attempt to think the technicity of man in relation to the logic of juridical inscription however, gives rise to an urgent question concerning the status of prosthetic difference in Derrida's writing. For if it is the case that deconstruction gives a certain priority to arche-writing in the emergence of the human, then perhaps it is the case that obscures a more fundamental relationship of technics to self-consciousness, and of self-consciousness to the non-organic conditions of its existence ('matter'). This is Bernard Stiegler's position, and I want to conclude by examining briefly the concept of 'organized inorganic matter' which he presents in the first volume of *Technics and Time*.

Stiegler and 'organized inorganic matter'

There is a sense in which all of what has been said above is concerned with the concept of materialism, that is, with the relationship between human life, inorganic matter and the technological means through which both are transformed in the process of production. The preceding sections have considered the possibility of maintaining a Marxist approach to the relationship between technological means of labour and productive activity: for if it is the case that the impact of digital, informatic and prosthetic technologies has been to intensify the production of surplus value while at the same time displacing Marx's dialectic of the real (the symbolic economy of alienation, the increasing disparity of fixed and organic capital, the immanent socialization of the mode of production), then it becomes imperative to determine what the ethical and political consequences of this transformation are. Heidegger's account of technology as the outgrowth of an instrumental orientation to Being marks a fundamental shift in the way in which the impact of technology on social relations is conceptualized. Instead of situating the effects of technological innovation within the dialectics of capital accumulation, Heidegger's essay contends that the use of technology should be understood in terms of its reduction of Being to the level of a resource and of man to a soulless consumer of commodities. This attempt to think the concept of technology does, of course, sustain the kind of millennial demands (for cultural transformation, for recourse to the original value of artistic praxis, and for the re-gathering of the German *Volk*) which are characteristic of Heidegger's analysis of

Dasein. However the recourse to fundamental ontology which characterizes his approach to the technological organization of man discloses something of the excessively transformative power of technics. For the idea of 'enframing' (*Gestell*) which is the core of Heidegger's essay on technology, suggests an unavoidable complicity between the physical being of man and the technological means through which he becomes embroiled in the satisfactions of mass culture.

This analysis, despite its recourse to heroic assertions of authenticity against the technological organization of culture, is important because it re-opens the question of technology and its relationship to the mode of production. Thus the Frankfurt School project was, from the beginning, a response to the emergence of technology as an autonomous power through which capitalism could exceed the limits which Marx postulated in *Capital*. Despite their explicit rejections of Heidegger therefore, Benjamin, Adorno and Marcuse's attempts to expound the logics of control that arise from the technological organization of culture, constantly return to the question of redemption, of how it might be possible to reconfigure Marx's revolutionary promise in a society which seems to have co-opted the idea of socialized production. The categories through which critical theory sought to trace the negative therefore sustain a fundamental opposition between the reified identities of the culture industry and the autonomous essence of man which is glimpsed in the technological mutilation of life. The question which emerges therefore concerns the possibility of a politics of technology. For if it is the case that the essence of humanity is an archaic ghost which haunts the technological body of capital, how then is it possible to determine a political response which does not simply collapse into nostalgia for man's original self-presence?

Derrida's response to this question is to maintain that the concept of humanity cannot be disentangled from the logic of representation and dispersal which is instigated by language, and that consequently the presence of humanity to itself has always already been fractured by the technological instruments which accompany the emergence of protentive self-consciousness. Derrida's concept of originary technicity therefore opens up an aporia; for the technological organization/ spectralization of life simultaneously intensifies the exploitative power of capital and of the revolutionary demand for justice and democracy (Derrida, 1994: xix). For Stiegler however Derrida's recourse to the promise of the law sets an artificial limit on the transformative possibilities of technology. His argument is that Derrida's account of the original relationship between language and the metaphysical categories that become explicit in the text (the *grammē*), conceals a technological relationship of consciousness to matter which is the underlying condition of language, writing and protentive imagination (Stiegler, 1998: 137). By making the trace of *différance* the condition through which inorganic nature is symbolically articulated, in other words, deconstruction begins with a level of hominization (language, writing, culture) which can only be explained by reference to a technological differentiation of hominids which is implicit in the concept of inorganic matter (*Ibid.*: 139). And so to understand how humanity has come to inhabit the space of technological society, and the political consequences of this occupation, we must recognize that the very possibility of 'the human' has evolved through an immense pre-history in which consciousness develops through the interactions of matter, tool and cerebral cortex:

> [T]he human invents himself in the technological inventing of the tool – by becoming exteriorized techno-logically. But here the human is the interior: there is no exteriorization that does not point to a movement from exterior to interior. Nevertheless, the interior is inverted in this movement; it can therefore not precede it. Interior and exterior are consequently constituted in a movement that invents both one and the other: a moment in which they invent each other respectively, as if there were a technological maieutic of what is called humanity. (*Ibid.*: 141–2)

Thus the human is, in his very origin, technological; and so the evolution of humanity from pre-hominid (Neanthropian) to hominid (Zinjanthropian) can only take place through the manipulation of inorganic matter.

Stiegler's approach to the question of the hominization proceeds on the basis of an original differentiation of the tool (specifically the flint axe) and the cerebral cortex of pre-hominids; a differentiation which transforms matter into a technological object, and which initiates the capacities of anticipation and memory without which the transition from the pre-human to the human could not take place. Technics, in other words, determines a process of 'exteriorization' in which humanity is no longer tied to the genetic codes of its species; for the 'double plasticity' of life and inorganic matter inscribes the concept of 'man' in a process of constant technological self-invention (Stiegler, 1998: 142). Stiegler calls this process epiphylogenesis: the mutual invention of matter as a technological object and of humanity as a process of exteriorization which is neither voluntaristic nor externally imposed. Thus the 'who' of humanity (its inscription in time, language and culture) emerges through a technical relationship to inorganic matter which is the condition of language, and which constantly re-differentiates/ destabilizes the categories through which social being is articulated (*Ibid.*: 178).

The law, in all of its positive determinations, simultaneously calls forth a fictive narration of its history, or what Derrida has called the 'law before the law'. This logic of juridical necessity is undeconstructible; for it is that which 'gives' the time and space of culture and which gathers humanity into the narratives of spirit, substance and history which constitute the presence of the social. The radical promise (*Zusage*) for which deconstruction takes responsibility therefore is the promise of humanity to the fictive limit of the law, that is, to the 'originary alliance to which we must have in some sense already acquiesced, already said *yes*, whatever may be the problematicity of the discourse which may follow' (Derrida, 1990a: 129). Thus for Derrida the horizon of deconstructive thought is the 'problematicity' that arises from the inscription of the law; for it is within this horizon that the ethical demand emerges as an irreducible responsibility to those who are excluded from the fictive representations of friendship, community and identity through which the law is enacted. This conception of a responsibility that begins with man's originary promise to the logos gives rise to a certain privileging of literary analysis; for it is through its critiques of the fictive configurations which ground the legitimacy of the law that deconstruction seeks to outplay the transcendental categories of conventional philosophy. Indeed Derrida's reading of Marx proceeds from what he conceives as the founding promise of Marx's writing to the disjuncture of the present violence of the law. According to Stiegler however Derrida's 'Heideggarian' account of the originary promise obscures the *more originary* relationship of organized inorganic matter; for by taking the 'fictive point' as it is narrated in philosophy as the undeconstructible condition of ethical responsibility, Derrida's thought is always engaged in the reproduction of ontology, even as it seeks to fold and transform its categories. Stiegler's version of deconstruction, on the other hand, attempts to think the idea of humanity in terms of a 'technological giving of time', that is, in terms of an originary technicity which predates and exceeds the limits of ontology, and which demands that every biopolitical innovation should be judged in terms of the play of affective, libidinal, utilitarian and destructive effects it produces (Stiegler, 1998: 276). So what is the political significance of such judgements?

In order to answer this question I need to return briefly to Deleuze and Guattari. As we have seen the narratives of *Anti-Oedipus* and *A Thousand Plateaus* set out a universal history which develops through: (1) the co-presence of the organic and the inorganic in the emergence of human self-consciousness, (2) the originally technical constitution of desire and the symbolic imagination and (3) the undetermined possibilities of becoming which are inscribed in this originally technological self-consciousness. What is important here, as Paul Patton makes clear in his account of the political significance of Deleuze's writing, is to determine how the liberation of desire through the technological organization of social and organic bodies, is able to designate an ethico-political demand (Patton, 2000: 103). One possible approach to this question is to argue, as Nick Land does, that the flows of schizoid desire which are put into play by technological capitalism are 'ethical' in the sense that they run counter to the nostalgic ideals of belonging which are characteristic of bourgeois culture (Land, 1993: 67). It follows therefore that 'politics' ought to be about intensifying the drive towards depersonalization and intensification through which capital overcomes its internal limits (Patton, 2000: 104). This, I would suggest, is close to the political gesture which Stiegler makes at the conclusion of *Technics and Time, 1*. The idea of organized inorganic matter configures the precedence of technics in the process of hominization; and so the socio-historical evolution of humanity gives rise to questions of 'transcendence' (innovation beyond the genetic programme of the species) which cannot be mediated through the conventional categories of the logos (spirit, culture, man). This aporetic designation of the human therefore gestures towards an ethics of self-invention which arises from the technological body of society, and which becomes political through the assertion of the transformative excess/*différance* which is the very origin of the human organism (Stiegler, 1998: 272).

Patton argues that techno-libidinal arguments of this kind are anti-political; for they determine an absolute opposition between the social machines through which desire is channelled into regulated flows and the anarchic bodies through which that desire becomes transgressive. His claim is that although there are elements of Deleuze and Guattari's work which encourage this kind of reading (particularly the account of the reactive power of the *Urstaat* in *Anti-Oedipus*), the political gesture of their writing consists in the attempt to show that the forms of desire which are liberated by particular social machines are dispersed into heterogeneous (and simultaneous) events of capture and liberation.

The possibility of an effective politics of desire, in other words, 'hinges on the nature of the forms of deterritorialization present in a given situation' (Patton, 2000: 106). Under the conditions of biopolitical capitalism the dynamics of 'de' and 're' territorialization are extremely complex, and require a critical distinction between contingent flows which are immediately integrated into the axiological regime of the state, and those which draw minoritized forms of desire into rhizomatic associations. Thus the fact that the capitalist machine functions by constantly transforming its technological instruments and by recapturing the contingent forms of desire which it puts into play, means that the politics of desire is always bound up with the juridical forms by which the state attempts to legitimize its domination of particular minorities. The war machines which are constituted through global flows of money, information and desire, in other words, *can* take the form of a total resistance to capital; however it could be argued that they function more rhizomatically by confronting its legal institutions with minority demands (aboriginal rights, for example) which have been silenced by conventional juridical codes (*Ibid.*: 121–32).

Patton's reading of Deleuze and Guattari is not too far distant from Derrida's account of the relationship between the technological body of capital and the law of anachrony to which a deconstructive Marxism would respond. For if we conceive the technological precipitation of desire as something which takes place within the axiological structure of capitalism, then the ethical questions that arise from the prosthetic reconfiguration of humanity bear directly upon the juridical organization of justice. This is not to say that there is a simple homology between the political gestures offered by Derrida and Deleuze; for the 'wildstyle' experimentation through which Deleuzians have approached the question of technology, has, I would suggest, tended to draw attention away from the ethical questions of silencing and erasure which are foregrounded in Derrida's reading of Marx. And so while it may not be the case that Deleuze and Guattari seek the absolute liberation of technological desire (as in Stiegler's account of the pre-history of human technicity), their configurations of the nomadic and the sedentary, the smooth and the striated, do perhaps encourage the multiplication of absolutely singular forms of resistance to the accumulative regime of capital. Such a dispersal of revolutionary desire does not, as Hardt and Negri suggest, constitute a crisis to which only a return to a Marxist ontology of socialized production could provide the solution. Rather, and this is where I think Derrida's reading of Marx outplays the recourse to absolute singularity which is implicit in both Deleuze and Stiegler's conceptions of technics, it is through the question of hospitality to 'who comes' that we are constantly returned to questions of justice, democracy and the law. In the section which follows I will develop the cosmopolitical implications of this ethic of hospitality.

Part III

Globalization and the New International

This section is concerned with the political consequences which arise from the global restructuring of capitalism. In the two previous sections I have attempted to sketch the transformative effects which digital, informatic, cybernetic and prosthetic technologies have had upon the reproduction of capital and upon the political project of Marxism. The guiding thread of my analysis has been a concern with the technological processes through which the M–C–M relation has been transformed, or more precisely, the processes of 'virtualization' through which capital has revolutionized patterns of consumption, the productivity of labour and the processes of commodification. For Marx the relationship between base and superstructure is founded upon a distinction between the accumulative regime of capital and the symbolic order through which that regime is represented; literary, philosophical and religious forms transfigure powers of expropriation which are ontologically prior in the history of 'ruling ideas'. This fundamental distinction is now far more difficult to defend than it was in Marx's time, and so the relationship between Marxism and postmodernism is perhaps best understood in terms of Derrida, Baudrillard, Negri and Deleuze's attempts to expound the complicity between capital and the general economy of the sign. This raises the three crucial issues I want to examine in this section. First there is the question of the breakdown of capital, for what is common to all of the 'postmodernist' theorists we will look at in this section is a sense that the technological evolution of capital is such that its capacity for expansion is no longer constrained by the limits which Marx sought to expound in *Capital*. Second there is the question of neo-colonialism, or the reproduction of 'master' and 'slave' economies through the technological powers which have facilitated the expansion of the international market. And finally there is the question of global revolution, or, more specifically, of the fate of the international fraternity of the proletariat under the conditions of global technological capitalism.

These questions are not new; indeed they are the ones which preoccupied the thinkers (Bernstein, Kautsky, Lenin, Luxemburg *et al.*) who took part in the so-called Second International between 1879 and 1914. Thus Chapter 10 will examine the ways in which Lenin and Rosa Luxemburg sought to develop Marx's account of the relationship between the imperialist stage of capitalism and the revolutionary constitution of the international proletariat. Chapter 12 looks at the transformations through which capital has evolved into a properly global system of exchange, and the ways in which the political consequences of this transformation have been theorized in the conventional literature on globalization. Chapters 13 and 14 bring me back to the relationship between Marxism and postmodernist theory, and it is here that I want to examine the critique of neo-liberal approaches to globalization which has emerged from the work of Baudrillard, Derrida, Negri and Deleuze. In particular, I will examine their respective attempts to show that techno-scientific capital has produced a new form of imperialism in which even the limited principles of responsibility exercised by the old colonial powers have been dispensed with, and every resource has become the *de facto* property of a decentred and ultra-mobile regime of accumulation. Finally I will return to the relationship between postmodernist configurations of politics within the regime of global capitalism and Marxist accounts of international class solidarity.

10
Colonialism and Imperialism

There is a sense in which the task of expounding the relationship between capitalism and imperialism fell to Marx's successors; for as Ernest Mandel has pointed out in his introduction to *Capital* Volume Three, Marx never developed a fully articulated account of the place of colonialism and military conquest in the formation of the world market (Marx, 1991: 45). He did however provide a historical account of the relationship between colonialism and mercantile capital which anticipated the debates about the growth of international markets and the acquisition of pre-capitalist milieu that were to become the focus of Marxist theories of imperialism. This argument can be briefly summarized.

Under the conditions of large-scale industrial capitalism circulation has completely mastered production; every commodity is produced as an exchange value which is determined by the average rate of profit in its particular branch of manufacture (Marx, 1991: 445). The establishment of this relation, however, presupposes the emergence of mercantile capital within the old feudal order: for it is only in so far as the growth of the money economy which is stimulated by the expansion of foreign trade has a 'solvent effect' upon traditional relationships of dependency and obligation, that it is possible for the merchant to emerge as an autonomous person whose wealth is independent of landed property. This prototypical form of capitalism begins as a 'pure carrying trade' that does not yet dominate production, and so the activity of the merchant is concerned exclusively with buying commodities cheaply on one market and selling them at a higher price on another. Colonialism therefore emerges from the growth of mercantile capital; the latter establishes colonies as cheap sources of labour (slaves) and raw materials and makes money by exporting them to more developed economies.

As Marx puts it:

> Commercial capital, when it holds a dominant position, is thus in all cases a system of plunder, just as its development in the trading peoples of both ancient and modern times is directly bound up with violent plunder, the taking of slaves and subjugation of colonies. (*Ibid*.: 448–9)

Commercial trade, in other words, does not of itself revolutionize the mode of production, for what the merchant class does is simply to buy up independent producers and set them to work under conditions that are generally more exploitative than those of the old regime. What it does do however is to establish the accumulation of capital as an end in itself, for the goal of the mercantile entrepreneur is always the valorization of his capital through the sale of commodities for more than their original price. The exact nature of the shift from the dominance of landed property to that of commercial trade, and from commercial trade to industrial capitalism does, of course, vary from country to country. The relative solidity of the feudal order may well stifle the growth of commercial capital in one place, while in another the mercantile class may sweep away the old regime much more expeditiously; also some nations, in seeking to retain the old 'carrying trade' with its subjugated colonies and regime of violent expropriation, will fail to develop the industrial base that would allow them to remain competitive in the international economy (*Ibid*.: 450). Once industrial capitalism has established itself as the mode of production in the most developed economies of the world therefore, commercial capital is subsumed under the logic of the M–C–M relation: it becomes an ancillary element in the reproduction of surplus value through the manufacture of commodities (*Ibid*.: 454–5).

This raises some important questions, particularly with regard to the fact that the 'discredited' practices of colonialism have, as a matter of historical fact, continued to co-exist successfully with the regime of industrial capitalism. For Marx the nature of this persistence is determined by the evolution of the mode of production, and so we need to look briefly at the account of the falling rate of profit and the cyclical crises in the realization of surplus value which he presents in the third volume of *Capital*. Put very simply Marx maintains that as the regime of industrial capitalism expands, so the force of competition in the various branches of production compels each individual capitalist to increase the number of commodities he produces. This is because any branch of production, so long as it retains the possibility of valorizing capital investment in the manufacture of commodities, will continue to attract new entrepreneurs, and because the consequent increase in production will always drive down both the social value of the goods produced and the amount of surplus value that accrues to the capitalist from the sale of each commodity. The only way any given firm can expand the mass of surplus value which it creates therefore is by investing in machine technologies which speed up the process of production and thereby increase the total number of commodities which the capitalist has to sell. This increase in expenditure on machinery (fixed capital) in order to expand the mass of surplus value however operates within certain absolute limits. For Marx the pressure of competition constantly forces up expenditure on the means of labour and thereby increases the proportion of capital invested in instruments whose value can be redeemed only very slowly. Thus the capacity to increase the *total mass* of surplus value is bought at the cost of diminishing the *rate* at which profit is created in each branch of production (Marx, 1991: 323). The very factors which increase the mass of profit generated by capitalist enterprise (cheapening of labour power, declining costs of machinery and raw materials), in other words, are those which determine the general decline in its rate of production (*Ibid.*: 331).

According to Marx the unfolding of this tendency of the rate of profit to fall expresses a fundamental contradiction between the development of productive forces and the regime of private appropriation. Industrial capitalism, as we have seen, develops by increasing the magnitude and complexity of the means of production and by reducing the amount of variable capital (wage labour) which it puts to work. This reduction is compensated for by a rise in the average rate of exploitation; for in so far as the productivity of labour is increased by each round of technological innovation, the mass of profit can be sustained, and even increased, with a declining number of workers (Marx, 1991: 355). The intensification of wage labour however cannot be sustained *ad infinitum*; the increased expenditure on fixed capital which is demanded of every enterprise leads to a situation in which wages are forced down to subsistence levels, working hours are constantly extended, unemployment becomes endemic, and the market is flooded with commodities which fewer and fewer people can afford to buy. Thus the tendency of the rate of profit to fall is an expression of the fact that the technological solutions which are adopted by capitalists to sustain the overall mass of surplus value, necessarily give rise to the crises of valorization which result from the under-exploitation of the means of labour. The fact that machines are deployed purely as instruments for the generation of exchange values, in other words, gives rise to an accelerated demand for their replacement which deprives them of their social function as producers of the means of subsistence (*Ibid.*: 357–8).

So, if it is the case that the ability of capital to valorize itself decreases with the development of the technological means of labour, then why, Marx asks, does the rate of profit not decline much more quickly? For it would seem as if the necessity to increase relative surplus value should lead to a rhythm of technological replacement which would outstrip the possibility of returning a profit in all but the largest joint-stock companies (Marx, 1991: 339). In chapter 14 of *Capital* Volume Three, however, Marx identifies six 'counteracting factors' through which capitalism manages to slow down the speed at which the average of rate profit declines, and thereby retain the spread of small and medium sized companies which are essential to its economic and political stability. The first four of these factors ('more intense exploitation of labour', 'reduction of wages below their value', 'cheapening the element of constant capital' and 'relative surplus population') are familiar; for they have already been identified by Marx as essential elements in the production of commodities in *Capital* Volume One.[1] Marx's account of the final two factors however ('foreign trade' and 'the increase in share capital') begins to sketch out the relationship between the internal and external markets through which capital expands, and to give some sense of the connection between capitalism and imperialism which was to become the focus of the Second International. His argument is that foreign trade has two primary effects: it lowers the cost of both fixed capital and the means of subsistence (*Ibid.*: 345). Thus the importation of raw materials from less developed economies allows the manufacturers of the means of labour (Department I) and of the means of subsistence (Department II) to reduce expenditure on fixed capital and thereby extract more surplus value from goods sold at the same price. In addition to this the technological disadvantage at which pre-capitalist nations find themselves in relation to the established industrial powers, means that the latter are able to sell their commodities to the former at a price that is well above the level established in their own domestic economies (*Ibid.*: 346). According to Marx therefore the growth of world trade bears the imprint of colonialism upon it from the very beginning; for as industrialized markets become increasingly monopolistic, so the opportunity for higher rates of profit and exploitation offered by pre and partially capitalist markets becomes essential to the reproduction of surplus value (*Ibid.*: 348).

Ultimately the global spread of capitalism has three material effects which follow from, and are reproduced by, the necessity to intensify the exploitation of colonial dependencies. First, the development of scientific, technological and economic infrastructures increases the cost of the raw materials imported from the colonies, and thus drives down the average rate of profit towards the lower levels established in more developed nations. Second, colonialism demands the establishment of an indigenous middle class who are capable of operating the bureaucratic and technological apparatus of imperial control. And third, the imposition of science, technology and bureaucratic reason sweeps away what, for Marx, is the stagnant regime of pre-capitalist production and establishes the foundations of rational capitalism. These three effects form the basis of the idea of revolutionary cosmopolitanism which Marx presents in 'The Future Results of British Rule in India'. He argues that 'old Asiatic society' is incapable of generating the scientific and technological conditions necessary for an industrial revolution, and that the shift towards the rational asceticism of the capitalist regime can take place only through the agency of the Western colonial powers (Marx, 1977c: 332). Thus the possibility of world revolution depends upon the spread of Enlightenment science, bourgeois asceticism and large-scale industrial production into every indigenous culture; for it is only insofar as the latter are forcibly subsumed under the regime of capitalist exploitation, that they can become active within the international body of the proletariat (*Ibid.*: 335).

Marx's construction of the relationship between the enlightened regime of techno-bureaucratic exploitation and the inveterate passivity of Asiatic society is, of course, highly contentious; for as Edward Said has pointed out, the concept of an 'Asiatic' mode of production which Marx deploys in his essay on British colonialism, is taken more or less unmodified from Hegel, Goethe and Schlegel's reflections on the essence of the Oriental character and Oriental civilization (Said, 1995: 21). Asiatic society, in other words, is conceived in terms of certain immutable traits – capricious despotism, feudal luxury, subsistence agriculture, lack of rational subjectivity – which consign it to the status of a primitive aggregation that awaits the transformative powers of bourgeois culture and capitalist industry. Such a society, according to Marx, 'has no history at all'; for in so far as its organization of production stands very close to the cyclical movement of nature, the absence of economic, political and technological differentiation has meant that it has been unable to 'act' historically, that is, to resist the 'successive intruders who have founded their empires on the passive basis of that unresting and unchanging society' (Marx, 1977c: 332). This *a priori* conception of 'Asiatic' societies as essentially passive carries within it the assumption that colonialism, despite the fact that it is based on the violent expropriation of indigenous populations and resources, is the instrument through which the inarticulate, subjectless culture of the Orient is inserted into the dialectics of world revolution. Marx's account of colonialism therefore raises serious questions about the erasure of cultural difference from the register of historical necessity: for if it is the case that world revolution is possible only through the socialization of productive forces achieved by industrial capitalism, and if that socialization is also the erasure of the 'primitive' forms of culture, religion and production which Marx associates with Asiatic societies, then world revolution would bring about the end of a culture whose very concept had predestined its disappearance from human history. I will return to these cosmopolitical questions shortly, but for the moment I need to look in more detail at the way in which the relationship between capitalism and imperialism was developed by Marx's immediate successors.

As I have said, one of the major questions which occupied the Second International was the breakdown of capitalism and the role of the working class in the establishment of international socialism. Lack of space means that I cannot do justice to the complexity of the debates which were fought out on the Marxist left between 1879 and 1914; what I can do however is to examine the opposing arguments of Lenin and Rosa Luxemburg on the historical forces which would shape the revolutionary transition from capitalism to socialism. In chapter 26 of *The Accumulation of Capital* Luxemburg argues that if we take Marx's assumption that social productivity is divided into two departments (Department I which produces the means of production and Department II which produces consumer goods), it is clear that the continued valorization of capital depends upon there being enough disposable wealth (wages + profits) to absorb the mass of commodities produced by Department II. Such an ideal unity cannot however be achieved under the actual conditions of a capitalist economy, as part of the surplus value which is produced by Departments I and II has to be used to generate the next round of production. This unconsumed portion of surplus value is utilized in two ways: (1) the production in Department I of more means of labour than are required by both departments and (2) the production of less value[2] in Department II than is accumulated by both workers and owners; and so the internal market of capitalism always recreates the vicious circle of falling demand and overproduction. Luxemburg's analysis maintains that Marx radically underestimated the extent of capitalism's dependency on undeveloped countries, under-exploited classes, and enclaves of craft manufacture and that consequently his account of the disordering tendencies which animate the 'free market' conceals the far more rapid temporality of decline which emerges as 'pre-capitalist milieu' are used up. Thus for Luxemburg there is an objective tendency for capitalism to break down; for the continued valorization of money through the commodity form depends upon the exploitation of new sources of labour, raw materials and consumers which, as they are colonized by the most powerful economies, precipitate the world market into increasingly severe crises of valorization (Luxemburg, 1968: 348–67).

Lenin's analysis of the imperialist phase of capitalism is in fact very similar to Luxemburg's. He argues that the kind of free market capitalism which predominated for most of the nineteenth century has given rise to the cartels, syndicates and trusts through which the largest corporations have monopolized the major branches of industrial production. This consolidation of industrial corporations is reinforced by the growth of finance capital; for without the enormous amount of credit which is provided by the banks (at an appropriate rate of interest), the constant development of the means of production which is required by monopoly capitalism could not take place. As the internal markets of the most economically developed countries become over-capitalized, so the export of capital to less developed nations becomes essential to the reproduction of corporate profits. Consequently the big corporations of each of the major industrial powers (Lenin specifies France, Germany, Britain and America) begin the process of partitioning the world: each nation acts to consolidate its military, economic and political presence in the colonies it has already acquired and to expand its influence over those which currently belong to its competitors. The outcome of this universal competition for resources is the total partitioning of the globe; for every territory which is, or might become, useful to the maintenance of a particular monopoly is appropriated by one or other of the major powers (Lenin, 1934: 81). Thus competition among imperial nations is always about *re-partitioning*; it is a violent struggle which constantly alters both the distribution of finite resources and the geopolitical organization of hegemony (*Ibid.*: 83–4).

The accounts of capitalist imperialism which are presented by Lenin and Luxemburg therefore are complementary rather than exclusive: both emphasize the link between monopoly capitalism and the competition for colonial territories, both provide an account of the growing dependency of finance and industrial capital on the exploitation of external markets and both regard imperialism as the final phase of the conflict between private appropriation and the socialization of the means of production. However, this basic agreement on the relationship between capitalism and imperialism does not extend to the politics of revolutionary change. Lenin's argument is that although the imperialist stage of capitalism is marked by increasingly violent conflicts, the crises that arise from the partitioning of the world do not necessarily produce the kind of revolutionary class consciousness which could bring about the transition to socialism. Indeed he claims that imperialism has led to the emergence of a constellation of ideological illusions which he groups together under the term 'opportunism'. Thus, as the financial oligarchies and industrial corporations accumulate more and more capital in the most prosperous nations, an increasingly large section of the working class is bought off by the promise of higher wages, a greater say in the government of the state and the possibility of exerting a moderating influence over the worst excesses of capitalism (Lenin, 1934: 94). The theoretical counterpart of this cooption of the working class is, for Lenin, to be found in Kautsky's notion of 'ultra-imperialism': the idea that the concentration of finance and industrial capital in the hands of a few imperialist nations marks the point at which it is possible to conceive of a cosmopolitan association of states which would function to preserve international peace and the equal distribution of resources (*Ibid.*: 106). Lenin's response to this providential Marxism is, quite rightly, to argue that the dynamics of monopoly capital are such as to exclude the attribution of idealistic motives (universal respect for humanity, the pursuit of perpetual peace[3]) to those nations who are struggling to expand their share of a totally partitioned world (*Ibid.*: 113). The only way to bring about the peaceful coexistence of humanity therefore is through the abolition of capitalism; and this, for Lenin, requires the strategic intervention and leadership of the communist party in the formation of revolutionary class consciousness.

There is a sense in which Leninist critiques of Luxemburg maintain that her account of social revolution commits the same kind of idealist fallacy as Kautsky; for even though she rejects the idea of reformism on the same grounds as Lenin, it has been argued that her belief in the breakdown of capitalism led her to maintain that revolutionary praxis would arise spontaneously from the conflicts inherent in its imperialist stage. The formation of the proletariat as a political subject, in other words, is presented as the necessary counterpart of capitalism's decline into permanent conflict over the last unexploited peoples, territories and resources. This reading of Luxemburg is rather tendentious: her position is not that the objective contradictions of imperialism simply 'go over' into the realm of practical collective culture, but rather that we can, given the historical tendency of the mode of the production, be justified in maintaining that *at some point* the privations to which the international working class are subjected will result in the worldwide abolition of capitalism (Kolakowski, 1981: 71). According to Lenin, however, such appeals to the long run of history retain a certain providentialism; for if the precondition of revolutionary praxis is conceived as an objective tendency in the mode of production, then the organization of class consciousness in relation to specific events (crises of legitimacy in particular states, catastrophic conflicts between imperialist powers, etc.) tends to be subsumed under the balance of conditions which, *as yet*, may not favour the success of the worker's revolution. For Lenin, in other words, the dynamics of revolutionary praxis must always be reformed in relation to the exigencies of the day; for if the possibility of action is missed on the grounds of its being 'untimely', then the moment of revolution will constantly recede into an infinite future of reform and opportunism (Lenin, 1976: 44–9).

So, what light do these arguments shed on the possibility of a Marxist politics that could operate in our late capitalist world? It is clear that Luxemburg's confidence in the breakdown of international capitalism was misplaced: the growth of the military-industrial complex, the division of the globe into 'First', 'Second' and 'Third Worlds', and the emergence of a knowledge-based information economy have all contributed to a longevity of capitalism which shows little sign of ending. Indeed the violent antagonisms which Luxemburg attributes to the scarcity of pre-capitalist milieu seem to have been managed more or less successfully by the media-techno-scientific reorganization of production. This, of course, is not to suggest that the techno-scientific expansion of the world market has superseded the 'complex machinery' of oppression which Lenin identified as the essence of capitalism; for the very technologies through which the conflicts of imperialism have been reconfigured, have given rise to new regimes of geopolitical exploitation whose logics we will need to examine closely. Thus if it is the case that the social, political and class constitution of capitalism has been radically altered by the development of its technological basis, then the question we will need to examine in the following chapters concerns the fate of Marxism *after* the violent conflicts of late nineteenth and early twentieth century imperialism. How, in other words, might a cosmopolitan socialist politics still be possible within the biopolitical networks of the global economy? Before proceeding to this question however I need to situate it in relation to contemporary debates about the nature and consequences of globalization.

11
World Markets and Global Transformations

In their book *Global Transformations: Politics, Economics and Culture* Held *et al.* identify three main perspectives in the globalization debate: the hyperglobalist thesis, the sceptical thesis, and the transformationalist thesis. Essentially the hyperglobalist thesis maintains that globalization is primarily an economic phenomenon, that an increasingly integrated world market exists today, and that the needs of multinational capitalism impose a neo-liberal economic discipline (low taxation, minimal welfare provision, privatization of public services) on all states who participate in the world economy (Held *et al.*, 2003: 4). This approach has, to a large extent, become associated with a neo-liberal idea of cosmopolitanism: the development of an integrated world market means that individual nation states have to develop coherent social and economic strategies, to ensure that individual talent is properly utilized and to pursue the particular advantages which they may have relative to other states in the global economy. And so the economic demands which are constituted through global competition are conceived as giving rise to morally and politically coherent states in which individual freedom is recognized as the key to economic success (Fukuyama, 2000: 5). It should however be recognized that the hyperglobalist thesis does not necessarily entail an attachment to neo-liberalism; for as Held *et al.* point out, it is perfectly consistent to maintain that the world market has become globalized, and that nation states are under increasing pressure to lower taxes and reduce welfare spending, without subscribing to the idea that this contributes to the greater happiness and wellbeing of humanity. Callinicos *et al.*, for example, develop a Leninist account of globalization as a new form of imperialist exploitation which is made all the more efficient by new techniques of integration, policing and military intervention (Callinicos *et al.*, 1995: 127–34).

The sceptical thesis, whose most coherent expression is presented by Hirst and Thompson in their *Globalization in Question*, maintains that if the concept of globalization necessarily involves an increasing level of openness in the world market, then it is far from clear that the current state of the international trade points to the existence of a qualitatively new regime of global exchange. Indeed they argue that if statistics for international trade, the movement of capital, and the migration of labour at the end of the twentieth century are compared with those for the period between 1875 and 1913, it seems as if the world market was actually more 'open' in the period of high imperialism than it is today (Hirst and Thompson in Held and McGrew, 2002: 335–40). This leads them to conclude that: (1) multinational corporations still transact the majority of their business in their 'home' economies, (2) the 'triad' America, Europe, and Japan has largely retained its economic hegemony in the world market, (3) the globalization of the labour market is constrained by the state controls and the regional bias of the multinationals, (4) there has been no 'great migration' of manufacturing to the developing nations of the south and (5) the emergence of a 'global culture' is unlikely in a world which is still marked by strong regionalization. Thus the hyperglobalist claim that nation states have been fundamentally compromised by social, cultural, economic and political relationships which exceed and intersect their territorial extent, is conceived as a gross exaggeration of the degree to which the world market has become an objectively constraining influence upon their sovereignty. The processes of integration that are at work in the world economy, in other words, are still significantly influenced by the economic and political autonomy of nation states; and so while Hirst and Thompson admit that qualitative changes have taken place in the organization of world trade, they contend that to mistake these changes for a paradigm shift, as the hyperglobalists do, is to lose sight of the fact that the concept of globalization has yet to be (and may never be) realized (*Ibid.*: 346).

The third perspective which Held *et al.* identify is the transformationalist thesis (Held *et al.*, 2003: 8–9). Unlike the sceptics transformationalists argue that there *has* been a qualitative shift in the organization of the world market: new technologies have increased both the range and the frequency of transactions between different regions of the globe, the mode of production has been fundamentally transformed by the emergence of the 'knowledge economy', regional cooperation (the EU,

ECOSOC, SADC, etc.) has begun to influence the conduct of nations in the global market, and international institutions (the UN, UNESCO, UNICEF, etc.) have come to exert an increasing influence over the legal, economic and political sovereignty of individual states. Thus to argue that these transformations do not alter the basic functions of states in the world economy is to refuse to acknowledge that the turnover of capital in different periods, while it can be expressed in similar statistical indicators, takes place through qualitatively different sets of social, economic and political relationships. According to the transformationalists therefore it is necessary to recognize that the world market has, over the last thirty or so years, achieved unprecedented levels of integration and interdependence, and that as a result of this transformation the practice of territorial sovereignty has been radically altered. Anthony Giddens in *The Consequences of Modernity*, for example, argues that while it is true that nation states remain the dominant actors in the global political order (due to the fact that they retain a virtual monopoly over the means of violence), their autonomy is intersected by the influence of multinational corporations, the international division of labour which they create and the rise of international institutions which seek to regulate the operation of the world market (Giddens, 1997a: 71–8). The state, in other words, is conceived as the site of a contestation between the neo-liberal orthodoxy of the multinationals, the ethical demands of international law and the political culture of the nation; and so far from being swallowed up by the functional imperatives of the international economy, the state is galvanized by the global influences to which it must constantly adapt and respond (Held *et al.*, 2003: 9).

The three perspectives which Held *et al* present in *Global Transformations* are discrete configurations of an old philosophical question, that of the nature and possibility of human progress. Kant, in his essay 'Idea for a Universal History With a Cosmopolitan Purpose', maintained that the ultimate purpose of creation was that human beings should live together in peace under the authority of the moral law, and that the apparent chaos of historical events was in fact the phenomenal form in which the cosmopolitan purpose of history is revealed to the reflective intellect. The structure of Kant's argument therefore refers empirical history to a transcendental purpose (the cosmopolitan federation of states) which exceeds the violent contractions and dislocations of ethical life which are characteristic of the secular existence of nation states (Kant, 1991: 51–63). According to Held *et al.* the neo-liberal form of the hyperglobalist thesis reproduces the structure of Kant's argument: for by maintaining that global integration is the immanent purpose of modernity, and that the exploitative practices it has determined are temporary phenomena which will disappear with the evolution of the system, hyperglobalism neglects any serious analysis of the tensions which afflict the relationships between global systems and nation states. It is in this sense then that the sceptical thesis can be seen as the obverse of hyperglobalism; for the concentration on economic indicators and the reluctance to admit that new technologies, institutions and regimes have substantively changed the world economy, is a reaction to the strongly teleological claims which are expressed by the hyperglobalists. Thus the sceptical claim that 'hyperglobalization' is not happening, and that a far more limited set of transformations has affected the sovereignty of the nation state, is based upon a confusion of globalization as an ideal with globalization as a conjunction of real effects that are being played out in the contemporary world order. The transformationalist approach[1] which is espoused by Held attempts to clarify this confusion: he maintains that we should conceive globalization neither as an instrument of cosmopolitan democracy nor as a kind of postmodernist ideology which obscures the real issues of governance which confront modern nation states. He argues that it is in fact a 'conjunctural' phenomenon in which the increasing speed and intensity of connections among nation states should be conceptualized in terms of the historically specific forms of domination, cooperation, conflict and regulation which they produce (Held *et al.*, 2003: 27–8). This, as we will see in moment, is not to reject the idea of cosmopolitanism out of hand; rather it is an attempt to think its possibility in relation to the transnational institutions and relationships which intersect the territory of the state (*Ibid.*: 444).

Held's version of cosmopolitanism is essentially a Habermasian account of the responsibilities that arise from what he has called 'thick' globalization, that is, the transformation of the world order which has been brought about by increasingly frequent and intensive contacts among nation states who participate in the extensive networks of the global economy (Held *et al.*, 2003: 21). Under these conditions, Held argues, the concept of ethics has to undergo a fundamental transformation: for in so far as the actions of the most economically, politically and militarily powerful states have profound consequences for vast numbers of people in the less developed nations of the world, the context of ethical discourse must be shifted from particular lifeworlds (the political cultures which evolve in specific nations) to the extensive space of global networks. In his article 'Law of States, Law of Peoples' he suggests that such a cosmopolitan ethics is already discernible in the structures of international law and international organizations which have emerged during the latter half of the twentieth century, and that these institutions, while they are clearly imperfect, gesture towards a set of ethical principles which ought to govern the conduct of all nations (Held, 2000, in Held and McGrew, 2004: 514). These principles are identified as:

1. equal worth and dignity;
2. active agency;
3. personal responsibility and accountability;
4. consent;
5. reflexive deliberation and collective decision-making through voting procedures;
6. inclusiveness and subsidiarity;
7. avoidance of serious harm and the amelioration of urgent need. (*Ibid.*: 515)

Held divides these principles into three 'clusters': 'constituting principles' (principles 1–3); 'legitimating principles' (principles 4–6); and the final principle of 'prioritizing commitment'. The first cluster 'sets down the fundamental organizational principles of the cosmopolitan moral universe', and is concerned with the relationship between the *right* of every rational human being to exercise his/her public reason in deciding how to act and what institutions to create, and the *obligation* which all such beings have to treat others with decency and respect (*Ibid.*: 520). Each individual, in other words, should consider the consequences of his/her actions – intended and unintended, distant and proximate – for other rational human beings. The second cluster is concerned with determining the kind of regulatory frameworks that follow from the designation of ethical responsibility which is set out in the cluster one. Essentially this involves a transformation of particular lifeworlds from nationally specific traditions of freedom, sovereignty, and obligation into more reflexive constitutions which are open to the demands of those whose life-choices are harmfully restricted by their structural position in the world economy. Such a transformation would, of course, require a radical reconstruction of international law and its institutions; for it is only in so far as states are made subject to deliberative procedures which involve all individuals in decisions concerning economic planning, the distribution of resources, legislation on climate change and 'the amelioration of [the most] urgent need' (cluster three, principle seven), that the idea of cosmopolitan justice can become effective. None of this, of course, is guaranteed to happen; but the fragile possibility which is configured in institutions like the UN, UNESCO and the European Court of Human Rights does at least form a basis from which to begin (*Ibid.*: 527).

This version of cosmopolitanism is very close to and yet crucially different from the position I will seek to defend in the final chapter of this section, that is, Derrida's account of the cosmopolitan ethics that arises from the impact of techno-scientific capital (and its forms of prosthesis, virtualization and supplementarity) upon the discursive structures of the nation. Without going into too much detail at this point, Derrida's argument is that the logic of inscription through which the legal, ethical, moral and political strictures of the lifeworld are formed, proceeds from a necessary limitation of the principles of justice which arise in particular nation states. In *Politics of Friendship*, for example, he concentrates on the ways in which the responsibilities of friendship have been constructed in Western philosophy, and in particular their limitation by the act of mourning those men whose martial deeds found and recall the authority of the nation (Derrida, 1997: 13–14). It is this limitation which, for Derrida, organizes the 'becoming political' of friendship: it marks the point in the Western tradition where the law of hospitality (unconditional openness to the stranger) becomes subject to the different modalities of violence by which the nation sustains itself against the foreigner/enemy (*Ibid.*: 20–1). This account of the violence that is implicit in the identity structures of the nation is important for three reasons. First, it problematizes the Habermasian basis of Held's cosmopolitan ethics; for if the communicative processes which are inscribed in particular lifeworlds are always marked by their restriction of the demand of hospitality, then the idea of cosmopolitanism always exceeds the 'international' forms of deliberation through which it is implemented. Second, Derrida's idea of cosmopolitan democracy as that which is always 'to come' is intrinsically related to his account of Marx's revolutionary promise: for as we saw in part one, the symbolic economy of capital constantly transforms the conditions under which the destitution of the stranger is erased from the register of international law, and so constantly re-forms the demand for radical change. Finally, this logic of inscription is further complicated by the technological instruments which have transformed the physical, psychical and spiritual constitution of humanity; for in so far as 'the other' to whom we are responsible is now the object of such 'spectralizing' powers, our responsibility to him/her is made all the more urgent and difficult.

I will return to these issues presently; for the moment however I need to specify the expository strategy of the next two sections. So far I have suggested that the 'sceptical' and 'hyperglobalist' theses which Held *et al.* identify in their introduction to *Global Transformations* are diametrical opposites each of whose pronunciations are informed by the extremity of the other's claims about the fate of the world order. The nominalism espoused by the sceptics, in other words, is a reaction to the cosmopolitan significance which theorists like Fukuyama attach to the social, political and economic institutions of liberal capitalism. The recourse to scepticism however is not the only possible response to the hyperglobalist thesis; Marxists like Callinicos and Ohmae have argued that while it is true that the world economy *has* been globalized, it is also true that the techno-scientific powers through which this has taken place serve to intensify the regime of imperialist exploitation. What I want to do in the following chapters however is to move beyond conventional Marxist–Leninist approaches to globalization and to examine the critical inflections which Negri, Deleuze, Baudrillard and Derrida have introduced into the hyperglobalist thesis.

12
Biopolitical Production and the 'New Science of Democracy'

In the previous section I argued that David Held's notion of cosmopolitan democracy is problematic in the sense that it lacks an adequate account of the technological transformations through which global capitalism continues to expand. New prosthetic, informatic, digital and communications systems, in other words, have fundamentally altered the topology of exploitation; and so the regimes of disciplinarity, subjection and policing which have emerged under the conditions of the global economy cannot be properly understood in terms of the categories which Held deploys in his account of international law. This is not, of course, to say that the rights of equal worth, informed consent and democratic inclusion which he seeks to uphold are worthless abstractions, but rather that the possibility of their being mobilized within the networks of global capitalism depends upon a clear understanding of the ways in which technological systems have become universally involved in the reproduction of human life as living capital. This 'biopolitical' transformation of capitalism is the fundamental concern of Hardt and Negri's Marxism; for they argue that in order to salvage Marx's revolutionary politics we must give up conventional notions of class solidarity and examine the processes of affective, linguistic and cultural composition which are put into play by the mobilization of life as capital. I will say more about Hardt and Negri's attempts to trace the emergence of the cosmopolitical subject which they call the multitude at the end of the section. For the moment however I need to look in more detail at the concepts of biopolitical production, immaterial labour and imperial sovereignty through which they conceptualize the global transformation of capital.

In Chapter 8 I examined Hardt and Negri's original formulation of the concept of biopolitical production in *Empire*. At this point I want to move the discussion on to the more detailed account of the relationship between the biopolitical regime and the production of common forms of communication, conceptual understanding and affective engagement which Hardt and Negri set out in the sequel to *Empire*, *Multitude: War and Democracy in the Age of Empire*. As we have seen Hardt and Negri's relationship to Marx is complex: on the one hand they are concerned to distance themselves from any simple repetition of conventional ideas of class politics, while on the other they maintain that Marx's idea of 'the proletariat' already includes a recognition that the techno-scientific powers of capitalism work simultaneously upon the accumulative regime of the bourgeois economy and upon the creative powers of 'living labour'. In *Multitude* this idea of a prescient Marx, who was already working through the idea of a collective body whose being and desire is constituted in the transformations of the mode of production, is set out in the first of three 'excursions' into the contemporary significance of Marxism. We need then to look briefly at the elements of this first excursus. Initially Hardt and Negri set out the four 'primary elements' of Marx's method which inform their own approach to the future of Marxist politics: (1) historical tendency, (2) real abstraction, (3) antagonism, (4) the constitution of subjectivity (Hardt and Negri, 2005: 141). Thus we need to look at the way in which *Multitude* seeks to establish the historical development, social effects and revolutionary potential of biopolitical production as the 'hegemonic tendency' of contemporary capitalism.

The exemplary form of capitalist production to which Marx constantly alludes in his economic writings is the highly individualistic, *laissez-faire* organization of productive relations which emerged in Britain at the beginning of the nineteenth century. By the time Marx had completed the first volume of *Capital* in 1867, production based on the valorization of capital still accounted for only a tiny portion of the total means of subsistence produced by labouring humanity: most of the world still remained in the grip of feudalist relations of one kind or another which retarded the scientific and technological development of the mode of production. Marx's method of analysis therefore began with the identification of the 'isomorphic elements' of capitalism, that is, the forms of scientific, technological, economic and political organization through which the production of commodities expands its domination over every kind of living labour. What is important here, according to Hardt and Negri, is Marx's identification of an historical tendency in the capitalist economies which had established themselves in Europe and North America: he argued that the rate of economic expansion in those countries which had developed a market economy and revolutionized the technological basis of production, had already established the hegemony of capitalism – even though the majority of the world's population still lived under pre-capitalist conditions (Hardt and Negri, 2005: 141). Thus the expansion of the world market, the growth of joint-stock companies and monopoly capital and the colonization of undeveloped economies, are produced as real effects of the historical tendency which Marx identified in the most advanced industrial nations of his day. For Hardt and Negri however a new set of isomorphic elements have emerged from within the capitalist machine and it is these which are designated under their concept of biopolitical production.

Hardt and Negri argue that capitalism has undergone a fundamental change in the last decades of the twentieth century, and that this change has to be understood in terms of the evolution of the technological basis of production. Their claim is that industrial labour is no longer hegemonic and has been displaced by the kind of 'immaterial' activity which creates products such as 'knowledge, information, communication, a relationship, or an emotional response' (Hardt and Negri, 2005: 108). The productive regime of capitalism, in other words, is shifting towards the total mobilization of human life: the technological-prosthetic organization of humanity as bits of information, biopolitical capital and cybernetic organisms, in other words, has produced a network of connections through which capital constantly expands its powers of expropriation. Thus, for example, the rise of the knowledge economy is dependent not only upon the emergence of communications technologies which allow the instantaneous transmission of information around the world, it also relies increasingly on encryption and biometric systems, new language regimes and complex interfacing between human subjects and technological systems. The isomorphic elements of this new regime have, according to Hardt and Negri, emerged as 'qualitatively hegemonic' in the world economy: America, Japan, Germany and all of the G8 nations are already bound together by their reliance on the expanding networks of biopolitical production, and by their need to coordinate the disciplinary order which preserves its efficient functioning.

Much of the conventional Marxist literature on Hardt and Negri's account of the shift from 'industrial' to 'biopolitical' production maintains that their analysis is simply an 'objective welcome' to the global-technological forms into which neo-liberal capitalism has migrated (Fotopoulos and Gezerlis, 2000: 7). This however is to ignore their insistence on the fact that biopolitical production is a regime which functions through the privatization of every element of the productive process (including the genetic structure of life itself), and that it serves to intensify the exploitative potential of the commodity form. The creative potential which is liberated by the emergence of the internet as a common resource, for example, constantly provokes the intervention of corporate law as a means of controlling access and enforcing copyright regulations (Hardt and Negri, 2005: 186–7). The logic of 'real abstraction' which Hardt and Negri undertake in *Empire* and *Multitude* therefore traces a double movement of liberation and exploitation: on the one hand the global networks through which capital circulates constantly extend the performative potential of the workers who operate within them, while on the other the international organization of law, sovereignty and violence serves to police every 'exception' from the rule of empire. The concept of 'full-spectrum dominance' which Hardt and Negri introduce in the first section of *Multitude*, for example, is the culmination of the counterinsurgent violence which states have exercised against those groups who resist its claims to sovereignty. They argue that after the cold war military policing of the world order by organizations like NATO and the UN has done little to protect the most vulnerable nations of the world, and that their strategic interventions have served mainly to protect the hierarchies of wealth and power upon which biopolitical capitalism still depends (*Ibid.*: 55). This account of the relationship between national sovereignty, international institutions and the regime of biopolitical production does, of course, have important consequences for the concept of globalization, and it is to these that we must now turn.

As we have seen the neo-liberal version of the hyperglobalist thesis maintains that there is a positive correlation between the development of techno-scientific means of production, the expansion of the global market and the spread of the rights and duties which are the counterpart of good government and entrepreneurial activity. What is good for the free market and the unimpeded flow of capital, in other words, is good for freedom and the universal rights of humanity. This argument however simply repeats the naturalistic fallacy which Marx identified as the cardinal error of classical economics; for by presenting the 'free market' as both the driving force behind and the realization of human freedom, it neglects the complicities into which the 'law of the market' must always enter in order to preserve its integrity. Thus, as Hardt and Negri rightly point out, global capitalism is not the opening up of the world market to 'pure' competition, as Rosa Luxemburg had maintained in *The Accumulation of Capital*, but rather a highly regulated expansion of cooperative relations between the economic power of corporate capital and the political power of nation states (Hardt and Negri, 2005: 167). The detail of their argument can be briefly summarized. Free competition requires the legal force of nation states; for without the complicity of national governments biopolitical capitalism could not have transformed the conditions under which exploitation and accumulation take place. The establishment of trade agreements and regional forms of cooperation therefore tend to reflect the ability of powerful nation states to rig the market; and so the 'vast array of legal authorities, normative systems and procedures' which come into being with the expansion of world trade, are, from the beginning, powers of imperial domination (*Ibid.*: 175). Finally, this regional inscription of empire prefigures the regulatory apparatus of the world economy: the International Monetary Fund and the World Bank, for example, are institutions which, despite their apparent commitment to cosmopolitan justice, are fundamentally constrained in their operations by the demand for an 'open' global market:

> The supranational economic institutions must work along with national officials and business leaders to reproduce the global economic order along with its international hierarchies, and the margin of flexibility on this point is small. This is the hard rock that will crush any serious reform. (*Ibid.*: 176)

Each level of inscription, in other words, interlocks with the others and determines the global organization of power, security and exploitation which Hardt and Negri have called empire.

So, what hope is there for cosmopolitan justice if its institutions are no more than regulative mechanisms for the global market? For Hardt and Negri, as we have seen, the expansion of biopolitical production institutes a double movement; for as the autonomy of human labour increases within the global networks of biopolitical production, so the corporations who own those networks become increasingly stringent in their enforcement of copyright law, patent ownership and rights to intellectual property (Hardt and Negri, 2005: 182–5). This then is the point at which the Marxian contradiction between the socialization of production and the privatization of the means of labour reaches its highest stage: for the social relationships which arise from immaterial labour simultaneously determine the forms of language, understanding and affective response which constitute the body of multitude, and the violence through which empire polices the acts of transgression though which that body determines its organization and purpose (*Ibid.*: 187–8).

Thus if we return to Hardt and Negri's excursus on Marx, we can see that the relationship between living labour and the structural antagonisms of capital are radically transformed in their account of empire: for while it is certainly true that they regard the multitude as a 'class concept', the forms of autonomous subjectivity which arise within the networks of biopolitical production are conceived as 'singularities' which have already exceeded the mechanisms of capture through which surplus value is expropriated (*Ibid.*: 150–3). Put synoptically the common bases of production which are put into play by the labour of the multitude are also the bases of their common subjectivity; and so the social, economic, communicative and affective praxis which evolves under the regime of immaterial labour, constantly extends their powers of representation and desire beyond the conventional forms of sovereignty which have come to dominate the realm of political recognition. The difference of different cultural identities therefore is given in events which belong to the ontology of the multitude, but which simultaneously determine and rescind its universality (*Ibid.*: 208).

Two important questions arise here. First, how does the multitude constitute itself as a revolutionary force within the regime of empire? And second, how would it be possible for the multitude, as an actual revolutionary power, to avoid repeating the logic of domination which is characteristic of conventional forms of sovereignty? With regard to the first question Hardt and Negri have argued that revolt is made possible by what exceeds the overcoding of desire, that is, the revolutionary surplus which is always created by the repressive interventions of the state. This surplus is the common being of the multitude; it is the 'wealth of intelligence, experience, knowledge, and desire' which emerges from the practical engagement of living labour in the processes of biopolitical production, and which constitutes the immanent possibility of revolt which haunts the regime of empire (Hardt and Negri, 2005: 212). Thus the concept of global composition which informs Hardt and Negri's account of the multitude, takes place through the articulation of singular events of resistance (events which are, by definition, dispersed across the global space of empire) into the shared forms of language, communication and affective engagement which are essential to the biopolitical regime. The anti-capitalist movement which emerged in the mid 1990s, for example, was never a unified political movement with a fully formed set of strategies and objectives. Rather, Hardt and Negri argue, it was composed of disparate elements (environmentalists, trade unionists, anarchists, feminists, etc. from a plurality of different nations) each of which was able to negotiate with the others on the basis of common forms of communicative and affective culture, and to extend that commonality through the pursuit of democratically agreed strategies of resistance. As Hardt and Negri put it:

> In conceptual terms, the multitude replaces the contradictory couple identity-difference with the complementary couple commonality-singularity. In practice the multitude provides a model whereby our expressions of singularity are not diminished in our communication or collaboration with others in struggle ... with, in short, the global mobilization and extension of the common. (*Ibid.*: 218–19)

The practical engagement of multitudinous desire, in other words, is conceived by Hardt and Negri as a properly human performance of identity in difference; and so the violence which may emerge from the constitution of the multitude as a body of collective desires, languages and affective relations (i.e. violence against the counter-revolutionary violence deployed through the apparatus of empire) maintains a fragile and perpetually contingent legitimacy (*Ibid.*: 342–7).

This brings me to the second question: how is it possible for the multitude, as an actual revolutionary power, to except itself from the logic of transcendental sovereignty? Hardt and Negri have argued that the multitude's interaction with itself, in the form of an increasingly differentiated concept of 'the human', is absolutely autonomous and has democracy as its essential object. This expressive/expansive articulation of desire is presented in the final section of *Multitude* as an ontological principle whose necessity can be realized only through the political self-consciousness which accompanies the global expansion of biopolitical production (Hardt and Negri, 2005: 334–49). Thus the cosmopolitan 'love' which coordinates the political activity of the multitude is different from the conventional forms of sovereignty which reduce 'the people' to mere reflections of the arrested desire upon which the concept of the state is founded. Each element of the multitude, in other words, arises as a singularity which has 'the common' both as its condition and its goal; and so the heterogeneous forms of resistance which arise within the networks of biopolitical production are, in the final analysis, expressions of an immanent identity which becomes increasingly self-conscious through the conflicts which provoke its self-communication (*Ibid.*: 339). The revolutionary praxis whose possibility Hardt and Negri expound in *Multitude* therefore is creative of an ever more inclusive, ever more democratic 'body without organs', that is, a community of free desire whose unpredictable events/singularities constantly reshape the ontological basis of revolutionary change (*Ibid.*: 340).

This idea of a cosmopolitical 'love' which expands and coordinates all of its racial, cultural, religious and ethnic singularities however raises some serious questions about the logic of political composition which is traced throughout the narrative of *Multitude*. As we saw in chapter 8, Hardt and Negri's idea of the multitude attempts to synthesize the performative demand which is implicit in Deleuze's concept of machinic differentiation with the ontology of living labour which Marx set out in the *Grundrisse*. This synthesis, I suggested, is problematic. For Deleuze, generality (the universal) takes place through the discrimination of resemblance and equivalence; yet neither of these registers are capable of expressing 'the miracle of repetition', that is, the free recurrence of what is singular in each particular thing or event (Deleuze, 2004: 1). Thus conventional philosophy proceeds by reducing every finitely existing thing – 'object x' – to the sum of the predicates through which it is represented; and so the appearance of every such object (man, animal, artefact, machinic assemblage, etc.) in the discursive regime of metaphysics, transforms it from an autonomous singularity into a particularized individual which is prepared for subsumption under its transcendental idea (*Ibid.*: 13). This process of representation reveals the inadequacy of the conceptual forms through which philosophy seeks to transform the world into the realm of 'good sense'; for every recuperation of the law of sufficient reason re-encounters the 'object x' as a singularized event which blocks the generality of the concept (*Ibid.*: 14). Repetition therefore is the inner principle of machinic differentiation; it is that which precipitates movement through the asymmetry of the cause with its effect, and which introduces an unrepresentable difference into the established patterns of mediation, transcendence and authority. And so from a Deleuzian perspective the terms through which Marx articulates the universality of human labour belong to a register of generality which, if it is conceived ontologically, obscures everything that is singular about the events which transgress the boundaries of empire.

Hardt and Negri's answer to the question of how the multitude can avoid becoming an authoritarian body with its own 'special apparatus' of domination therefore is called into question by their apparent misconstrual of Deleuze's concept of difference. As we have seen Deleuze's claim that 'in every case repetition is difference without a concept' gestures towards a community of singular differences whose challenge to the striated space of empire is determined precisely by the fact that they cannot be totalized. The lines of flight which are precipitated by the 'civilized capitalist machine', in other words, give rise to their own undecidable questions about the organization of struggle, the contemporaneity of different media of resistance, and the constitution of revolutionary authority. Indeed, Deleuze argues that the core of Marx's idea of revolution is not the realization of an essential freedom which belongs to a fully integrated system of 'social production', but rather a free movement of difference which demands that we, as desiring singularities, confront the violence upon which representation and integration are founded (Deleuze, 2004: 259–60). In the final sections of *Multitude* however the communicative relations through which the multitude becomes aware of itself as a differentiated unity of free singularities are endowed with an ontological significance that exceeds the complex economy of events (silencing, liberation, dispersal, erasure, hospitality, etc.) which arises from the networks of biopolitical capitalism:

> [T]he common appears at both ends of biopolitical production: it is both the final product and the preliminary condition. The common is both natural and artificial; it is our first, second and nth nature. There is no singularity, then, that is not established in the common, there is no communication that does not have a common connection that sustains and puts it into action; and there is no production that is not based on commonality. (*Ibid.*: 348–9)

For Hardt and Negri this idea of the multitude as an ontological power which engenders itself through its own collective activity, recalls Marx's account of the formation of working class solidarity through the negative effects of capital: for as biopolitical production establishes itself as the hegemonic regime, so the forms of national, cultural, religious and ethnic identification which have divided the proletariat are mediated through an evolving consciousness of the common foundation of productive activity (*Ibid.*: 351). Thus the immanent subjectivity of the multitude arises from the counter-revolutionary powers of empire, and determines itself as a universally transformative body with its own ontologically grounded rights of self-determination, defensive violence and collective decision-making (*Ibid.*: 353).

This brings us back to Lenin, or, more precisely, to Lenin's account of the historical rights of appropriation which belong to the proletariat during the transition from capitalism to communism. Put simply Lenin's argument in *State and Revolution* is that the national power struggles which are precipitated by the imperialist stage of capitalism demand the establishment of an administrative apparatus to guide the activity of the revolutionary working class; and that once the dictatorship of the proletariat is established, this apparatus (the Politbureau of the Communist Party) should take responsibility for the liquidation of the reactionary elements who threaten the future of the world wide revolution (Lenin, 1976: 62–8). Hardt and Negri's response to the claim that their arguments fall back into a Leninist position which asserts the absolute right of the oppressed ('the poors') in relation to the counter-revolutionary powers of empire, is that the ontology of the multitude is always mediated through a revolutionary self-consciousness whose object is the extension of human desire beyond the violently acquisitive regimes of capital accumulation (Hardt and Negri, 2000a: 351). Thus, if violence results from the exodus of living labour from the networks of biopolitical production, this tends to come from the reactionary powers of empire and to provoke what Hardt and Negri conceive as the nomadic, cosmopolitical strategies of resistance which are proper to the networked existence of the multitude (*Ibid.*: 264).

This line of argument however gives rise to some serious issues about the politics of difference. Hardt and Negri maintain that labour within the regime of biopolitical production creates the shared basis of communication, affective response and technological expertise which constitutes the ontological foundation of the multitude. Thus the revolutionary potential of the mode of production is realized as a 'plane of immanence' which includes *all* of the singularized forms of desire that are engendered by the networked organization of labour, and which constantly exceeds the disciplinary and acquisitive regimes of empire. This construction of historical materialism however follows a logic of composition which, having dismissed the provocation of Deleuzian difference as an 'indeterminate horizon', is brought into a dangerous proximity to Lenin's construction of the rights of the revolutionary proletariat (Hardt and Negri, 2000a: 28). Indeed, the final sections of *Multitude* read like an obsessive attempt to exorcise the ghost of Lenin through ever more complex accounts of immanent identity, utopian desire and defensive violence (Hardt and Negri, 2005: 328–58). What is at stake here, of course, is what Derrida has called the inheritance of Marx: for if it is the case, as Hardt and Negri claim, that Marxism must continue to be an ontologically grounded project which encompasses the whole of the international proletariat/multitude, then the prescience of *Capital* and the *Grundrisse* lies in the fact that Marx conceived living labour as an organic force which will always inhabit the technoscientific expansion of capitalism. Thus the composition of the multitude as a subject which embodies the socializing power of biopolitical production is a process whose revolutionary power is grounded in the ontology, or, as Marx would express it, the historical tendency, of the mode of production. For Deleuze, on the other hand, revolutionary socialism remains an idea which is constantly reconfigured through the events which arise from the mutations of the capital; and so the logic of composition which Hardt and Negri maintain is proper to the biopolitical organization of desire, is always dispersed across contingent events, alliances and aesthetic gestures which oppose and transform the space of capital, but without determining a sovereign body whose political powers would lapse into the repressive logic of resemblance and equivalence.

This brings us, finally, to the questions of hospitality and cosmopolitan justice. As we have seen Deleuze and Guattari maintain that under the conditions of biopolitical capitalism the dynamics of de and re territorialization are extremely complex, and require a critical distinction between the contingent flows which are immediately integrated into the axiological regimes of the state, and those which draw minoritized forms of desire into rhizomatic associations. Thus the fact that the capitalist machine functions by constantly transforming its technological instruments and by recapturing the contingent forms of desire which it puts into play, means that the politics of desire is always bound up with the juridical forms by which the state attempts to legitimize its domination of particular minorities. The war machines which are constituted through global flows of money, information and desire, in other words, *can* take the form of a total resistance to capital; however it could be argued that they function more rhizomatically by confronting its legal institutions with minority demands (aboriginal rights, for example) which have been silenced by conventional juridical codes. This is close to the concept of hospitality which informs Derrida's reading of Marx; for as we see in a moment, his attempt to remain faithful to the revolutionary promise of Marx's writing is focused upon the events of silencing and erasure which are produced by the global-technological organization of capital, and which go unregistered in the conventional structures and categories of international law. Before proceeding to this discussion however I want to examine the fatal complicity between capital, technology and simulation which Baudrillard has developed in his later writing, and which presents biopolitical production as the total erasure of 'the real' (body, sexuality, gender, class, etc.) from the regime of global accumulation.

13
Transeconomic Capitalism

The hyperglobalist thesis covers a multitude of sins: for although it is generally associated with a neo-liberal approach to the scrapping of national constraints on the mobility of capital, we have seen that this particular vision of the wealth producing, democratizing effects of the market is not the only way of theorizing the shift from a regional-industrial to a global-postindustrial organization of the world economy. Indeed, the orthodox Marxist position is that the very processes which are identified by neo-liberals as the means to international justice and equality – that is, the expansion of new media technological systems, the increasing mobility of virtual capital, the shift from 'heavy' to 'light' manufacturing – simply intensify the logic of exploitation which Lenin set out in his account of the imperialist stage of capitalism. As Hardt and Negri have pointed out however, this line of argument tends to under-play the transformative effects of new technologies on the geopolitical space of capitalism, and, as a consequence, to impose a model of class struggle upon social, political and economic relationships to which it is no longer appropriate. And so the project which they pursue in *Empire* and *Multitude* attempts to redetermine Marx's account of the revolutionary potential of capitalism through the techno-scientific processes (virtualization, digitization, prosthesis, informatics, etc.) which have globalized the commodity form of production. Thus for Hardt and Negri immaterial labour transforms the life and desire of humanity across the networks of biopolitical capitalism; and so 'the multitude', as they conceive it, is a practical subject whose 'being' is immanent in the global-techno-scientific organization of production. This version of 'hyperglobalism', as we have seen, turns upon the credibility of the claim that it is possible to recuperate the revolutionary subjectivity of Marx's proletariat through techno-scientific powers which appear to be

144

the instruments of a new, more intensive regime of exploitation. The present section therefore will be concerned with Jean Baudrillard's account of this regime, and particularly his contention that new media technologies have expelled every trace of revolutionary immanence from the symbolic order of capitalism.

Baudrillard, as we saw in Chapter 4, stresses the point that Marx's theory of revolution has an impeccable logic to it; for if it were true that capitalism functioned simply to distort the power of living labour to produce a properly social humanity, then world revolution would indeed be an historical inevitability. The problem with Marx's analysis however is that the approximation between the object (capitalism) and the concepts which Marx's deploys (exchange value, living labour, alien-ation) has never been a matter of ontology; indeed, for Baudrillard, the real significance of Marx's writing lies in its disclosure of the contingent nature of theoretical descriptions of a system whose essence lies in its powers of self-transformation. Capital, in other words, has never oper-ated simply as a mechanism which distorts the productive essence of humanity; rather it has, from its very inception, functioned through a symbolic order which exceeds Marx's ontological designations of man as 'living labour' and the producer of all value. Thus from as early as *The Mirror of Production* Baudrillard has insisted that the standpoint from which Marx launches his critique of capital is a reflection of the produc-tivist ideology of classical economics, and that the concept of productive humanity through which Marx presents the dialectics of revolutionary transcendence, serves to obscure the general economy of play, donation, eroticism and the sacred which is presupposed by capitalist relations of production (Baudrillard, 1975: 105). Thus Baudrillard attempts to open up historical materialism to the exorbitance of the symbolic; for he argues that it is only through the possibilities of unregulated donation, sacrifice and service that arise in 'primitive' societies, that the regulated exchange of capitalist relations is possible. The act of pure expenditure which Baudrillard calls the gift, for example, is the original possibility which inhabits capital from its emergence as mercantile credit through to the 'fictitious' circulation of money which Marx identified as part of the historical tendency of the rate of profit to decline.[1] For Baudrillard however this migration of capital into the realm of the virtual serves infinitely to defer the point at which it is no longer able to valorize itself as surplus value (Baudrillard, 2004: 21–3).

Symbolic Exchange and Death seeks to extend this account of the relationship between capital and the symbolic order through which it expands. As we have seen, Baudrillard argues that once the encoding of reality exceeds the dialectics of value which Marx and the classical economists sought to impose upon it, each discrete sphere of production is opened up to every other: the code, in other words, institutes an 'ecstasy of communication' between different elements of the symbolic order of the social (the erotic, the aesthetic, the political, the ethical), and thereby reduces each to a conductive node within an ever expanding, ever accelerating system of exchange/accumulation. This drift into the hyperreality of the code is not, according to Baudrillard, simply a concomitant of structural changes in the organization of capitalism; rather it makes possible the emergence of capital as an autonomous power of investment, intensification and dispersal which constantly transforms the conditions of its reproduction (Baudrillard, 2004: 8–9). Thus, if it is the case that capitalism presupposes the encoding of man and nature as the condition upon which the commodity form is founded, then the logic of failing utility which Marx attributes to the M–C–M relation need never reach crisis point; for the ability of capital to invest and transform the symbolic order of 'the social' constantly defers the point at which crises of over-production, under-consumption and unemployment would determine their proper dialectical result (*Ibid.*: 56). The effect of this viral form of capitalism is, according to Baudrillard, the complete evacuation of transcendence from social relationships: for once every designation of the lifeworld is taken into the regime of third order simulation, the logic of communicability which has come to dominate the performance of labour, sexuality, gender and race constantly overwhelms the accumulation of our common, transcendent humanity (*Ibid.*: 60).

The concept of third order simulation which Baudrillard sets out in *Symbolic Exchange and Death* presents the total collapse of 'the real' (that is, the particularized and heterogeneous forms of being which are roughly drawn together in the normative tradition of the lifeworld) into the play of simulacra through which the social becomes utterly transparent. This process is, of course, a technological one; for it is only in so far as new media technologies (the Internet, satellite communications, digital television, virtual networks, etc.) have become thoroughly enmeshed with social relationships, that the logic of simulation can enter its fatal third stage. The ethical questions which arise from the fracturing of humanity into races, genders and cultures, in other words, are preempted by the pure transparency which they achieve in the realm of the hyperreal: for once the simulacrum has split off from the objects it is supposed to represent, 'all content is neutralized by a continuous process of orchestrated interrogations, verdicts and ultimatums' which have become the exclusive conditions through which 'the real' is apprehended (Baudrillard, 2004: 63). For Baudrillard however the very extremity of the transformations which are precipitated by the hyper-real is what re-intensifies the primitive relations of symbolic exchange: for as the system of operational simulation goes on perfecting itself, so it becomes increasingly susceptible to the intrusion of radical acts (of donation, sacrifice, love) which arise from its own weightlessness. These acts, according to Baudrillard, spring from the sense of mortality which haunts every system which 'fails to inscribe its own death'; for in so far as the hyperreal refers only to its own signifying economy, the experience of death is always simultaneous with the escalatory play through which each system expands itself (*Ibid.*: 4). A few years after the publication of *Symbolic Exchange and Death* however Baudrillard withdrew, at least in part, from the idea of an unaccountable excess which arises from the operational logic of simulation, and began to explore the possibility that such a logic is capable of operationalizing even its most extreme effects.

In his essay 'The Procession of Simulacra', Baudrillard argues that the 'excessive transparency' which has become the dominant form of communication in highly mediated societies, has brought about an even more severe dislocation of the image and the referent than the one he described in *Symbolic Exchange and Death*. This fatal severance of the symbolic order from what Marx would have called the economic infrastructure, is presented in Baudrillard's essay as the transition from third to fourth order simulacra. In the former case, the image corresponds to the stereotypical productions of the culture industry which 'mask the absence of a profound reality' in the reified societies described by Benjamin, Adorno and Marcuse; in the latter, the image has become 'its own pure simulacrum' and has succeeded in shifting the entire operational logic of the social into the realm of the hyperreal (Baudrillard, 1999: 6). The constant refraction of the images through which reality is 'known', in other words, reduces the substantive institutions of ethical life to 'weightless' appearances which are constantly transformed in the play of simulation; and so the system of moral, legal, economic and political norms through which 'the social' expands its hyperfunctionality, is no longer encumbered by any reference to what lies beyond its autonomous self-generation. Everything, in other words, is taken up into a constantly accelerating play of operational signs, none of which bears witness to the immanence of 'man' in the symbolic presentation of the real.

The loss of the real which Baudrillard presents in 'The Procession of Simulacra' however is not simply an entropic movement which threatens to engulf the whole productive organization of society; rather, it gives rise to the kind of disordered hyper-expansion of capital which Baudrillard, in *The Transparency of Evil*, calls 'the transeconomic' (Baudrillard, 1995b: 26–35).[2] His argument can be briefly summarized. The virtual space which is created by the liberation of the image from its reference to the real, allows capital to accumulate outside of the fragile relations of cooperation, exchange and exploitation that are constituted in the 'real' world economy. Thus, for Baudrillard, Marx was right in his diagnosis of the catastrophic effects that vast sums of money flooding into established branches of production would have on the turnover of capital and the stability of the world market. Once new image technologies have transformed the symbolic economy of the real however, transeconomic capital is able to migrate into virtual forms (Third World debt, speculative corporations quoted on the stock exchange, Eurodollars) which allow it to avoid the catastrophic effects of over-capitalization, and to retain its power of decisive intervention in real and potential markets. Speculative capital has, for example, been able to flood gene and bio-technological research with massive amounts of money in order to secure future rights of exploitation, while at the same time sustaining more reserved investment in established branches of production (*Ibid.*: 27). The hegemonic organization of the world economy therefore is sustained through an infinite extension of the indebtedness, for in the long run it is more profitable for First World economies to maintain the conditions of total exploitation than it is to demand actual repayment of the Third World debt.

Baudrillard, with his usual dose of irony, maintains that this is the 'best possible outcome' for a system of social relationships which is dominated by the operational power of fourth order simulation; for without the migration of capital into the virtual forms he has specified, the already unstable structure of the real would collapse into total chaos (Baudrillard, 1995b: 28). Capital, in other words, 'goes into orbit' around the simulated forms of being and identity through which the social bond has been operationalized, and migrates strategically into a world without immanence, transcendence, or finality:

> The fact is that all the functions of man's body, so far from gravitating around him in a *concentric* order, have become satellites ordered eccentrically with respect to him ... once transcendent he has become exorbitate. (*Ibid.*: 30)

'Economics' therefore has become pure speculation; it is that which is utterly empowered by the virtual accumulation which allows it to exploit any and every effect of biopolitical capital, and to do so in a way which transforms but does not destroy the vestiges of community and identity through which the 'real' economies of nation states continue to function. Political economy, according to Baudrillard, has become 'viral'; it has gone beyond 'the law of value, the law of the market, surplus value, all the laws of capital', and developed into an utterly mutable power which is able to expand itself through any conjunction of simulacra and its effects (*Ibid.*: 35). Thus the transformation of political economy into a speculative power with no organic rules of operation marks the point at which transcendence is totally evacuated from the object; for once capital has gone into orbit, it constantly precipitates new effects of the hyperreal which further evacuate the system of reality. This is the true meaning of hyperglobalization: the total simulation of mind, body, gender, love, sex and the aesthetic through which capital sustains its orbital power over the production of the real.

The other side of this viral activity of capital is the increasing inertia of the masses: for as the system goes into hyperreality, the organic context of their action is lost and their being is shifted from a structural-historical presence which has to be mediated by the state (as, for example, with Gramsci's concept of hegemony), into a formless negative which is produced by the surfeit of operational simulacra (Baudrillard, 1995b: 32). The masses, in other words, are no more than the shadow cast by the hyperreal; they are the negativity which results from the ever expanding production of simulacra through which viral capitalism exceeds the organic laws of political economy. For Baudrillard the system of fourth order simulation has succeeded in erasing both idealist transcendence and materialist immanence: for there is nothing which appears in the realm of the hyperreal which radiates the light of moral teleology, or which signifies the type of compositional power which is configured in the dialectics of historical materialism, however these are conceived. The expansive relationship between capital and the hyperreal therefore is such that the global networks which it creates are never able to bring about anything other than the accelerated dispersal of 'man' into the simulated forms through which his being is capitalized. Even the disciplinary interventions through which dominant economies maintain their hegemony have become part of the logic of simulation; for according to Baudrillard's analysis international institutions function to preserve a 'peace' whose condition is the simulated conflicts which are played out between the caricatures of 'democracy' and 'fundamentalism' (Baudrillard, 1995b: 75–80).[3] Obviously this would have profound consequences for the politics of globalization. For if it is the case that the media-technological organization of the world market has transformed it into a virtual space in which sovereignty, nationality and culture have been reduced to mere simulacra, and if this transformation has produced the 'orbital' accumulations of capital which have come to control the reproduction of the real, then it really would seem as if the best possible outcome of transeconomic capitalism is the stasis and conformity which it produces.

In Chapter 12 I argued that Hardt and Negri's account of the relationship between biopolitical capitalism and the revolutionary body of the multitude crucially underestimates the virtualizing, aestheticizing and disaggregating powers of immaterial labour. As we have seen they argue that the operational codes of technological capitalism are unable to master the being of productive humanity because, as they understand it, it is constantly re-formed by the cooperative processes through which 'the social' is produced. Living labour, in other words, has become a practical-technological activity whose powers of composition are spread across the virtual networks of biopolitical production. What this means in terms of the politics of globalization is that the multitude occupies a position which is both inside and outside of the forms of immaterial labour through which biopolitical capitalism expands. For while it is certainly true, as far as Hardt and Negri are concerned, that capital has 'virtualized' the productive relations upon which it depends, this regime has also intensified the communicative and affective bonds which constitute the ontological desire of the multitude for justice and democracy. The system of technological encoding which Baudrillard takes to be increasingly hermetic, in other words, is understood as constituting an ever more diversified, ever more self-conscious community of desire which is spread throughout the virtual body of capital. Despite its rather forced construction therefore the revolutionary logic which Hardt and Negri present in *Multitude* does at least gesture towards real events of conflict and injustice which are produced within the system of technological simulation, and which should lead us to question the vast, self-productive interiority which Baudrillard calls transeconomic capitalism.

What is at stake here is the possibility of salvaging a Marxist account of politics from the powers of virtual investment, accumulation and ownership which capital has acquired under the regime of biopolitical production. Hardt and Negri's approach to these powers, we have seen, is to treat them as the media through which the immanent commonality of human beings is realized: the communicative, cooperative and affective networks of immaterial labour, in other words, produce an increasingly diversified humanity whose common desire forms the basis of a radical transformation of the economic and political regimes of empire. For Baudrillard, on the contrary, the technological means through which biopolitical production becomes hegemonic bring about an operational organization of 'the human' which is both absolutely functional for the commodity form, and absolutely fatal to the possibility of global revolution: all of the faculties of living labour are enhanced, exaggerated, and intensified in ways which open them up to the strategic interventions of capital, and which rupture the organic ties which have constituted the 'being' of humanity. The last vestiges of cosmopolitanism therefore are visible only in the mass charitable events – 'Live Aid', 'Live 8', 'USA for Africa' – through which the West seeks to discharge its responsibilities to the Third World (Baudrillard, 1995a: 67). Clearly this encounter between Baudrillard's conception of the transeconomic effects of simulation and Hardt and Negri's account of revolutionary ontology is one which offers no hope of dialectical or dialogical consensus. In the section which follows however I will argue that the impossibility of an accommodation between these two positions is what constantly re-opens the question of cosmopolitan democracy, and that the concept of hospitality which Derrida presents in his later writings on politics, religion and ethics, is what sustains the practical demand for justice which is inscribed in Marx's notion of the New International.

14
The Politics of Hospitality

The law of hospitality is what lies at the core of Derrida's reading of Marx: it is the quasi-transcendental idea which is traced through concepts of 'democracy to come', 'inoperative community' and 'revolutionary promise' which are expounded in *Spectres of Marx*. Derrida's initial approach to the question of inheriting Marx's ideas, an approach which he briefly sketched in *Positions* in the early 1970s, is to regard his texts as a provocation to 'transformative reading': for in so far as the *The Grundrisse* and *The Communist Manifesto* depict capitalism as an open system which constantly exceeds its contemporary limitations, the critique of capital must evolve beyond the categories (the labour theory of value, the primacy of class antagonisms, the immanence of socialized production, etc.) which have become sacred to the Marxist canon (Derrida, 1980: 63). For Derrida, in other words, our inheritance of Marx ought to be informed by the statute of limitations which he put on his own writing (Derrida, 1994: 13); for if it is the case that the possibility of the M–C–M relation depends upon its ability to transform the techno-scientific and ideological conditions of its reproduction, then the critique of the commodity form must always question the adequacy of its powers of ethical and political representation. The possibility of such a non-iterative response to the machinic operations of capital, operations which have come to encompass the entire physical, affective, and spiritual life of Man, is given through the figure of the other: the spectral body which haunts the operational languages, corporate networks and virtual accumulations through which the world has become capitalized. As Derrida puts it in the 'exordium' to *Spectres of Marx*, the other who is silenced, erased and exploited is what 'secretly unhinges' the smooth operations of global-technological capitalism: he/she always arrives back on the agendas of academics, political activists and international institutions as a demand (for hospitality) which re-opens the question of justice and democracy 'to come' (*Ibid.*: xix). Before I proceed to examine the relationship between Marxism and hospitality more closely however, I want to return briefly to Derrida's account of the conditions under which 'ethics' and 'politics' emerge as possible forms of praxis.

In 'Violence and Metaphysics: An Essay on the Thought of Emmanuel Levinas', Derrida undertakes his first explicit analysis of the themes of alterity, difference and ethical responsibility. Levinas's thought is configured around the absolute demand which is inscribed in the expressive morphology of the human face, or, more, precisely, the capacity of the face to disclose the suffering of the other as an absolute and immediate demand for care. This demand that we should be hospitable to the other who comes to us, whoever he or she my be, exceeds every legal, economic or political inscription of responsibility; for each of the latter, according to Levinas, imposes a limitation upon what is, by definition, the illimitable duty of care which each of us owes to the other. As Levinas puts it in *Totality and Infinity*:

> The relation between the Other and me, which draws forth in his expression, issues in neither number nor concept. The Other remains infinitely transcendent, infinitely foreign; his face in which the epiphany is produced and which appeals to me breaks with the world that can be common to us, whose virtualities are inscribed in our nature and developed by our existence. (Levinas, 1994: 194)

As incarnated, sentient individuals therefore we are always already engaged with the other as an alterity which forms us as subjects; for without the originary demand of the face, 'the social' (love, friendship, family, etc.) could not have come into being as the concrete organization of hospitality. And so the concept of ethical community which Levinas develops exists only in the absolutely excessive obligation which the other places upon every human being; it is the infinitely recurrent demand for compassion which springs from the designation of social relationships as legal, economic and political expressions of being/totality. Such a community cannot be reduced to the metaphysics of being or spirit, for its only 'outcomes' are the unpredictable acts of care which spring from the suffering of the other, and which transform the regulated violence of the sociopolitical order. According to Levinas therefore the epiphany of the face is the origin of a divine law of hospitality which exceeds all of its sacred incarnations, and which solicits an obedience to God which is immediately respect for man as a desiring, incarnated, vulnerable being. The central argument which Derrida presents in 'Violence and Metaphysics' is that the question of ethical responsibility remains *proximate* to the Heideggarian question of Being; for the possibility of taking responsibility for the other has always already been determined through the ontological designation of the essence of Man. His argument is that if, as Levinas claims, the ethical demand springs immediately from the inscription of infinity (God) in the face of the other, then the pure desire which haunts the systemic organization of discrete subjects (ipseities) cannot determine itself in any specific command. Levinas's ethico-phenomenology, in other words, collapses into a kind of 'empiricism' which seeks a pure unmediated contact with divine alterity, and which obscures the logics of mastery and domination which are put into play by the societal designation of human essence (Derrida, 1990: 151–2).[1]

It is, however, important to remember that Derrida's insistence upon inscribing the possibility of ethics within the general economy of being is not simply a defence of Heidegger *against* Levinas. Rather the significant point here is that Derrida's exposition of *Totality and Infinity* situates the origin of the ethical demand not in the epiphanic figuration of the face (which ultimately refers to the pure identity of the human in its resemblance to the face of God), but rather in the processes of inscription and supplementation through which cultural identities are, in general, sustained.[2] *Of Grammatology*, as we have seen, sets out a highly detailed account of the relationship between the moderating power of nature and the corruptive influence of civil society which is developed in Rousseau's philosophy. Derrida argues that Rousseau's attempt to strip away everything from human nature which was not put there by social convention, is informed by the idea of an absolute past in which humanity lived within the confines of primitive drives and instincts which its physical constitution, as devised by God, was perfectly adapted to satisfy (Derrida, 1976: 180). This originary relationship between man and nature is presented as a timeless harmony in which the fecundity of the latter keeps the instinctual life of the human beings in a state of untroubled satisfaction: sexual desire is cyclical and tied exclusively to the demands of reproduction, responsibility for the offspring falls exclusively to the female who will look after her children for as long as they cannot fend for themselves, and the harmonious fulfilment of desire through the body of nature produces a spontaneous feeling of pity towards the suffering of others. Rousseau's speculative anthropology narrates the loss of this primitive harmony: the expulsion of humanity from Eden takes the form of God's imposition of the seasons upon mankind, which in turn imposes the necessity of language, cooperation and the law upon the 'natural' being of humanity (*Ibid.*: 216–29). Thus the affections and institutions of civil society which are the object of Rousseau's critique (private property, luxury, jealousy, envy, promiscuity, greed) are presented as having silenced the 'voice of nature' which God has inscribed in the very heart of humanity. One of the fundamental points which Derrida makes in his exposition of Rousseau is that the origin, that is, the natural being of humanity, already has a certain conception of difference inscribed within it: the moral chaos of civil society is due, to a large degree, to the unfettering of feminine sexual desire from the bonds of procreation and the care of children. The independence which wealth has allowed certain women to attain (as well as the provocations of a symbolic order which has ruptured the proper limits of female sexuality), in other words, has disturbed the 'natural' order in which the business of the world is conducted through the rationality and restraint of male citizens. Thus the very chaos into which human affairs have descended marks the point at which human nature 'ascends toward itself in the inalienable immediacy of self-possession', and begins to reassert its proper restraint upon sexual desire, gender differences and the performance of 'the feminine' outside of the family (*Ibid.*: 297).

The project of deconstruction is concerned with the metaphysical foundations of the real (presence), and seeks to expound the operations of the textual/philosophical resources through which established forms of 'community' (love, friendship, fraternity, obligation, gender, sexuality, etc.) are constituted as expressions of 'being'. So, if we return to *Of Grammatology* we can discern an expository strategy which seeks to disclose the tropes through which Rousseau narrates the 'absolute past' of the state of nature. Rousseau's text, in other words, presents the self-coordinated cycle of desire/satisfaction which is configured in the state of nature, as the prefect expression of human virtue: the natural differentiation of 'man' and 'woman' into discrete expressions of a properly equilibrated distribution of being appears as that which comes before the corruptive influence of language and society upon the virtuous distribution of desire. Three important points emerge here. First, Derrida maintains that it is impossible to determine the nature of the absolute past; for the textual resources which are used to articulate its simple presence/identity are always part of a redemptive logic which transforms the state of nature into the spectral 'other' of human history. The source of our humanity, in other words, takes its meaning from the 'chain of supplements' through which its presence is distributed in narratives of natural virtue (Derrida, 1976: 152–7). Second, the association between the metaphysical resources of the text (that is, the articulation of certain necessary relations between different orders of being, such as masculinity, race, animality and the feminine) and the hegemonic relationships which have founded Western culture, is a necessary one. Thus Derrida's claim that there is 'nothing outside of the text' should be understood as maintaining a problematic and contingent identity between the resources of philosophy and the cultural forms of love, friendship, gender, sexuality and community which come to predominate at any given time. This, finally, brings us back to Derrida's account of ethical responsibility. The distribution of being through the logic of cultural inscription, he maintains, always determines a distribution of violence in which certain 'others' are excluded from the register of democracy; and so the possibility of justice is sustained as a performative demand for hospitality to whoever is unnamed, and unnameable, within the established structures of recognition.

The law of hospitality which Derrida traces throughout the text of *Politics of Friendship* is the law of unconditional openness to the stranger whose arrival disrupts the satisfactions of (my) political identity and cultural belonging. These satisfactions, as we have seen, derive from a certain genealogical determination of the political, that is, the structuring of duty and consent around the collective act of mourning (Derrida, 1997: 94). What is significant here, and what continues to be a fundamental element of Western democracy, is the reproduction of blood and birth as the necessary conditions of belonging to the nation, and of responding 'in one's being' to its demands. This construction of belonging has, of course, always been complicit with the worst excesses of political rhetoric, and with the violence and xenophobia, nationalism and ethnocentrism (*Ibid.*: 99). However, if we are to understand this economy of violence, we must recognize that the remembrance through which the political sphere is founded is the remembrance of illustrious fathers. The possibility of suppressing the demand of the other *begins* with the masculine confrontation with being (a confrontation which Derrida has already remarked in Rousseau's account of sexual difference in the state of nature) which is dramatized in the mythology of nationhood. And so what is hidden in the Greek act of commemoration is the erasure of the feminine, or, more precisely, the suspension of responsibility to 'she who comes' in the fraternal injunction: 'fight for the freedom won by your illustrious fathers' (*Ibid.*: 109). This, for Derrida, inevitably begs the question of democracy; for in so far as fraternal citizenship begins with the erasure of the feminine (female desire, sisterhood, the minor voice), we are immediately referred to the legal, economic and technological foreclosures through which the other retains its ethico-political demand for hospitality.

This brings me back to the political problematic which is presented in *Spectres of Marx*. Derrida argues, as we have seen, that if the question of 'living in' the resources of the text cannot be closed (if it is re-opened by every 'empirical' differentiation of community, belonging, identity, friendship, hospitality, etc.), then the question concerning technology (the relationship of 'the human' to its supplements) is simultaneous with the questions of ethics, justice and politics which arise from the techno-scientific evolution of capital. What this means is that we can treat 'capitalism' neither as a fixed set of socioeconomic conditions, nor as a teleological organization of human desire which will ultimately transcend its negative effects. The term should be understood as registering an open-ended relationship between power, technology and exploitation; a relationship which constantly transforms itself and which precipitates the events of suffering (of the other/others) to which Marxism is originally responsible (Derrida, 1994: 13). The ethical demand which is traced throughout *Spectres of Marx*, in other words, haunts the symbolic economy through which biopolitical capitalism presents itself as the living expression of human freedom and desire. Thus the question we identified in part two, that is, the possibility of discerning the revolutionary promise of Marxism within the media-techno-scientific space of simulation, re-emerges within Derrida's account of hospitality. For Baudrillard, this question has long since been decided; the evolution of increasingly sophisticated media technologies has brought about a fatal collapse of the real, in all its social, ethical and political diversity, into the autonomous play of simulation. Public space has become the sphere of universal communicability in which every event is encoded by the performative demands of the media: the sheer conductivity of the image is such that the possibility of receiving the ethical demand of the other has always already been dispersed into a play of simulations which sustain the hyper-functionality of global accumulation. Thus the demand for cosmopolitan responsibility does not disappear, but rather is circulated through images of destitution which are designed to contain the guilt of Western societies within the established parameters of donation and responsibility (Baudrillard, 1995a: 67).

So, is it really true that new media technologies have erased the ethico-political demand from the symbolic order of the social? And further, is it the case that the kind of radical cosmopolitanism which Derrida expounds in his later writing, is destined always to collapse into simulations of responsibility which are complicit with the system they seek to question? In order to respond to these questions I need to examine the concept of spectralization which Derrida sets out in *Spectres of Marx*. In a passage which repeats Baudrillard's concern with the transformative power of new media technologies, Derrida maintains that:

> Electoral representivity or parliamentary life is not only distorted, as was always the case, by a great number of socio-economic mechanisms, but it is exercised with more and more difficulty in a public space profoundly upset by techno-tele-media apparatuses ... by the new modes of appropriation they put to work, [and] by the new structure of the event and of its spectrality that they *produce*. (Derrida, 1994: 79)

The public sphere, in other words, has, since the early decades of the twentieth century, been subject to the effects of media and communications technologies, effects which have tended to rupture the relationship between 'the public' as an organ of the body politic and 'the state' as the embodiment of legitimate political power. Thus, the massification of politics which occurred in Europe between the wars was, for Derrida, dependent upon the media-technological transformation of public space; for it was only in so far as the inscription 'ethical substance' in the institutions of the lifeworld was radically altered by the technological reproducibility of the image, that 'the masses' were created as an entity which could by manipulated by the populist aesthetics of fascism and communism (*Ibid.*). These effects, according to Derrida, are amplified by the complicity between media technologies and capital; for as the political institutions of bourgeois democracy are broken down by the accelerated rhythms of information and communication, so the power of liberal capitalism to simulate the performance of ethical responsibility is increased exponentially. Thus, the international institutions which evolve through the global expansion of capitalism (the IMF, the World Bank, NATO, UNESCO, etc.) are always *to some extent* complicit with the neo-liberal ideology of market forces, radical individualism and the rights of free enterprise (*Ibid.*: 80). However, and this is a point of differentiation between Derrida and Baudrillard, the processes of spectralization through which media-informatic capitalism expands its regime can never effect a total operational control of the spectre: for the effects of silencing, erasure and geopolitical dislocation which haunt the global regime of accumulation, constantly return to the play of simulation as the trace of the real which is (re)inscribed in the melodrama of appearance.

It is this logic of return which informs Derrida's inheritance of Marxism. In the preceding discussion we have seen that the being, or presence, of social relationships has always been sustained through the resources of the logos, and that consequently the cultural self-identification through which each of us enacts our belonging to a particular community, has always been performed within the economy of cultural inscription. Thus the concept of ethical responsibility which emerges from deconstruction begins with the designation of the symbolic economy culture; for the ontological differentiations which spring from the structures deployed in the textual resources of metaphysics are what originally inscribe the demand of the other/others in the hierarchical order of the social. Thus, if it is the case that 'spectralization' is originally part of the symbolic economy of the culture, or, more precisely, if it is true that there has always been a disturbing excess of the symbolic which breaks the immediate identification of the individual (subject, ipseity) with its community, then the question arises as to the transformative significance of this break. We have seen that for Baudrillard the unrepresentable finality of death, which he presents in *Symbolic Exchange* as a destabilizing power which upsets the established order of social and political life, eventually cedes place to the operational power of fourth order simulation. The power of new media technologies to simulate the conditions of social, political and biological life, in other words, has become complete enough to control every manifestation of the real (destitution, suffering, love, gender, sexuality, etc.) within the symbolic order of the social. For Derrida however, the ghost of the other, the ghost who comes to rupture the established bonds of community and self-identity, can never be exorcised by the operational logic of simulation: indeed the increasing power of neo-liberal ideology to synthesize the life, economy and imagination of every part of the globe, is precisely what precipitates 'a suffering that suffers still more, and more obscurely, for having lost its habitual models and language', and which is the spectral/messianic demand to which Derrida's Marxism seeks to respond (Derrida, 1994: 81).

This, of course, is not the Marxism of Marx; for the suffering of the other which founds the demand for hospitality, cannot be gathered into the logic of class composition which informs the dialectics of historical materialism. Indeed, one of the central arguments of *Spectres of Marx* is that the logic of spectralization is universal, and that Marx's efforts to determine a perfectly harmonious balance of social need, desire and satisfaction is an especially powerful determination of the logic of presence. It is at this point therefore that the question of materialism re-emerges. Conventional Marxists such as Eagleton, Ahmad and Callinicos have claimed that Derrida's version of 'Marxism' abandons every substantive category which Marx deployed in his critique of capital, and that the concepts of class, state, ideology and mode of production are jettisoned in favour of idealist notions of 'otherness' and 'hospitality' which cannot form the basis of a revolutionary politics.[3] In the section which follows I will argue that each of these authors makes the questionable assumption that Marx's categories can be applied, largely unmodified, to the global-techno-scientific organization of capitalism which has come to dominate our own living present, and that they misrecognize the messianic demand which is configured in *Spectres of Marx*. For the moment however I want to return to the reconstructed conception of materiality that we have explored in the previous two chapters, that is, the idea of machinic desire which is developed by Deleuze and Guattari in their work on capitalism and schizophrenia and by Hardt and Negri in their account of biopolitical production.

Fidelity to Marx's revolutionary promise, according to Hardt and Negri, demands that we reconceptualize the relationship between the technological means of production and the composition of revolutionary desire. The theoretical strategy which is pursued in both *Empire* and *Multitude* attempts to articulate a concept of prosthesis which brings together Marx's account of the 'real subsumption' of living labour and Deleuze and Guattari's notion of the transgressive potential contained in every strategic overcoding of desire. They argue that Marx's account of the progressive evacuation of knowledge and dexterity from the processes of industrial production contains a speculative element within it; and that the way in which his argument is staged, gestures towards an expansive relationship between labour and technology which will emerge once technology is freed from the constraints of commodity production (Hardt and Negri, 2000: 25). The possibility of this prosthetic expansion of human labour and desire is, for Hardt and Negri, immanent in the technological development of capitalism; and it is in their descriptions of the unfolding of an increasingly articulate, increasingly autonomous 'multitude' of producers, that they draw upon Deleuze and Guattari's account of the contingent 'lines of flight' which arise from the imposition of repressive disciplinarity. What is important here is Hardt and Negri's attempt to synthesize the account of living labour which is presented in *The Grundrisse* with the radical contingency which is configured in Deleuze and Guattari's concept of machinic desire. Ultimately the synthetic operations which are conducted by Hardt and Negri in *Empire*, attempt to bring Deleuze's account of the radical difference under the control of certain 'ontological' characteristics of human labour and sociality, that is, characteristics which are *produced in common* through the constantly expanding regime of biopolitical production (*Ibid.*: 28). The material reality of Deleuzian desire, in other words, is determined through the concrete praxis of the multitude; for the regime of immaterial labour in which it participates (despite the parasitic regimes of empire which seek constantly to privatize, appropriate and overcode every aspect of productive activity) produces a globally networked, communicative body of desire whose 'being' is simultaneously the substance and practice of democracy (Hardt and Negri, 2005: 196–202).

This reconstruction of Marx's materialism however is problematic. As we have seen Deleuze and Guattari's account of the three kinds of social machine does not present a simple diachronic progression from 'primitive' to 'despotic' to 'civilized capitalist' forms of society. Rather their exposition traces a play of immanence (each machine is defined as a predominant territoriality which produces flows and intensities that exceed it) and dispersal (every excess of desire constitutes a trajectory which threatens the existing mechanism of capture) in which 'progress' is always displaced by unpredictable effects of desire. It is in this sense that capitalism has 'haunted all forms of society'. For what is named here is not an historically specific mode of production (in Marx's sense), but rather the very condition of history, that is, the excessive flows of desire which are put into play by every territorial machine and against which every machine reconfigures its strategy of capture (Deleuze and Guattari, 2000: 140). What capitalism designates, in other words, is the power of desire to precipitate unpredictable flows, breaks and intensities within every regime of domination – the 'schizophrenic desire' whose multiple trajectories outplay the state and its mechanisms of capture (*Ibid.*: 260). The difference between Deleuze and Guattari's account of transgressive desire and the one set out by Hardt and Negri therefore, is that the fugitive events of love, transgression and affiliation which the former conceive as the ungraspable horizon of an infinitely extensible regime of capture, are taken by the latter as disclosing the ontological commonality which is immanent in the multitude. Thus the 'force' of Hardt and Negri's reading of *Capitalism and Schizophrenia* lies in its determination to reduce the sheer heterogeneity of the events which arise from the global constitution of capitalism, to a logic of ontological composition through which multitude determines its cosmopolitan sovereignty.

The question which is at issue here is that of ontological violence. In both *Empire* and *Multitude* Hardt and Negri make a sustained attempt to synthesize Marx's ontology of living labour with Deleuze's conception of the unforeseeable events (of difference) which arise from the machinic desire. We should be clear that this project attempts to bring together two radically incommensurable universes: the first determines the possibility of ethics, justice and democracy through the movement of an immanent identity (the multitude) within the techno-scientific networks of global capitalism, the second attempts to maintain the integrity of the event, and to seek justice in the 'minor' lines of flight which depart from established regimes of sovereignty. The 'community' which is implicit in Deleuze and Guattari's account of such nomadic flights, in other words, is, to use Jean-Luc Nancy's term, an 'inoperative' one: it is a dispersed association of ideas, sensations, affections, languages and representations which has no permanent 'being', and which exists only in the contingent acts of departure which it precipitates. From this perspective, Hardt and Negri's attempt to subsume the events of difference which arise from the global expansion of capitalism under the immanent identity of living labour, must always be haunted by the force of its own composition; for what they conceive as the 'ontological' movement of the multitude, always proceeds through the designation of sovereign forms of the right, the good and the true. There is a sense then in which Derrida's Marxism occupies the same conceptual universe as Deleuze and Guattari's account of schizophrenic desire; for their idea of the nomadic lines of flight which arise from the techno-scientific organization of capital, lies close to Derrida's understanding of the contingent events which haunt the prosthetic transformation of public space and the transcendental structures of cultural identity. However, this is not to say that their analyses are the same; indeed, as I indicated in the previous section, the crucial difference between the two positions is what I take to be the ethical reserve which is configured in Derrida's conception of hospitality to who comes.[4] Thus we need to examine Derrida's concept of 'the law of hospitality' and its inscription in the political gestures which are made in *Spectres of Marx*.

The law of hospitality, as Derrida conceives it, is a messianic demand which haunts the symbolic economy of being; and so in its contemporary form, it is the absolute responsibility to the other which arises from the circulation of ontological figures (race, gender, fraternity community) through the prosthetic/mediatic economy of capitalism.[5] Whoever comes to us in true destitution is always 'unnamed' in the institutional structures through which he or she is received; for the nature of such destitution is that it has no direct language of appeal beyond the fact of its suffering, and that it must represent itself to cultures which have already designated it as something 'outside' the bounds of their responsibility. The figure of the 'asylum seeker' is exemplary here; for he or she appears before the tribunal of the nation as a potentially dangerous stranger whose race, language and religion have, before proceedings even begin, marked him or her as hostile to the values and traditions of the host culture. This transaction between the 'host' (Derrida uses the term in *Of Hospitality* to designate the position of those nations whose military, economic and political power has given them a virtual monopoly over the world's resources) and those who come in destitution however, is never entirely closed; for the fact that every culture is a discursive accumulation of linguistic usage, established traditions of ethical life and formal legality, means that the coming of the stranger is always a disruptive event which recalls the demand for hospitality. As Derrida puts:

> We will always be threatened by this dilemma between, on the one hand, unconditional hospitality that dispenses with law, duty, and even politics, and, on the other, hospitality circumscribed by law and duty. One of them can always corrupt the other, and this capacity for perversion remains irreducible. It *must* remain so. (Derrida and Dufourmantelle, 2000: 135)

The ethical demand of hospitality, in other words, is messianic in the sense that it can neither be erased from the operational logic of simulation (Baudrillard) nor gathered into the ontological configurations of immaterial labour (Hardt and Negri). Rather the demand is radically intensified by the effects produced by global capitalism; for it is dispersed across the inter-ethnic wars, forced migrations and military interventions whose catastrophic frequency is part of the operational logic of the biopolitical regime (*Ibid.*: 139).

So, if the global space of media-techno-scientific capitalism is marked by an exploitative violence which is all the greater for having exceeded the register of conventional Marxist categories, what are the political demands which follow from Derrida's messianic designation of the law of hospitality? This brings us back to *Spectres of Marx*, or, more accurately, to the idea of the 'New International' which Derrida introduces at the conclusion of chapter three (Derrida, 1994: 84–6).

In many ways Derrida's account of a cosmopolitical association of revolutionary ideas recalls Jean-Luc Nancy's concept of the 'inoperative community'. Nancy's argument is that if the social bond is understood in classically idealist terms (i.e. as a transcendental unity which can, at least potentially, mediate all of the essential characteristics of human nature), then an unavoidable contradiction arises: namely that the autonomy of ethical substance (*Sittlichkeit*) is always related to a 'beyond' which cannot be known or predicted. The idea of community therefore always exceeds its 'operative' designation as spirit, substance or absolute subjectivity; and in so far as it arises from what cannot be included in the established transactions of the social (the absolute excess of death and the erotic which Bataille sets over against the logic of Hegel's phenomenology, for example), it exists only as 'a *relation* to the absolute, and imposing on the absolute a relation *to* its own Being instead of making this Being immanent to the absolute totality of beings' (Nancy, 2004: 6). The inoperative community, in other words, disrupts the recuperative logic of totality; it exists as a performative relationship which is constantly re-distributed through the events (of silencing, aesthetic transfiguration, eroticism, poiesis, love, etc.) which arise from the social, economic and political inscription of Being. For Derrida, the unpredictable 'beyond' which returns to the dialectics of social totality is configured through the demand of the other; for as we have seen, the world created by biopolitical capitalism is one in which the prosthetic supplementation of 'the human' (and all its conditions of life) is such as to give rise to an open-ended series of questions about the ethics of hospitality: Is it right to use bio and genetic technologies to help alleviate famine in the Third World? Does this kind of 'aid' simply perpetuate a relationship of dependency? Is it true that international institutions have functioned only to facilitate the First World exploitation of natural and human resources? What are the international responsibilities of the West to those 'others' who come in anger and destitution?

Such questions (the list, of course, is always incomplete and, in a radical sense, uncompletable) are the responsibility of the New International; for they arise out of the 'operative' regime of accumulation and gesture towards the infinite horizon of democracy to come which is opened by the arrival of the other. This, as we saw in chapter eleven, is quite close to David Held's account of cosmopolitan justice; for both Derrida and Held insist that while it is true that international institutions will always be imperfect, their imperfection marks the possibility of improvement in the actual condition of international law.

As I have already indicated however, the Habermasian basis of Held's theory leads him to underplay the aporetic structure of the questions which arise from biopolitical capitalism: for the level of communicative rationality which is assumed to have accumulated in the network of international institutions, is conceived as having brought about a relatively permanent increase in the ethical culture of humanity (even if this culture may suffer periodic recessions and reversals). For Derrida, on the contrary, the arrival of the other (the nomad, the migrant, the asylum seeker, the 'guest worker', the mutant, the clone) is dispersed across radically heterogeneous events which throw the lifeworld into crisis; his or her destitution immediately calls into question the universality of ethical life and demands that the host culture respond in ways which go beyond defence of the border and the expulsion of the unknown (Derrida and Dufourmantelle, 2000: 123). This demand for hospitality is what founds Derrida's conception of the New International; for the spectres of the other, as they are dispersed across the prosthetic, informatic and telematic systems of global capitalism, constantly reopen the question of democracy to come, and of how such a democracy is to be enacted (Derrida, 1994: 84).

So, who is part of this New International? And how is it to be constituted as a political force? In answer to the first question, Derrida maintains that the gesture of affiliation which he makes towards Marx constitutes:

> [A]n untimely link, without status, without title, and without name, barely public even if it is not clandestine, without contract, 'out of joint', without coordination, without party, without country, without national community ..., without co-citizenship, without common belonging to a class. (Derrida, 1994: 85)

Thus, the constituency of this New International is, by definition, 'inoperative': it is made up of those 'friends' (artists, philosophers, poets, political activists) who seek no community beyond their mutual precipitation of the ideas, aesthetic representations, literary testimonies and radical gestures of hospitality through which the difference of the stranger is received. Such gestures, according to Derrida, are not simply the posturing of a bourgeois avant garde; rather their impact retains something of the transformative status of the unforeseen (the event of the other), and acts as a provocation to the established regime of international law (*Ibid.*). This constituency 'without name', of course, is not the International as Marx, or Lenin, or Luxemburg conceived it; for despite the differences of emphasis which we have noted, the idea of class as the material basis of political action remains constant throughout their respective theories of revolutionary change. Indeed, as we will see in the next section, much of the criticism provoked by *Spectres of Marx* has focused on the apparent depoliticization of Marxism which results from Derrida's impiety towards the eschatological organization of class, state and mode of production. Terry Eagleton, for example, has argued that Derrida's failure to determine the substance of his 'New International' should be seen as proof of the incompatibility of deconstruction – as a method of literary criticism – with the strategic necessities of class organization which are the *real* concern of Marxist politics (Eagleton in Sprinker, 1999: 85). Thus the question which will concern us in the following section brings us back to concept of class politics; for we must consider to what extent the critical tropes of machinic desire, simulation and *différance* are essential configurations of a new critique of capital, and to what extent such a critique has transformed the concepts of resistance, solidarity and revolution which are possible under the regime of global-technological accumulation.

Part IV

Marxism, Postmodernism and the Political

As we have seen, 'postmodernist' readings of Marx have sought to follow the transformations of the mode of production beyond the dialectical limits which Marx sought to impose upon them. And so if there is a general idea which links the theorists I have examined, it is a concern with the power of capital constantly to exceed the established boundaries of accumulation, and to alter the social, political and technological terms under which surplus value is realized. This concern, however, has not taken the form of a flat contradiction of Marx's critique of capital; and so in the preceding chapters I have attempted to situate postmodernist configurations of power, identity and autonomy within a broadly Marxist constellation. What I want to do in this final section therefore is to examine the diverse political demands which have arisen from postmodernist configurations of Marxism, for as we have seen, the voices which are supposed to speak the language of 'the postmodern' are by no means united in their political aims or affiliations. In particular I will examine: (1) the powers of capital which Marx identifies in his account of the historical trajectory of the capitalist mode of production, (2) the disparate conceptions of post-ontological Marxism which are presented by Baudrillard, Derrida and Deleuze, (3) conventional Marxist critiques of the postmodernist ideology and (4) the idea of a Marxism 'without reserve' which arises from Derrida's deconstruction of historical materialism.

15
Marx and the Powers of Capital

For Marx what is distinctive about capitalism is the fact that commodities are produced not for the purpose of consumption but for the purpose of reconverting them into money. The bourgeois entrepreneur, in other words, produces commodities as things destined for sale on the open market which will realize more capital than was originally invested in their manufacture. Marx refers to this transformation of money into money through the realization of surplus value as the Money–Commodity–Money, or M–C–M, relation. This relation arises out of a more primitive organization of productive activity in which the use-value of commodities functioned as the exclusive condition of exchange. Once money has emerged as a universal equivalent capable of purchasing any of the means of subsistence however, the 'simple circulation of commodities' based on the satisfaction of social need is displaced by the distributive powers of capital. The principal difference between the M–C–M relation and the barter economy therefore is that the latter begins with the need of the individual producer to secure enough of the means of subsistence to fulfil his/her needs, while the latter begins with the dispersal of commodities in order to allow the reflux of money to the capitalist (Marx, 1990: 249).

According to this analysis, once the old system of exchange, or the commodity–money–commodity (C–M–C) relation, has established money as the universal expression of value, the M–C–M relation is able to emerge as the dominant mode of production and distribution (Marx, 1990: 256). Thus the movement of capital becomes self-valorizing; for it simultaneously engenders its monetary expansion through the production of commodities and the expansion of its productive capacity through the reinvestment of surplus value in the form of profit. Implicit in this relation is the demand constantly to decrease the time taken to transform raw materials into commodities which can be offered for sale. Every capitalist, in other words, labours under the same necessity to make his enterprise as efficient as possible; for if the production of his commodities is slower than the average rate, there will be insufficient surplus value produced for his enterprise to remain competitive. It is this hard necessity which Marx identifies as the driving force behind the introduction of machine technology into the productive process: for if capitalist B does not follow capitalist A in employing machines in his enterprise, he will be unable to maintain his share of an ever expanding market. Before turning to the effects of such technologies on the process of production however, I want briefly to consider Marx's account of the ways in which the M–C–M relation has functioned to destabilize the established boundaries of communal life.

The regime of landed property, or feudalism, appears in Marx's analysis as the precursor to capitalism: it is the regime under which the accumulation of wealth in the hands of the aristocracy leads to the establishment of monetary tokens as a universal equivalent which is exchangeable for all commodities. Initially the use of such tokens is limited and takes place within the old system of barter; however, as the productivity of the estates slowly increases, so the use of money is established as the medium through which surplus produce is exchanged. This simple circulation of commodities is extremely durable, and supports a regime of social and political obligations in which the labour of the serf is closely tied to the absolute authority of the feudal lord. As such the productive activity which takes place under feudalism is largely undifferentiated: it is part of a subsistence economy whose technological basis is limited to the use of metal implements in agriculture, and whose product is embedded in system of ties and obligations which, for all practical intents, precludes the possibility of major economic or technological innovation. For Marx, the importance of the C–M–C relation as it is determined under feudalism is that it opens the possibility of a new type of capital accumulation; for the emergence of money as a universal equivalent prefigures the appearance of the mercantile form of capital which reproduces itself through the purchase and resale of commodities and raw materials. This type of capital, as we have seen, becomes increasingly powerful as better ships and more reliable forms of navigation intensify international trade: more and more commodities are offered for sale to the landed aristocracy, who, in purchasing those commodities, deplete their own capital and add to the stock acquired by the merchant class. It is this growing accumulation of money acquired through trade which, according to Marx, leads to the antagonism between town and country: as the cities become established as centres of mercantile activity, so the economic power and political authority of the landed aristocracy is compromised. Ultimately the decay of the feudal estates into regimes of violent extortion leads to a mass exodus of surfs into the towns; for the increasing prosperity of the mercantile economy provides a constantly expanding demand for day-labourers which is supplied by the influx of cheap labour from the country (Marx, 1977b: 70).

It is the accumulation of mercantile capital and the expansion in the range and diversity of the work which services that capital which, for Marx, is the precondition of the growth of manufacturing. Initially the manufacture of commodities is of less importance to the accumulation of capital than the trade in raw materials; merchants, in other words, make the majority of their profits from the importation and distribution of goods which are used in cottage industries. Thus the fragility of 'manufacture', conceived as the centralization of labour, tools and raw materials in one place which is governed by a strict regime of discipline and time-keeping, arises from the intense competition among merchants from different nations: for immediately a particular branch of production begins to emerge in a particular nation, its survival is dependent upon the continued existence of foreign markets which could, at any moment, be ruined by fluctuations in labour and commodity prices (Marx, 1977b: 76). This means that without the patronage of the mercantile class, who were able to lobby for state protection of indigenous manufacturing, industrial capitalism could not have emerged; for while it is true that such patronage was born out of self-interest (more industrial manufacture means more need for more raw materials), the outcome of this relationship furnishes the conditions of a fundamental shift towards the domination of industrial capital. What is important here is that the historical tendency which Marx identifies, that is, the establishment of a world market that has come under the sway of a small group of nations in which trade and manufacture are most developed, has a radical impact upon the social fabric of every nation state. The spread of international competition and free trade, in other words, results in:

> The destruction as far as possible of ideology, religion, morality, etc. and where it could not do this, made them into a palpable lie. It produced a world history for the first time, in so far as it made all civilized nations and every individual member of them dependent for the satisfaction of their wants on the whole world, thus destroying the former natural exclusiveness of separate nations. (*Ibid.*: 78)

The development of manufacturing as the dominant type of accumulation therefore is destructive of the separate forms of social obligation, religious worship, traditional authority and public morality which make up the substance of the nation state. For as the industrial basis of capitalism begins to establish itself in the most prosperous economies, so the pressure of the international market begins to transform fundamentally the social and political structures of all 'civilized nations'.

This then is the point at which civil society, as the realm of self-seeking individualism, realizes its concept (Marx, 1977b: 57). We have seen that for Marx the fundamental problem with Hegel's *Philosophy of Right* is the fact that he attributes a spiritual significance to the division of humanity into the disparate, egoistical subjects which are ranged against each other in civil society. His argument is that while Hegel successfully identified the dislocating impact of trade and entrepreneurialism upon the structures of feudal authority, he failed to recognize that this unregulated individualism is without transcendental limits and that it is constantly exacerbated by the drive for profit which accompanies the development of the free market. Thus the bourgeois citizen and the independent wage labourer become abstract figures whose mutual dependence is conceived as the expression of the implicit and evolving unity of ethical life (Marx, 1977c: 27). For Marx however the *Philosophy of Right's* recourse to the old guild corporations as bulwarks against the 'penurious rabble' of day labourers cannot possibly suffice as a solution to the contradictions of atomistic individualism. The essence of civil society as it develops under the influence of the M–C–M relation is the subsumption of every ethical tie ('ethical' in the sense of an obligation which is not entirely determined by the demands of competition) under the regime of capital: for the rights, duties and obligations which arise within the sphere of public legality are determined by the increasing power of capital to destroy the established forms of social obligation. This, of course, is not to say that Marx regarded the *ancien regime* with any sense of nostalgia; his perspective on the feudal order was clearly one of a thoroughgoing modernist who had no time for the 'stupefied seclusion' of the rural economy (*Ibid.*: 318). However, the establishment of civil society as the realm of bourgeois rights and freedoms marks the point at which capital begins to determine itself as an independent power which constantly transforms the social, economic and political conditions of its reproduction (Marx, 1977b: 58). Thus the communal ties which bind human beings together are constantly ruptured by the fetishistic pursuit of surplus value and the compulsion to secure a living wage in a fluctuating labour market.

For Marx the constitution of civil society as the realm of legal rights and freedoms is the counterpart of a phenomenological transformation of the commodity form. The simple circulation of commodities which precedes the M–C–M relation is embedded in the old feudal economy, and so the circulation of money functions primarily to secure those commodities which are necessary to a certain level of communal subsistence. With the emergence of bourgeois civil society however the relationship between material objects and their producers is inverted; for as the M–C–M relation becomes dominant, the exchange of commodities takes on the appearance of a *social* relationship which gathers together all of the disparate forms of productive activity. The logic of exchange which has come to dominate social relations, in other words, becomes fetishized; commodities take on a life of their own in which they 'appear as autonomous figures which enter into relations both with each other and with the human race' (Marx, 1990: 165–6). Thus, as soon as the products of organic labour become commodified, the spatial, temporal and institutional dimensions of society are radically transformed: the old feudal association of church and state is displaced by an expansive power of production (capital) whose appearance in the form of the commodity gives it a fetishistic power over every institution of ethical life. This is not to say that established traditions and institutions simply collapse under the pressure of capital accumulation, or that the abstract freedoms of bourgeois society are incapable of determining any sense of community or social cohesion. Rather the point is that Marx's account of the fetishism of commodities discloses a virtualizing relationship between the commodity form and the 'substance' of social relations; for he argues that even before the introduction of industrial technologies into the productive process, the emergence of the M–C–M relation as the dominant form of exchange, marks a fundamental alteration in the dynamics of representation, desire and authority.

There is a sense in which the M–C–M relation has always been technological; for as we saw in chapter six the possibility of the commodity form presupposes the establishment of a certain level of technical development prior to the emergence of trade and manufacture as the dominant forms of capital accumulation. The feudal economy, in other words, stands upon metallurgical processes of manufacture (tools, agricultural implements, utensils, etc.) which have intensified the productive power of humanity and transformed its relationship to itself and to nature. Marx however maintains that it is not until the emergence of bourgeois civil society that the technological transformation of the labour process, and of the social and political institutions which support it, can really gather pace. As we have seen, the historical appearance of manufacture presupposes the establishment of trade and the mercantile economy, for it is not until the cities have established their independence from the feudal estates that it is possible for the manufacture of commodities to emerge as a viable form of capital accumulation. Initially the distinctive characteristic of manufacture is its reorganization of the division of labour: the means of subsistence are no longer produced by individual workers who perform all of the tasks necessary to complete a particular commodity; rather the workshop emerges as the place where labour is gathered together in a system of 'organic cooperation', and where each individual undertakes one or two repetitive operations in the production of a single type of commodity. It is this cooperative regime which provides the basis for the introduction of machine technology; for as the tasks performed by wage labourers become ever more simplified, so the way is opened for the introduction of machines which replicate their actions (Marx, 1990: 495). These machines make their first appearance as part of the cottage industries which precede the emergence of workshop manufacture, but it is not until mathematical and scientific principles are applied to this productive regime that they can emerge as a real productive force. The motive power for this kind of production is supplied initially by a variety of different sources: wind, water, draft animals, or the worker himself. Yet these sources belong to a smaller scale and slower temporality of production than the one which is implicit in the technological basis of manufacture. And so it is through the combined force of economic and technological necessity that they are replaced by the thermodynamic technology of the steam engine (*Ibid.*: 497).

So, how is this technological transformation of the labour process related to the disembedding of social and political relationships which is already implicit in the M–C–M relation? In *The Grundrisse* Marx introduces a distinction between what he calls the 'formal' and the 'real' subsumption of labour (Marx, 1993: 690–5). The formal subsumption of labour, according to Marx, designates a system of organic cooperation in which the worker retains a certain level of autonomy; for while it is true that he or she is employed in minute and repetitive tasks, it is also the case that instruments of production are not yet sophisticated enough to appropriate all the traditional skills and knowledge from the labour process. Once industrial technologies are applied to the workshop however, the temporality of production is transformed. Marx argues that machines are the very embodiment of the fixed capital through which every enterprise must seek to speed up its production of commodities, and that as such, the regime of industrial production is one which functions to absorb the knowledge, virtuosity and skill of the worker under the self-activating operations of the machine (*Ibid.*: 694). The real subsumption of labour therefore has an essential link with the mounting speed at which commodities are produced and exchanged; for it is the evacuation of all but the most basic knowledge and skill from the labour process which determines the exponential rise in productivity that is characteristic of industrial capitalism.

For Marx, a number of important consequences follow from the increasing power of capital to absorb the differentiations of organic labour, consequences which draw together the earlier and later strands of his thought. First, the labour of the workforce is reduced to pure repetition; for as machines become increasingly sophisticated, so fewer workers are required to perform less demanding tasks in the automated production of commodities. Second, the social and political life of human beings, both bourgeois and proletarian, is reduced to the exercise of abstract rights which are the ideological counterpart of commodity production. Participation in the public sphere (civil society), in other words, is limited to transactions between the abstract categories (wage labour, capital, exchange value, profit) which have come to determine the social being of humanity. Third, capitalist enterprise becomes increasingly concerned with technological innovations which push up the rate at which surplus value is produced. This leads to a situation in which the 'moral' obsolescence of machinery, that is, the point at which its productivity falls below the general level established by competition among individual capitalists, occurs before it has produced enough commodities to pay for itself (Marx, 1992: 237–61). Finally, the over-representation of fixed capital (in the form of machinery) in the productive process leads to the migration of money into the 'fictitious' forms of shares, bonds, and equities; for as the difficulty of realizing a profit is compounded by the over-production and under-consumption of commodities, so the non-material forms of accumulation offered by the banks and the stock exchange become increasingly important to the turnover of capital (Marx, 1991: 525–42).

According to Marx's analysis, this process of technological abstraction takes place within certain absolute limits which are determined by the labour theory of value. If we follow his account of the historical tendency of the capitalist mode of production, there is a sense in which the idea of community which is present in his work from the *Economic and Philosophical Manuscripts* onwards draws its force from the cooperative labour which first differentiates human beings from their pre-hominid ancestors. This labour, whose social expression Marx calls 'primitive communism', is what first makes human beings human; for it simultaneously provides for the basic needs of the community and establishes the possibility of forms of cooperation which develop the higher faculties of the species (language, reasoning, imagination, etc.) (Marx, 1977a: 72–4). What is important here is that, for Marx, the concept of socialized production is embedded in the origin of human society; and so the force it acquires in his account of the 'abstract' nature of capitalist relations derives from its status as a concretely integrated community of production, consumption and desire. The increasing level of alienation which takes place through the dominance of the M–C–M relation and the deployment of machinery into the labour process therefore is an effect which belongs specifically to the abstract relations of capital: for it is only in so far as the last vestiges of living labour have been subsumed under the operational powers of private accumulation, that the (revolutionary) demand for socialized production returns to the inverted world of the commodity form (Marx, 1990: 618). This however raises two fundamental questions. First, do all of the abstract forms through which capital expands (knowledge, credit, prosthetics, informatics) contribute to the alienation of productive humanity? And second, is it true that the intrinsic value which Marx attributes to human labour has remained immanent in the global-techno-scientific evolution of capitalism? It is these two questions which will occupy us in the following chapter.

16
A Post-Ontological Marxism?

In the preceding sections I have tried to defend two 'postmodernist' theses: first, that the techno-scientific transformation of the mode of production has extended the power of capital to reproduce itself beyond the dialectical limits which Marx sought to impose; and second, that if we are to inherit what Derrida has called the 'spirit' of Marx's revolutionary politics, we must seek to transform the fundamental categories of historical materialism. This brings me back to the question of ontology. As we have seen, the postmodernist critique of Marxism has in general focused on the violence which plays around materialist constructions of historical necessity; and so the Marxist discourse of social being (i.e. the immanence of man's communal productivity within the exploitative regime of capital) is expounded as a totalizing power which draws its authority from the interlacing of performative concepts (class, resistance, identity, value, production, solidarity) with the negative evolution of the mode of production. This tendency to treat the operative regime of capital as the true foundation of politics has been a recurrent theme in the preceding chapters: the concepts of simulation, *différance* and machinic desire which I examined in a number of different theoretical contexts, all present 'capitalism' as a regime which indefinitely defers the revolutionary exchange between the object (the commodity form and its institutions) and its 'alienated' forms of subjectivity. If there is to be a 'post-ontological' Marxism therefore its political responsibility lies in attempting to think the techno-scientific development of the mode of production outside of neo-liberal ideas of freedom, and to trace the lines of communication which might be possible among those contingent forms of resistance to which global capitalism has given rise. This is not to say that the ontological apparatus of Marxism has quietly passed away, and in the following chapter I will try to respond to those critics who regard the postmodernist critique of materialism as a dangerous piece of ideology which neglects the strategic importance of class. For the moment, however, I want to examine the technological transformations which capitalism has undergone since the early 1970s, and to specify the relationship between those transformations and the concepts which have been elaborated by Baudrillard, Deleuze, Derrida and Negri.

The most systematic account of the relationship between new informatic, prosthetic and media technologies and the restructuring which capitalism has undergone since the end of the 1970's is given in Manuel Castells's *The Rise of the Network Society*. In the first chapter of the book he specifies the five characteristics of what he calls 'the information technology paradigm': (1) information is the 'raw material' of digital communications technologies, (2) such technologies have become utterly pervasive of the social, cultural and economic organization of advanced capitalist societies, (3) the interpenetration of the social and the informatic determines a 'networking logic' in which each system or institution is connected to every other (4) this universal connectedness gives rise to increasing flexibility in the organizational structures which make up the network society. The fifth characteristic which Castells identifies in his typology is the 'growing *convergence of specific technologies into a highly integrated system*' which gathers together all specific fields of research and development under the umbrella of the information technology paradigm (Castells, 2000: 70–2). This requires some exposition. Castells's claim that new informatic technologies work upon information as their raw material really concerns the positive feedback capacity of such technologies; the faster information is processed and distributed, in other words, the quicker the technological basis of the knowledge economy is pushed forward by new innovations. This mutual precipitation of knowledge and technology becomes the operative paradigm of all social relationships; for once information technologies are sufficiently developed, their encoding of 'the real' determines a network of interconnections in which each institution constantly transforms itself in relation to the others. Thus, for example, the expansion of the information economy occurs through the proliferation of new areas of expertise (chaos theory, micro-electronics, fractal geometries) which impact upon the curricula of schools and universities, thereby reshaping the cultural, economic and political expectations of those who work within the network society. Finally, the information technology paradigm has even appropriated the biological conditions of life; for once the mathematical code of DNA became available to computer scientists, it was then possible for them to model computational programmes on the infinite versatility and adaptability of the human g-nom (*Ibid.*: 73).

Castells makes it clear that his description of the information technology paradigm should not be considered in abstraction from the economic restructuring of capitalism which took place after the inflationary crises of the 1970s. According to his argument IT companies fundamentally alter the rules of capital investment; for the fact that a large proportion of their profits are given over to research and development means that the returns which corporate investors can expect are, relatively speaking, quite small. However, the high value at which these companies are quoted reflects a rational expectation on the part of investors, namely, the expectation that the future of capitalism is inextricably bound up with the technological innovations which these companies will produce in the future. It is better, in other words, to get into the market early than to have to pay an exorbitant price of admission further down the line (Castells, 2000: 152). Once financial capital begins to invest heavily in the expectation of commercial opportunities which information technology will provide in the future, the operational logic of the market undergoes a radical change; for the acquisitive regime of capital, instead of remaining tied to the traditional form of the commodity, is limitlessly expanded by the very technologies in which it has begun to invest. Thus the idea of 'value' is uncoupled from the limitations of materiality; it is created and recreated through informatic technologies which open up an infinite horizon for the accumulation of capital (*Ibid.*: 160). The old idea of profit, with its connotations of fiscal responsibility and restraint, is displaced by an exorbitant corporate greed which is unconfined by the spatial and temporal limitations of industrial production, and which spreads through the global-financial networks which it creates.

This is not to say that there is no longer any 'material' production of commodities; Castells's claim is rather that such productivity has been subsumed under the information technology paradigm:

> While finance capital has generally been among the dominant fractions of capital, we are witnessing the emergence of something different: capital accumulation proceeds, and its value making is generated, increasingly, in the global financial markets enacted by information networks in the timeless space of financial flows. (Castells, 2000: 503–4)

Thus the major financial markets of the developed world transform the material forms of labour which Marx considered to be the essence of the commodity, into virtual codes through which capital maintains its ability to expand, diversify and mutate. This process is both universal and reductive: for if we allow that the information technology paradigm will always function in terms of the latest innovations in its operational powers, and if this process serves to reproduce the convergence of interest and practical cooperation among trans-national corporations, then the value of the material labour which is performed in particular national economies is inevitably set upon a downward trend. Indeed the overall effect of the migration of capital into the informatic networks which have come to dominate the world market has been to render labour 'disaggregated in its performance, fragmented in its organization, diversified in its existence [and] divided in its collective action'(*Ibid.*: 505). So if, as Castells maintains, the circulation of capital takes place through a 'meta-network' which arbitrarily determines the value of everything (labour, technological innovation, product image, research breakthroughs, natural resources, human capacities), must it not also be true that the information technology paradigm has taken control the of process of cultural valuation? The implication is clear in Castells conclusion to *Network Society*; for he argues that the volatile axes of confidence, trust and investment which constantly transform the geopolitical terrain of capital, have produced a global-informatic 'culture' which offers little more than a celebration of abstract individualism and the distractions of mass consumption (*Ibid.*: 508).

Castells's analysis of the information technology paradigm has made it clear that the restructuring of productive relations which it determines is ultimately an intensification of the power of capital to reproduce itself (Castells, 2000: 13). Indeed his entire account of the network society is concerned to expound the infinitely complex ways in which capital and technology have become entwined, and the impact this virtualization of the commodity form has had upon the social, economic and cultural existence of humanity. So what, we might ask, is Castells's relationship to Marxism? The fragmentation of labour and loss of cultural identity which results from the informatic restructuring of capital is presented by Castells as something which demands a deepening of our powers of political reflection, and yet his analysis remains strictly withdrawn from evaluative judgements of the geopolitical effects whose causality he describes (*Ibid.*: 26). This methodological position is partly explained by a determination not to overload his account of the network society with a battery of evaluative concepts which would obscure its difference from the socio-economic forms which have preceded it. Thus a convention-ally Marxist approach, in its haste to specify the dialectical significance of the new commodity form, would exclude Castells 'profane illumina-tion' of the possibilities which have arisen from the present conjunction of capital and information technologies.[1] He does however give a qualified approval to David Harvey's version of Marxist critique; for his attempt to make a causal connection between the ideological functions of postmodern culture and the condensation of space and time through which the global economy operates,[2] is acknowledged as having prefig-ured the analytical project of *Network Society*. So, while it is certainly true that there are significant differences between Harvey and Castells (most notably the latter's claim that Harvey attributes a historically determin-ing power to logics of accumulation which informatic capitalism has radically transformed), it is, I think, fair to say that their respective accounts of the relationship between capital, culture and technology inhabit the same conceptual universe. Both maintain that the cultural supports of selfhood and moral attachment are threatened by the extreme volatility of global markets, and both agree that 'postmodern' art, literature and theory are no more than the ideological reflex of this ongoing process of cultural fragmentation (*Ibid.*: 493). What I want to argue however is that Castells's analysis of the information technology paradigm is, in Harvey's sense of the term, postmodern; for his account of the operational powers which it brings to the global economy cannot be articulated without recourse to the notions of virtuality, simulation and prosthesis which configure the postmodernist engagement with techno-scientific capitalism.

Thus, if it is the case that Castells's description of informatic capitalism has deployed ideas which derive from postmodernist theory, and if these ideas provoke ethical reflections which cannot be reduced to the logic of ideological legitimation, then the informatic economy which he describes has, by definition, to be a rather more complex conjunction of effects than the one described in *Network Society*. Castells writes as if the information technology paradigm, having come into being, is able to determine the infinite perfection of the social, political and technologi-cal conditions of its reproduction: for while he certainly does not hold out the prospect of such a 'timeless' future as an ideal, there is a sense in which *The Rise of the Network Society* repeats Max Weber's account of the fatal intrusion of instrumental reason upon traditional forms of social solidarity (Castells, 2000: 214–15).[3] Networks of informatic exchange, in other words, are treated as having extended the logic of rational appro-priation into the realm of the virtual; for as the cultural life of humanity expands through the new powers of imagination and prosthesis made possible by media networks, so the dominance of the informatic code becomes increasingly perfect. This is why, according to Castells, it is vital that the 'horizontal' operation of the internet should be defended against colonization by media corporations: for if it is transformed from a dialogical medium which solicits disparate forms of expression into a centrally administered network which constantly extends the flow of cultural simulacra, then the chance of alternative messages emerging from within the informatic loop would be reduced to almost nothing (*Ibid.*: 405). Such a demand for resistance however sits uneasily with the discourse of simulation through which Castells has presented the fate of mass culture; for we might legitimately ask, in the spirit of Baudrillard's concept of the hyperreal, where the resources of such resistance are to come from if the conditions of symbolic representation are already determined by media and informatic codes.

The importance of Baudrillard's determination to think through the effects of new media technologies lies in the fact that his theorizations of virtual capital, global space and the loss of identity push the encoding of the real beyond any putative residue of human culture or political solidarity. Thus when he claims that under the present regime the image has 'no relation to any reality whatsoever', and that it has become 'its own pure simulacrum', his intention is to configure the inexpressible absence which runs throughout the system of informatic exchange: politics, in other words, has become weightless in the sense that the forms of symbolic representation through which it is carried on, are all reversible simulacra which are deployed as solicitations to the nameless indifference of the masses (Baudrillard, 1999: 6). The issues which defined twentieth-century modernity (racism, feminism, socialism, ecologism) have all passed into the realm of the hyperreal where they are presented as the 'natural' counterparts of anything from neo-fascism to New Age spiritualism (Baudrillard, 1995b: 3–13). So, while I do have reservations about Baudrillard's thesis, there is a sense in which his conception of the hyperreal indicates the urgency of the political questions which arise from the information technology paradigm; for the play of simulacra into which politics has descended is conceived not as a possibility which might be resisted, but as the accomplished outcome of the complicity between capital, technology and informatic code. Every form of 'difference' is presented in a symbolic order which has already determined its place in the economy of the hyperreal, and so the unaccountable, the truly 'other', is finally erased (*Ibid.*: 124). Baudrillard's concept of simulation therefore pushes the logic of encoding to the point where the conduct of politics has lost all reality; and so it is at this point that the *question of the political* becomes absolutely urgent. In Castells's work this critical point is played out in his vacillation between the politics of cultural resistance and a kind of Weberian pessimism; for in so far as he fails to think through the total effect of simulation on mind, body and culture, he is left with the fading hope of what may arise from the closed system of information technology paradigm (Castells, 2000: 406).[4]

This is not to say that Baudrillard's approach to the political gestures towards a new transcendence that would redeem the real from its fatal descent into simulation. Indeed his later work, particularly *Fatal Strategies* and *The Transparency of Evil*, returns to the theoretical strategy of pushing the logic of simulation beyond the catastrophic effects which it has already produced.[5] Please provide notes for Note number 5. Thus AIDS, cancer and crack addiction are conceived not as contingent pathologies which it might be possible to ameliorate, but as effects that arise from the loss of the real and which actually portend the emergence of even more extreme phenomena. Such catastrophic thinking is not simply nihilistic voyeurism; for the whole point of confronting the political rationality of the system with its most extreme consequences, is to produce unexpected events of disorder in its hyper-functional expansion (Baudrillard, 1993: 125). The morality of this approach would consist in forcing the advocates of any given system of reference (genetic technologies for example) to specify the ultimate ground of their legitimacy; for even though the logic of simulation has, according to Baudrillard, become total, the art of imagining its most catastrophic possibilities remains possible (*Ibid.*: 127). Ultimately, however, it is necessary to go beyond the limits of reading Baudrillard 'in his own terms' (Butler, 1999: 1–22). For while it is true that much of the criticism of his work is almost wilfully misguided, I have argued that, in the end, the politics of simulation lies in the relationship of the virtual to the categories of being which it transforms and reproduces. The capacity of new media technologies to alter the terrain of public space and cultural recognition, in other words, gives rise to events which are not already encoded and which always re-open the question of who is excluded by the mediatic staging of the real. This notion of responsibility to the other, as we have seen, is the basis on which Derrida attempts to re-configure the revolutionary demand of Marx's thought. Before considering the political implications of this strategy however, I want to return briefly to the concept of machinic desire through which Deleuze and Guattari conceive the general economy of capitalism.

Castells's theory of the information technology paradigm sets out the conditions of an increasingly close relationship between informatic encoding, the circulation of capital through virtual networks, and the reciprocal transformation of the genetic and computational systems which have engendered the network organization of the world economy. The more the biological basis of production becomes integrated into the technological systems of the virtual economy, in other words, the greater are the innovative possibilities on which that economy is able to draw (Castells, 2000: 73). Thus the 'knowledge economy' is not simply added to the existing form of rational appropriation; for the whole range of productive activity, including the most basic forms of manual labour, is now quantified in terms of the productivity made possible by the informatic regime. What is important here is the absence which is implicit in this analysis; for while I agree with Castells's assertion of the predominance of information systems in the turnover of capital, *Network Society* fails to give a proper account of the way in which the emergence of these systems presupposes the technological transformation of the human. Obviously Castells's response to this complaint would be to argue that his analysis is not concerned with theorizing the history of the relationship between the human and the technological, and that his primary objective is to determine the nature of the regime which is shaping the contemporary organization of capitalism. However, the lack of a theoretical account of technology is something which places crucial limitations on the political significance of *Network Society*; for in the absence of a determinate idea of the processes through which human desire is dispersed and intensified by the techno-scientific regime of capital, Castells is unable to offer any remission from the logic of disenchantment which pervades his work.

As we saw in Chapter 8, the account of the three kinds of social machine which Deleuze and Guattari set out in *Anti-Oedipus* does not present a simple diachronic progression from 'primitive' to 'despotic' to 'civilized capitalist' forms of society. Rather their exposition seeks to trace a play of immanence (each machine is defined as a predominant territoriality that produces flows and intensities which exceed it) and dispersal (every excess of desire constitutes a trajectory which threatens the existing mechanism of capture) in which the logic of progress is always displaced by unpredictable effects of desire. It is in this sense, they argue, that capitalism has 'haunted all forms of society'. For what is named here is not a historically specific mode of production in Marx's sense, but rather the very condition of history, that is, the contingent flows which are put into play by territorial machines and against which they reconfigure their respective strategies of capture (Deleuze and Guattari, 2000: 140). What Deleuze and Guattari are referring to here is the excess of desire which is dispersed and intensified by the social and political assemblages of the state; for even in the most primitive forms of territoriality intensities are produced which exceed the dominant system of encoding and anticipate the asceticism which founds the barbarian despotic regime. This machinic conception of desire is important because it demands a radical transformation of the way in which we think about the evolution of capital. First of all the M–C–M relation which lies at the core of Marx's conception of the historical tendency of capitalism, is uncoupled from the labour theory of value. The logic of absolute impoverishment which accompanies his account of the decline in the general rate of profit, in other words, is replaced by the idea of open-ended system in which work, satisfaction and desire are constantly transformed by the technological evolution of the means of production. This, of course, is not to say that the 'civilized capitalist' regime is presented by Deleuze and Guattari as an ideal form of social organization; for the unpredictable flows of desire to which it gives rise always produce reactive movements in the state apparatus which seek to reestablish the repressive distribution of power, discipline and property (*Ibid.*: 260). As the capitalist machine expands, its mechanism of capture becomes increasingly diffuse; the networks through which money, knowledge and information are conducted give rise to nomadic assemblages of technological innovation and aesthetic performativity which, from the point of view of the state, require increasingly 'total' systems of cathexis and counterinsurgency (Deleuze and Guattari, 2004a: 465). Yet the constitution of the state as the object of mass oedipal desire can never be completed; for even though the activity of conative bodies has become embroiled in the repressive mechanisms of heteronormativity, the technological revolutions through which capital transforms its productive regime give rise to contingent and unpredictable flows of desire. Thus, for Deleuze and Guattari, it is the efflorescence of minor 'war machines' and the strange intensifications of mind, body and community which they produce, which sustains the possibility of the political.

Deleuze and Guattari's account of desire discloses two possible configurations of Marxist politics within the techno-scientific organization of the network society. The first of these, which I will call 'post-ontological', is structured around the impact of new technologies on the reproduction of social solidarity, both as a repressive strategy of capital and as a transcendent community of 'minor' ideas and desires. The fundamental assumption of this approach is not an exclusively Marxist one, for the claim that the techno-scientific organization of capitalism is destroying the basic structures of social identity crosses the political spectrum of theory. Emile Durkheim, for example, maintained that the central problem of modernity was the speed at which economic and technological transformation had weakened the traditional institutions of social solidarity without putting anything in their place (Durkheim, 1992: 247). The point which has emerged from Baudrillard and Deleuze and Guattari's work, however, is that the concept of social ontology has been radically transformed by the techno-scientific evolution of capitalism: both argue that informatic exchange and prosthetic supplementation have reached a degree of intensity which has erased the historical experience of 'the real' (that is, the 'organic' functions of sex, gender, class, power) from our immediate experience of the present. In Baudrillard's work this erasure is presented as the emergence of a total system in which there is nothing outside of the escalatory logic of simulation; everything is transformed into a reversible sign which can be used in the solicitation of silent and unresponsive majorities. According to Deleuze and Guattari however the symbolic economy of the real carries within it the possibility of events which cannot be diffused into the hermetic circle of simulation: for if the inertia of the masses demands a proliferation of media technological interventions, this is because the re-encoding of their desire gives rise to new possibilities of artistic expression, political symbiosis and spontaneous resistance. Such possibilities however are fugitive events which cannot be re-gathered into an orthodox Marxist ontology; and so if there is line of flight which connects Marx with Deleuze it lies not in the recuperation of class identities, but rather in the demand for a permanent critique of the technological powers through which capitalism apprehends and utilizes the contingent flows of desire to which it gives rise (Deleuze and Guattari, 2004b: 224). I will return to this in a moment.

Before I proceed to look at the implications of this post-ontological version of Marxism however, I want briefly to recall the terms of its opposite formation; that is, the return to materialism which is presented in *Empire* and *Multitude*. We have seen that for Hardt and Negri the technologies through which the productive regime of capital evolves cannot be regarded as external to the bodily and intellectual constitution of the masses. Within the networks of informatic exchange labour and desire have become virtualized: they are no longer quantifiable in the substantive form of the commodity and have passed over into the 'immaterial' forms of language, innovation and technique through which biopolitical capital expands (Hardt and Negri, 2000: 366). The political subjectivity of the multitude, in other words, is intrinsically bound up with the virtuality of its labour; for the direct engagement of their sensations, desires and practices within the networks of social capital, means that they have become 'machines of innovation' which resist both the transcendental structures of imperial authority (responsible citizenship, moral individualism) and the reduction of desire to the acquisitiveness imposed by dominant culture industries (*Ibid.*: 355). Thus if there is to be a new proletarian politics Hardt and Negri argue that it must proceed from this power of self-composition: for it is only in so far as immaterial labour carries within it moments of solidarity, cooperation and resistance which exceed the possessive organization of production, that it is possible for new common forms of resistance and autonomy to become effective (*Ibid.*: 358).

So, the question here is again one of ontology; for in Hardt and Negri's account of immaterial labour the new forms of intellect and desire which arise from the informatic encoding of the real are understood as expressions of a common substrate desire which belongs to the concept of productive activity. Thus Marx's account of the real subsumption of labour under the technological regime of capitalism is conceived as a prescient anticipation of the powers of technology to diversify the experience of 'the common' which underlies the social being of the multitude. The prosthetic, informatic and cybernetic modifications which form their universal being, in other words, are articulations of a deep cooperative structure which is sustained and intensified by the networks of biopolitical production. This connection between Deleuzian desire and Marxist ontology, as we have seen, is problematic; it proceeds as if the contingent events (of resistance, symbiosis, etc.) which arise from the new paradigm are actually forms of repetition which belong to the Marxist ontology of living labour, use value and socialized production. The difficulty here however is that even in its most basic assemblages, the concept of machinic desire disturbs the organic composition of labour; and so the possibility of the transition from 'primitive' to 'despotic' to 'civilized capitalist' societies, as Deleuze and Guattari conceive it, is opened by the immanent play of difference/desire to which even the original system of capture gives rise (Deleuze and Guattari, 2000: 217–22). What this means is that the art of synthetic judgement which Hardt and Negri practice in their pursuit of the common basis of the multitude, has always been superseded by the virtual operations of biopolitical production, and that their account of revolutionary praxis remains embroiled in the questions of historically necessary violence which have always haunted the concept of the proletariat.

So, if we allow that Hardt and Negri's account of the multitude is incompatible with the operational network of biopolitical capitalism, we are left with three possible versions of a post-ontological Marxism. The first of these is configured in Baudrillard's account of the relationship between capitalism and simulation, or, more precisely, in his concept of the hyperreal. His argument is that once media and information technologies have become the exclusive condition under which reality is encoded, the reproductive power of capital is freed from every restriction: nature becomes an infinitely exploitable resource, poverty, unemployment and debt are transformed into new forms of leisure, consumption, and lifestyle, and power appears only in the fugitive events of transformation and war through which the system expands itself. This concept of the hyperreal configures the worst possible outcome of the relationship between capital and technology; for by conceiving every possible event as a refraction of the informatic code, Baudrillard pursues the line of skepticism and disenchantment to its absolute conclusion (Abbinnett, 2003: 102–10). Indeed, he regards with profound scepticism Deleuze and Guattari's attempts to conjure revolutionary associations out of the virtual flows of capital; for he argues that the gesture towards communicability which is made in the idea of schizoid desire, itself reflects the expanding economy of reversible simulacra (Baudrillard, 2004: 23). Thus, the ethos of critique which Baudrillard pursues is a kind Nietzschean excess, which, in its attempts to expose the worst effects of the hyperreal, must always decline the temptations of community, identity and value that would mark its complicity with the system of simulacra. Such a purification of revolutionary critique, I have argued, misses something of the spirit of Marxism; for in its constant provocation of the hyperreal it is unable to discern the moments of silencing, liberation, abuse and erasure which haunt the networks of global capitalism.

This brings us back to Deleuze and Guattari's configuration of Marxist politics. As we have seen the political import of both *Anti-Oedipus* and *A Thousand Plateaus* is structured around a Spinozan account of the real: the social assemblages through which desire is captured determine the conditions under which individuals are made subject to the powers of legality, territoriality and normativity which 'make it possible to experiment with something beyond history' (Deleuze, 1995: 170). The social machines through which desire is channeled into predictable flows, in other words, constitute a historical continuum through which the forces of political reaction are recapitulated: these powers however are always shot through with the untimely forms of desire which Deleuze and Guattari call 'becoming'; for it is only in so far as social machines have subjected the mass of desiring bodies to the strictures of normative orthodoxy, that it is possible for contingent lines of defection to emerge which are not subject to the law of repetition. Like Spinoza therefore Deleuze and Guattari situate the possibility of transforming the world within the very structures which constitute its being; they conceive a revolutionary potential in every extension of the historical continuum of reactionary powers, and present those powers as ontologically threatened by the necessity of their articulation as social models. In *A Thousand Plateaus* this concept of revolution is articulated in three directions: the 'lines of flight' which proceed from the extension of technocracy (particularly the expansion of information networks), the minor forms of becoming, interaction and symbiosis which evolve under technological capitalism, and the ways in which minor assemblages ('war machines') are able to affect the spatial and temporal continuum of legitimate authority (*Ibid.*: 172). What is important here is that each of these expository strategies converges upon the idea of the fold which, for Deleuze and Guattari, configures the possibility of a revolutionary movement within the established structures of being and identity. Put very simply, the fold is the passage which is made by desiring subjects towards the outside of normative space; it is the transgressive movement which is immanent in the structural-institutional organization of their desires. Thus if there is a connection between Marxism and Deleuze and Guattari's account of the techno-prosthetic expansion of capital, it lies in the revolutionary provocation of the fold; for everything that 'is' is conceived as a prefiguration of what might come to be.

So, what exactly is it that might come to be? Negri, in a late interview with Deleuze, asked if he saw 'some way for the mass of singularities that we all are to come forward as a constitutive power', and whether he felt that there was a 'note of tragedy' in the constitution of war machines that are without hope of total transformation (Deleuze, 1995: 171–3). Such questions, of course, anticipate his attempts (with Micheal Hardt) to derive a more 'Marxist' principle of unification from Deleuze and Guattari's thought, and to restage the dialectics of class struggle in terms of the immanent identity of the global multitude. This reversion to identity politics however misses the essential point of *Capitalism and Schizophrenia*, which is to show that capital, understood as a media-techno-prosthetic system, is able constantly to exceed its apparent limits, but that in so doing, it folds reality in a way which configures new revolutionary subjectivities. However, this does not entail an underlying commonality of purpose; for while it is true that Deleuze and Guatarri maintain that lines of flight which depart from the living present give rise to a quasi-community of transgressive desire (the 'body without organs'), this community lives only in the effects it produces in the techno-political organization of capitalism. Such effects take a variety of forms – artistic 'fabulation' of dissident desires, prosthetic modifications of the body, architectural contortions of public and private space, theoretical challenges to legal and philosophical conventions – all of which provoke the dispersal of desire into further lines of flight and moments of defection. There is therefore no conceivable end to this process, and certainly no possibility of machinic desire reaching its fulfilment in the body of Hardt and Negri's multitude; for the concept of an 'end', in Deleuzian terms, always transforms the relationship between major and minor desires and changes the terms of all future transformations.

This brings me finally to Derrida's version of post-ontological Marxism. In Deleuze and Guattari's account of the flows of transgressive desire which are precipitated by technological capital, the 'body without organs' arises as an unpredictable dispersion of desire across the networks of the capitalist machine; and so the answer to the question of 'who comes' in response to the suffering of the destitute is entailed in the very possibility of their being minoritarian desires. The fact that there are minorities which disrupt the spatial and temporal organization of capitalism, in other words, gives a certain *a priori* legitimacy to each expression of difference, and to the contingent effects of becoming, symbiosis and viroid dispersal to which it gives rise (Deleuze and Guattari, 2004a: 465). Although there are similarities between Derrida and Deleuze and Guattari's respective approaches to the question of inheriting Marx, it is this conception of minority which marks the difference between them. In the first chapter of *Spectres of Marx* Derrida begins to flesh out the relationship between Marxism and ontology, or, more precisely, the relationship between the question of being and the spirit of radical critique which springs from Marx's break from Hegelian philosophy. He argues that while this break is problematic (we have seen that something of the ghost of Hegel clings to Marx's dialectics of socialized production), what arises from the 'event Marx' is a demand to register the suffering, exclusion and silencing which haunts the ideological recuperation of identity. The living present, in other words, is always the site of reaction: it is the point at which old ghosts (fascism, religious fundamentalism, authoritarian socialism, Islamophobia) return to but-tress the ethical substance of society, and to reinvigorate the bonds of communal life. Yet this logic of reaction, as Marx himself pointed out in *The Eighteenth Brumaire*, is never one of pure repetition; the spectres of past epochs return in supplemented and intensified forms whose political powers are qualitatively different from their original expres-sions (Marx, 1977c: 301). Now, for Derrida, the political responsibility which arises from this return cannot be discharged in the moments of pure minoritarian departure which are mapped in *A Thousand Plateaus*; rather it is a dual responsibility which tracks between pure difference of the other and the structural-historical organization of justice, law and hospitality (Derrida, 1994: 28).

In Derrida's thought it is this disjuncture of law and legality, of justice and ethical life, which opens the possibility of the political; for it is only in so far as the present is characterized by the return of old powers of representation and identity, that it is possible for those who are not 'of the law' to come forward as a political demand (Derrida and Duformantelle, 2000: 135). The lasting significance of Marx's critique therefore is his recognition of the way in which capitalism transforms the temporality of the political; for he conceives the antagonisms which arise from the commodity form as effects that are constantly transformed by techno-scientific innovations in the mode of production (Derrida, 1994: 13). As capitalism develops towards its fully industrialized expression therefore organic labour is reduced to its most basic, homogeneous functions; and so the labour aristocracies and status groups which had remained part of the socioeconomic organization of production are steadily erased, leaving the way open for new and more extreme forms of exploitation (women's labour, child labour, colonialism) (Marx, 1990: 588–672). For Derrida, the question which arises here is one of difference. According to Marx the proliferation of those 'others' who are drawn into the mecha-nism of exploitation is a process whose outcome is determined by the fact that the reduction of labour costs which it produces, takes place within certain finite limits: in the end, capital has exploited everyone and everything to the point that the contingent differentiation of the exploited passes over into the universal body of the proletariat. Obviously this is something of a caricature; for as any conventional Marxist would point out, *Capital* provides a theory of the social, eco-nomic and political tensions that arise out of the commodity form of production, not a comprehensive description of *all* the conditions necessary for the overthrow of world capitalism. The work of the Marxist critic therefore is to elucidate the revolutionary possibilities that arise from the historical development of the mode of production, possibilities which are always unevenly dispersed across different cultures, different levels of technological development and different structures of economic and political cooperation. Yet for Derrida even this version of historical materialism still evaluates political conflicts in terms of their relationship to the body of universal desire which Marx names 'the proletariat', and so we need to look briefly at the consequences of maintaining this approach to the question of politics.

The final phase of Derrida's writing career is concerned primarily with the relationship between hospitality and politics: *The Other Heading, Politics of Friendship, Of Hospitality* and *Spectres of Marx* all attempt to expound the relationship between the ethical demand of the other and the transformation of the social, economic and political conditions through which this demand is staged. In *Spectres of Marx* the question of hospitality is referred directly to the media-techno-scientific transformation of capitalism; for the kind of virtual technologies whose effects Castells describes in *The Rise of the Network Society* have fundamentally altered the conditions under which we, as human beings, encounter one another in the public sphere. Derrida's analysis of this transformation however goes beyond the logic of disenchantment which pervades Castells's writing, and proceeds to designate the most extreme effects of networked capitalism. He argues that the spread of inter-ethnic wars, the global operations of the criminal economy, the impotence of international law and the constant inflation of Third World debt do not simply recapitulate Marx's fundamental categories, but rather that they are new phenomena whose extremity is peculiar to the informatic organization of capital (Derrida, 1994: 83). The proliferation of inter-ethnic conflicts in the Third World, for example, should be understood as an effect which results from the hyper-exploitative powers of new media networks; for their constant eruption is due, at least in part, to the increasing importance of locality ('land and soil') once the substance of a particular culture has been evacuated into the global flows of knowledge and capital. Such conflicts, in other words, are not just the hangover of a colonial past which have yet to become conscious of their true place in the dialectics of world revolution. In their contemporary form they signify the emergence of dislocated alterities which, having been utterly deprived of their powers of cultural, economic and political self-determination, are left to violent assertions of indigenous rights and ethnic identities. This, for Derrida, marks the emergence of a new ethico-political responsibility; a responsibility which is promised to the fate of those who are summoned, like ghosts without substance or language but still with the power of 'speaking', by the virtual expansion of capital into every facet of life, culture and being (*Ibid.*: 23).

So, who comes in response to this demand which Derrida describes as a 'can be' or a 'may be' which forbids transformation into 'substance, existence, essence, or permanence' (Derrida, 1994: 33)? This question lies at the core of Derrida's reading of Marx, for it opens up the dialectical apparatus of class struggle to the question of those others who come, destitute and without adequate means of representation, to the disparate projects of the living present. Let me summarize. For Marx the 'others' who emerge from the historical evolution of capitalism are generated by the progressive alienation of productive humanity, and as such, the history of racism, patriarchy and cultural imperialism can always be mapped on to the dialectics of class struggle. The historical constitution of the proletariat therefore is conceived as the outcome of processes of gathering which are initiated by the mode of production, and which its powers of ideological and technological self-transformation can, in the end, only intensify. Thus the constitution of revolutionary subjectivity and the structural contradictions of capitalism are dialectically related; for the heterogeneous elements of the proletariat have, at the very least, a common experience of exploitation which founds their identity. According to Derrida however, this articulation of revolutionary desire with the techno-scientific development of capital is unavoidably problematic: for if we allow that this development has utterly transformed the regime of commodification, then the possibility of gathering the disparate forms of suffering which arise from those conditions becomes the present-archaic responsibility of orthodox Marxism, in all its theoretical and political forms. The 'whole totalitarian inheritance of Marx's thought', in other words, is bound up with the demand that every presentation of difference should be given its proper place in the restricted economy of class struggle (*Ibid.*: 104–5). Derrida's reading of Marx, on the other hand, gestures towards a 'democracy to come' which is configured in the transformative power of the other/others: for it is those who come from beyond the cultural, economic and legislative horizon of the West, who always reopen the question of hospitality in relation to the formal structures of cosmopolitan justice (*Ibid.*: 115).

Spectres of Marx therefore attempts to trace the 'spirit' of Marx's writing as a severe ethical stricture which demands that Marxist critique begin with the question of its own ontological and metaphysical assumptions (Derrida, 1994: 10–11). The concept of class, for example, should be conceived as a contingent set of economic relations which may, at any given conjunction of events, operate as the focus of political action, but which lacks the social and historical primacy which Marx attributed to it. Thus the recuperation of the economic foundation of politics is never simply 'given'; rather, if it is possible at all, it comes through the racial, sexual, cultural and gendered alterities that arise from the networked operations of capitalism, and which appear as unforeseen moments of difference (Derrida in Sprinker, 1999: 235–40). This, of course, has given rise to a whole raft of neo-Marxist criticism, for it is claimed that what Derrida's conception of the 'spirit' of Marx has done is to deprive Marxist politics of its entire armoury of concepts and strategies. Thus Terry Eagleton, Aijaz Ahmad, Alex Callinicos and Perry Anderson have all contributed different versions of the claim that postmodernism in general, and deconstruction in particular, is really no more than neo-liberalism in disguise. In the following chapter I will give a brief response to these criticisms and examine the kind of political action to which a deconstructive Marxism might give rise.

17
The Protocols of Class Politics

The purpose of this chapter is to examine a set of realist protocols[1] which have, I will argue, established the terms of legitimate affiliation to Marx's thought and politics. Put schematically these protocols are (1) the ultimate recuperability of class struggle within the global-technological transformations of capitalism, (2) the redetermination of proletarian solidarity through the strategic interventions of Marxist theory, (3) the invocation of history as both the loss and the recovery of the revolutionary dialectics of class and (4) the referral of political agency to the structural antagonisms which determine power relationships within the mode of production. These protocols operate within a particularly influential strand of Marxist thought, that is, the kind of radical modernism which is espoused in the work of Aijaz Ahmad, Perry Anderson, Alex Callinicos, Terry Eagleton and Tom Lewis, to name only a few. Obviously constraints of space mean that I cannot undertake a comprehensive survey of the work of each of these authors. What I can do however is to register the effects of a particular encounter between Marxism and deconstruction, that is, of Michael Sprinker's solicitation of responses to the publication of Derrida's *Spectres of Marx*. The collection of essays, published in 1999 under the title *Ghostly Demarcations*, includes contributions by Ahmad[2] and Lewis[3] which, I will argue, exemplify the Marxist conventions I have sketched above. Callinicos is absent from Sprinker's collection; however his spirit is frequently invoked by Ahmad and Lewis, and I will examine the article on *Spectres of Marx* which he published in *Radical Philosophy* in 1996, as well as other interventions he has made in the Marxism-postmodernism debate. My intention is to clarify the terms through which Ahmad, Callinicos and Lewis have reconstructed the political effectiveness of class and through which they have determined the rules of Marxism's proper engagement with postmodernism in general and deconstruction in particular.

I want to begin by re-specifying the significance of Derrida's distinction between 'restricted' and 'general' economy, for it is this distinction which initiates the possibility of an ethical relationship which exceeds the recuperative dialectics of class solidarity. The encounter between Hegel and Bataille which Derrida examines in his essay 'From Restricted to General Economy: A Hegelianism without Reserve', is one which seeks to open Hegel's philosophy to the original condition of its possibility. This origin appears in the *Phenomenology of Mind* as the life or death struggle through which self-consciousness emerges from its subjugation to nature. In order for this transformation to take place, it is necessary for both combatants to survive; for if one or both are killed, the possibility of 'consciousness' finding the confirmation in the other which marks the transition to 'self-consciousness', is negated. Thus the two distinct forms of being which institute the historical drama of signification, the Master and the Slave, are established through the moment of capitulation in which the latter accepts enslavement in return for his life (Hegel, 1967: 228–40). In the *Phenomenology of Mind* therefore, productive negation (*Aufhebung*) works through what Bataille calls the 'logic of servility': the progress of self-consciousness takes place through a teleological movement which rends the historical forms of ethical life, but only in so far as what is destroyed is conserved in higher, more self-consciously universal, expressions of spirit. Everyday consciousness, in other words, is always ready to be taken up in the logic of signification; its experience is always prepared for the conserving destruction of the *Aufhebung* and the recuperation of absolute knowledge. What Bataille attempts however is to bring the unpredictable excess of mortality into the very centre of the Hegelian logos. Sovereignty, as he conceives it, expends itself 'without reserve', for its events occur as moments of spontaneity which immediately withdraw from the system of recuperable meanings (Derrida, 1990: 265). The relationship between the general economy of mortal desire and the restricted economy of absolute knowledge therefore is one in which the received meanings of the logos are constantly at risk from the excessiveness which defines 'being towards death'. And so the 'sovereign' forms of writing to which Bataille refers have no meaning beyond immediate occurrence; their performativity is simply the transmission of unforeseeable effects which disrupt the movement of spirit towards its self-realization (*Ibid.*: 273–5).

What Derrida takes from Bataille's insistence upon the events of mortal excess which make the Hegelian system waver, is the need to subject every form of restricted economy to an analysis of the conditions under which it determines its own necessity. In Bataille's thought the irrecuperable excess which disrupts the order of the logos is the sovereign relationship of mortal beings to their own death: for the performativity through which the recuperation of meaning is made possible (the pure expenditure of the life or death struggle), is also that which imports a non-dialectical contingency (what Derrida names *différance*) into the heart of the Hegelian system. Two important issues emerge here. First there is the question of ethics: Bataille's notion of mortality as the basis of performative independence is related to what he calls 'major writing'; it is expressed through forms which withdraw from the economy of signification and which disseminate accidental effects across the established relations of objective morality, or *Sittlichkeit*. For Derrida, this account of a sovereignty which is sustained through the unforeseeable events which arise from the closure of the system, bears upon the possibility of an ethics of difference; for it raises questions about how the autonomy of the other is to be received, about what our responsibilities to him or her might be, and about the relationship of ethical obligations to the formal structures of the law.[4] The second question concerns Marx's critique of Hegel, or more specifically, his attempt to expose the internal logic of absolute knowledge to the material dynamics of capitalism. The *Critique of Hegel's 'Philosophy of Right'* begins by questioning the concept of ethical substance: Marx argues that Hegel's account of the unfolding of increasingly universal forms of work, satisfaction and desire proceeds from the assumption of a transcendental reality which is implicit in the empirical existence of family, state and civil society (Marx, 1977c: 27). To assume such a rational trajectory however is to misrecognize the relationship between state and economy. For the acquisitive individualism which Hegel conceived as the moment of abstract difference (civil society) that finds its appropriate sublation in the juridical structures of the state, actually arises from the material-historical contradictions of capital accumulation. Hegel's concept of ethical life, in other words, abstracts democracy from its foundations in 'the real men, the real people' who live under the yoke of private property, and transforms it into a speculative concept which legitimizes the acquisitive regimes of capital (*Ibid.*: 28).

The nature of Marx's break from Hegelian idealism is crucial to understanding the antagonism between deconstruction and the left. Derrida makes it clear that for him, Marx's attempt to determine an absolute break between the ideological ghosts of Hegelian spirit and the dynamics of 'real individuals and the material conditions of their lives', is itself a provocation of the disturbing effects of general economy (Marx, 1977c: 160). The exorcism which Marx attempts in *The German Ideology*, in other words, cannot be separated from the anxiety which accompanies the calling forth of ghosts; for as soon as the material reality of Man is announced, its enunciation is contaminated by ideological forms which disrupt the seamless articulation of his being (Derrida, 1994: 110). The temptation at this point would be to draw some crude distinctions between Ahmad, Callinicos and Lewis's inheritance of the self-certainty of Marx's critique of Hegelianism and Derrida's account of a 'hauntological' Marxism which responds to the excessive mutability of technological capital. It could, for example, be argued that all of the former are committed to a materialist dialectic in which the agency of the oppressed is taken to be immanent in the contradictory organization of private property relations, while Derrida's freedom from the constraints of historical-material necessity means that he is able to encourage every conceivable 'line of flight' from the technocratic regimes of capital. In what follows, however, I will argue that the concept of general economy which is developed in *Spectres of Marx* opens the possibility of radicalizing the protocols of orthodox Marxism.

At the beginning of the chapter I claimed that there are four realist protocols which define the orthodoxy of orthodox Marxism: the recuperability of class struggle, the redetermination of proletarian class solidarity, the invocation of historical teleology and the recourse to fatal contradictions in the mode of production. What is important here is that these protocols have become the basis of a particular way of handling the most disquieting ideas which have arisen from postmodernist thought and, by implication, of neutralizing their ethical and political implications. Thus the critique of deconstruction which has emerged from the more conventionally Marxist essays in *Ghostly Demarcations* (particularly those offered by Aijaz Ahmad and Tom Lewis), begins by treating Derrida's thought as if it is already part of the counterrevolutionary apparatus of new liberalism, and that his remarks on the ethics, hospitality and the technological transformation of capital are, by implication, no more than ideological distractions from the real strategic tasks of Marxist politics. We need therefore to examine the elements of this critique.

The fundamental claim of Lewis's essay, that deconstruction has abandoned all commitment to the concepts of 'social class' and 'mode of production', is directly concerned with Derrida's reconfiguration of Marxism around the demand of hospitality (Lewis in Sprinker, 1999: 139). He argues, quite rightly, that *The German Ideology* was determined to put an end to the endless 'ghosting' of humanity into the egological forms which Stirner opposed to Hegelian idealism. What Marx demanded, in other words, was a recognition that Stirner's categories were themselves expressions of the abstract social relations through which capital frustrates the creativity of real individuals. For Lewis, Derrida's attempt to expose Marx's exorcism of Stirner to the disturbing effects of general economy instigates a dangerous descent into political indeterminism. His particular concern is with Derrida's attempt to transform Marxism into a 'messianic' responsibility which simply registers the catastrophic mutations of global capitalism without intervening. For in so far as Derrida understands the fundamental structures of Marx's politics as having arisen from 'a reaction of panic ridden fear before the ghost in general' (Derrida, 1994: 104–5), he can only conceive of actual socialist movements and regimes in terms of their struggles to conquer the spectres of difference/alterity which haunt them. Lewis therefore maintains that Derrida maps the analytical strategies of Marxism (immanent critique, structural analysis, negative phenomenology) directly on to his critique of the metaphysics of being; and in so doing, inscribes the Stalinist/totalitarian fear of difference at the centre of Marxist theory and politics (Lewis in Sprinker, 1999: 145).

Ahmad's essay 'Reconciling Derrida' pursues a similar argument. Ahmad contends that there is a complicity between deconstruction and the liberal democratic hegemony whose geopolitical contours emerged after the collapse of the Soviet Bloc. Derrida's determination to pursue the 'ethical' questions which arise from the techno-scientific reorganization of capitalism, in other words, betrays a fundamental lack of historical imagination: for had he bothered to consider the historical circumstances which have allowed this reorganization to take place (that is, the failure of working class organizations in liberal democracies to resist the functionalizing, consumerist tendencies of late-capitalism), he would have recognized that such questions can only detract from the strategic imperatives of class struggle (Ahmad in Sprinker, 1999: 97). Ahmad, therefore, contends that *Spectres of Marx* simply follows the depoliticizing effects of media technological capitalism without reference to the immanent power of class solidarity – either as it *should* have been constituted during the political upheavals of 1989 or as it *ought* to be solicited, channelled and constituted in our historical present.

There is, therefore, a homology between Ahmad and Lewis's remarks on the historical effectiveness of class which requires some unpacking. In Lewis's article the emphasis is placed on showing that the collapse of the October Revolution into Stalinism can be accounted for by a Marxist analysis of the position of the Soviet economy in the geopolitical order of early twentieth-century Europe. The mechanisms of 'state capitalist totalitarianism', in other words, were constituted not through an obsession with the ghosts of metaphysical alterity, but by the economic and technological backwardness which was inherited by the newly formed socialist regime. Leaving aside the crudity of Lewis's exposition of the 'method' of deconstruction, the structure of this argument entails a founding moment of prohibition which is similar to the one that Derrida identified in Bataille's reading of Hegel. For what Lewis maintains is that if the empirical conditions which prevented the realization of a genuinely socialist society had been different (i.e. if the historical dialectics of class solidarity had not been disrupted by the general economy of effects produced by the state of the world market), then it is possible that the conditions of socialized production could have been realized. What is at work in both Lewis and Ahmad's objections to Derrida's critique of Marxist 'science' therefore is a logic of immanence which draws the contingency of historical events back into the dialectical strictures of universal suffering and collective agency. For in so far as they both maintain that the constitutive power of class is always reinscribed in the general economy of capital, their critiques of *Spectres of Marx* begin by positing the referents of a trans-historical identity which Derrida's concepts (hauntology, spectralization, the *arrivant*) have called into question (Derrida, 1994: 11).

A slightly different version of this argument is deployed in Callinicos's article 'Crisis and Class Struggle in Europe Today'. His claim is that the struggles between left and right which have been precipitated by the economic crisis that has afflicted Europe since the early 1990s is not subject to a strong historical determinism. It may well be that the liberal democratic order will survive through its ability to integrate disparate elements of left and right-wing populism, or that there will be a steady drift to the right which is precipitated by the electoral success of neo-fascist parties. Yet to conclude matters here would hardly be true to the principles of Marxist critique; and so Callinicos attempts to reconfigure the dialectics of class solidarity through the 'whiff of Weimar' which has returned to the political arena of contemporary Europe. The spectre of fascism as a mass political movement, in other words, is introduced in an attempt to radicalize the present, and to galvanize the working classes of all European democracies into rejuvenating socialist and communist alliances (Callinicos, 1994: 27). This apparently messianic appeal to the crises and opportunities of the day however retains the structure of dialectical iterability that is present in Ahmad and Lewis's responses to *Spectres of Marx*. According to Callinicos the return of the spectre of fascism is determined by the deterritorializing power of global capital; for the lack of stability which has come to characterize the European economy has solicited dangerous old appeals to divine election, racial purity and national culture. None of this would provoke any dissent from Derrida (Derrida, 1994: 81–4). And yet there are important questions concerning the possibility of historical repetition which arise at this point. In Callinicos's account of the crisis of European politics, the conditions of the appearance of the spectre of fascism are given little attention; indeed the images, mythologies and psychological cathexes which he invokes seem to spring unmodified from their place in European history. This unwillingness to address the conditions under which the spectre of fascism reappears (i.e. the transformation of public space through new media and informatic technologies, the rise of 'biopolitical' regimes of production, and the emergence of new forms of aesthetic distraction) is significant because Callinicos deploys the threat of its return as rejuvenating the politics of class struggle. Derrida's 'hauntological' reading of Marx, however, is concerned precisely with the possibility of this logic of reinscription (Derrida, 1994: 10). What the term hauntology designates is an infinitely mutable play of effects (distraction, supplementation, dispersal, erasure, silencing) which defer the operation of the signifiers through which class solidarity is recuperated. Thus while it is true that the return of unquiet ghosts to the present belongs to the original responsibility of Marxism, it is neither ethically nor strategically judicious to re-gather them into the conventional oppositions of class struggle. In the end we must take responsibility for the unforeseeable effects which their manifestations produce in the temporal economy of the present.[5]

This brings me to the second point of encounter between deconstruction and Marxist realism: the supposed complicity of Derrida's critique of metaphysics with the ideological and technological regimes of liberal capitalism. Let me give a brief summary of the arguments presented by Ahmad and Lewis in *Ghostly Demarcations*. Lewis's article claims that deconstruction, conceived as a reading strategy which seeks to disclose the logic of presence through which culture, identity and law are sustained, looks suspiciously like the moment of ideology which Marx referred to in *The Communist Manifesto* as 'true' socialism (Lewis in Sprinker, 1999: 146). Derrida's pursuit of the truth of humanity's participation in the onto-theological resources of philosophy, in other words, repeats the 'one-sidedness' of the French socialists whose ideas of 'Human Nature' and 'Man in general' remained withdrawn from the realities of class struggle (Marx, 1998: 31). And so the spectre of Marx which Derrida evokes is a purely messianic presence which demands the revision of neo-liberal forms of hegemony but without ever engaging with their material structures (class, superstructure, state). For Ahmad, this spectral Marxism is no more than a 'Third Way' politics – 'not fundamentally different from more sophisticated, less cruel forms of liberalism' – whose revolutionary power is dissipated in hopeless revisionism and infinite mourning (Ahmad in Sprinker, 1999: 103).

These arguments misrecognize the questioning of ontology which runs throughout Derrida's thought. In *Spectres of Marx* Derrida argues that if the question of 'living in' the resources of metaphysics cannot be closed (if it is re-opened by every 'empirical' concept of community, belonging, identity, friendship, and hospitality), then the question concerning technology (the relationship of 'the human' to its supplements) is simultaneous with the questions of ethics, justice and politics that arise from techno-scientific capitalism. What this means is that we can treat 'capitalism' neither as a fixed set of socioeconomic conditions, nor as a teleological organization of human desire which will ultimately transcend its negative effects. The term should be understood as registering an open-ended relationship between power, technology and exploitation; a relationship which constantly transforms itself and which precipitates the events of suffering and erasure (of the other/ others) to which Marxism is originally responsible (Derrida, 1994: 13). What is important here is Derrida's continued insistence that responsibility to 'who comes' precedes the particular legal and contractual forms in which it is expressed, and that this responsibility is constantly reconfigured in the dynamics of capitalism and technology. The fact that he is unwilling to revert to the dialectical categories of relatedness which Ahmad and Lewis take to be essential to Marxist politics therefore, does not mean that deconstruction is *ipso facto* complicit with the ideological forms of liberal capitalism, or that it is a type of messianic resignation that awaits deliverance from the evils of the world. Rather the ethical responsibility which is announced in *Spectres of Marx* both exceeds and includes the dialectical temporality of class relations; for it is immediately given over to questions (about cosmopolitanism, international law, the rights of the foreigner) which disrupt the functioning of global-techno-scientific accumulation and configure new and contingent forms of solidarity (*Ibid.*: 37).

So, how can such questions become socially transformative? How, in the absence of the dialectical foci through which Ahmad, Callinicos and Lewis conceive the effectiveness of class relations, can they solicit resistance to established structures of political authority? From what has preceded it is not difficult to anticipate Ahmad, Lewis and Callinicos's objections to Derrida's 'gesture of fidelity' to the idea of international socialism (Derrida, 1994: 90). The gist of their arguments can be briefly summarized. The possibility of overthrowing the global hegemony of liberal capitalism depends upon the compositional power of class struggle. And so if the idea of a Worker's International is to have any political significance, it must function to focus the disparate struggles of the international working class: it must seek to organize the real commonalities of experience that underlie the racial, religious, cultural and gender differences which fracture its revolutionary potential. The New International as Derrida conceives it however has no substance; it has degenerated into a neo-Kantian form of cosmopolitanism which tries to configure revolutionary resistance through indeterminate concepts like 'hospitality', '*différance*' and 'the other'. Indeed both Ahmad and Lewis complain that Derrida's stripping away of the class content of the International degenerates into an academic aestheticism which refuses to sully itself with the realities of class struggle (Ahmad in Sprinker, 1999: 104–5; Lewis in Sprinker, 1999: 149). The spectre of the International which Derrida invokes, in other words, is presented as having no possible articulation with the experience of the masses, and it exists merely as an ideological phantasm whose revolutionary demands remain withdrawn from the material dynamics of historical transformation (Callinicos, 1996: 40; Eagleton in Sprinker, 1999: 85).[6]

What arises here, of course, is the very question which Derrida puts at the centre of his account of cosmopolitan responsibility and the New International: the question of hospitality. If we stick to the line of argument pursued above, then Derrida's precautionary remarks on class solidarity can be no more than ideological impediments to the gathering of cultural, religious, ethnic and gender differences into the strategic organization of the international working class. If, however, we are prepared to take his argument seriously, then we must consider the question of how the general economy of effects through which global capital functions (deterritorialization, informatic exchange, commodification of culture) can be gathered into the universal discourse of class struggle. The responses which are given by Ahmad, Callinicos and Lewis are hardly adequate, for they simply revert to the realist protocols which Derrida's account of media-techno-scientific capitalism seeks to question. In conclusion therefore I propose to move the discussion towards a set of issues, the technological condensation of space and time, the transformation of public space, and the aesthetic porosity of the 'postmodern' individuals, which provoke the question of politics beyond the established narratives of class and international class solidarity.

Conclusion

So where does this leave us? Isn't it true that deconstruction of the last traces of class solidarity has confirmed that Derrida's Marxism is no more than a messianic gesture towards an unnameable future? This suspicion is the guiding thread of Jameson's essay on *Spectres Marx*, for it inscribes a certain reserve, a certain prohibition, with regard to Derrida's account of the general economy of capital. Let me summarize the argument. Postmodernism is conceived as the 'cultural dominant' which emerges from globalization of the market, and deconstruction, despite its insights into the spectralizing powers of technological capitalism, remains complicit with the postmodernist desire to live in the pure immediacy of the present (Jameson in Sprinker, 1999: 59). Derrida's attempt to free Marxism from the deterministic elements of materialism ends up abandoning any sense of historical explanation; the play of spectres which he sets against the logic of revolutionary condensation becomes completely dissociated from the dialectics of subject and object, base and superstructure which determine the temporality of the mode of production. The ethical demand through which Derrida configures the 'spirit' of Marxism is therefore incapable of becoming properly political; for if there is no historical critique of the subject-object relations through which capital functions as a totality, then the other will always be without the chance of reception which is configured in the allegorical forms of class solidarity. Thus the 'weak messianic power' which is solicited by Derrida's New International is conceived by Jameson as the ghost of Benjamin's hope for redemption in the darkest times of history. For by collapsing the violence of historical repetition into the temporality of the spectre, Derrida's Marxism remains complicit with the unbounded present of postmodern culture (*Ibid.*: 62).

This, however, is to misconceive the political significance of hospitality. Jameson's critique of deconstruction maintains that the categories of trace, supplementarity and *différance* which Derrida deploys in his reading strategies, configure the kind of schizophrenic subjectivity which is at play in postmodern culture. Yet Derrida has always maintained that the law of hospitality to which deconstruction seeks to respond 'appears as a paradoxical law, pervertible or perverting' (Derrida and Duformantelle, 2000: 26). What this means is that the absolute obligation to receive the destitute and the powerless which is the foundation of ethical responsibility, is always already embroiled in the legal-contractual designations of friendship, community and identity which regulate the transactions of the lifeworld. The possibility of justice depends upon this structure of difference: for it is only in so far as the law of 'absolute hospitality' remains heterogeneous with and yet indissociably proximate to the categories of 'hospitality by right', that we are able to assume political responsibility to the future, to the idea of democracy to come. In the disjointed time of global capitalism this classical question – the question of hospitality to the stranger who comes, to the 'barbarian' who has no recognizable name and who does not speak our language – returns with great urgency; for the corporate powers which have come to dominate the global economy have produced a world of nameless, sub-legal migrants, nomads and refugees (*Ibid.*: 45).

The law of hospitality to which Derrida makes Marxism responsible therefore is not an abandonment of the political realities of the present, nor is it the collapse of class politics into a neo-Kantian International which does no more than disseminate the mourning work of deconstructionist intellectuals. Rather Derrida's Marxism demands fidelity to the *question* of class: it attempts to sustain the demand of absolute hospitality in relation to the cultural, ethnic and religious forms through which economic power is differentiated. Thus if we return to Callinicos's account of the relationship between race and class in contemporary Europe, we can raise some issues which complicate the logics of gathering/ repetition through which he expounds the condensation of politics into the struggle between left and right (Callinicos, 1994: 27–8). In particular we would need to pay close attention to the logics of autochthony through which liberal democracies have staged the integration of race, class and gender; we would need to consider the excessive play of desire through which the global economy has overloaded this staging; and we would need to remain open to the chance of hospitality which is offered by existent forms of class affiliation – the chance that the 'socialist culture' of the European democracies can be transformed by the unaccountable event/desire of the other (Derrida and Duformantelle, 2000: 123–4).

The 'gesture of affiliation' which is configured in Derrida's idea of the New International therefore is a gesture which commands without material necessity; it is that which gathers heterogeneous acts of dissent into fragile associations whose responsibility to the other exceeds every contractual bond of fraternity. This, of course, is *not* Marx's International; for Derrida's 'inoperative community' of the oppressed is revealed only in acts of ethical responsibility which exceed the subject positions inscribed in Marx's account of class. The point I have tried to make however is that Ahmad, Callinicos and Lewis's condemnations of *Spectres of Marx* on the grounds that it fails to begin with the materiality of class relations, miss the critical significance of Derrida's Marxism. What he is attempting to do is to *accompany* Marx; to open up historical materialism to a highly differentiated notion of class which begins with the thought of its own contingency. This is not Marxism as it is conventionally understood – yet why should this immediately be conceived as a weakness? Might it not be the case that the ethical performativity which Derrida demands in relation to questions about technological prosthesis, the spectralization of the real and the rights of the stranger are precisely the questions which open up the future of Marxist politics? Thus while it is certainly true that the idea of a revolutionary community 'without status, without title, and without name' raises an unfamiliar political problematic, this should not be dismissed purely on the grounds of its complication of Marx's revolutionary dialectics (Derrida, 1994: 85). In the end it is the techno-scientific development of capital which has transformed the temporality of class relationships; and so what Derrida has attempted is to open up the political and intellectual affiliations which have constituted 'orthodox Marxism' to the general economy of effects (prosthesis, spectralization, virtuality) through which capital transforms the 'material' conditions of its reproduction.

All of this, of course, has a disturbing fragility about it; a fragility which Derrida never sought to conceal but rather to disseminate through the weakness of the weak and the chance ethical responsibility. Such responsibility, as we have seen, forbids determination as an operative community or apparatus; and so the charge that it is no more than an ideological fantasy or a contentless demand which haunts the collective conscience of the liberal left belongs to its very presence in the world. Thus the return of the other in Derrida's reading of Marx has provoked a dual response. On the one hand the extremities of dispersal and repetition which are configured in Deleuze and Baudrillard's thought spring from the conviction that the spirit of Marx has long since departed into virtual networks which have swallowed every last trace of transcendence. The difference between them is that Deleuze seeks redemption through the pure nomadic 'becoming' of minorities, while Baudrillard's position seems to entail that we can do little more than register the descent of the real into ever more extreme phenomena. Conventional Marxism, on the other hand, seeks to determine the underlying reality of the processes of virtualization through which capitalism has continued to expand, and so the spirit of Marx is always drawn back to the realist protocols I enumerated above. The question of ethical responsibility as Derrida conceives it however remains absolutely proximate to the logics of composition, dispersal and redemption through which Marx's critique is constantly reconfigured; and so its very weakness – the weakness of the other, the perpetual *arrivant* – is what may give futurity to Marxism and to the idea of radical democracy (Derrida, 1994: 28).

Notes

Introduction

1. Anderson, P. (1998) *The Origins of Postmodernism*, London: Verso.
2. Jay, M. (1984) *Marxism and Totality: The Adventures of a Concept from Lukacs to Habermas*. Berkeley, CA: University of California Press.
3. A rather more subtle 'aporetic' version of the necessity articulated in Hegel's account of ethical life is given in Gillian Rose's *Hegel Contra Sociology*.

1 Materialism and Ideology

1. For a more detailed discussion of the relationship between the abstract forms of moral consciousness in the *Phenomenology of Mind* and the idea of Morality expounded in the *Philosophy of Right*, see chapter 1 of my *Truth and Social Science: From Hegel to Deconstruction*.

2 The Reification of Culture

1. Benjamin put his essay 'The Work of Art in the Age of Mechanical Reproduction' through a number of different drafts, the earliest of which dates from 1935. The version from which I have quoted was written in 1939 and appears in the collection of Benjamin's essays edited by Hanah Arendt and published under the title *Illuminations*.
2. The manuscript of *Dialectik der Aufklärung* was completed in 1944, although it wasn't published until 1947 by the Dutch publishing house Querido.
3. *Capital* Volume One, chapter 32, 'The Historical Tendency of Capital Accumulation'.
4. For Marx the equilibrium between the purchasing power of wages and the value of commodities produced in any given cycle of production cannot be assumed to be an automatic function of the market. In fact the proportionality of production and consumption which makes the turnover of capital possible is extremely difficult to achieve. What Marx's reproduction schemas attempt to show therefore is that equilibrated growth is the exception rather than the rule under capitalism, and that the growth of the economy itself is implicated in the onset of stagnation. The overproduction of consumer goods by capitalist enterprise ('Department II') gives rise to increasing unemployment among the workforce ('Department I') which in turn leads to the chronic under-consumption which deepens the general crisis in the turnover of capital (Marx, 1992: 565–81).
5. Gillian Rose, in her *Melancholy Science*, makes it clear that it is not just the infantilizing productions of the culture industry which perpetuate domination of monopoly capital, it is also the 'subjectivist philosophies' whose categories legitimize received ideas of free will, legal rights and individual sovereignty (Rose, 1978: 52).

3 The Rise of Ludic Aestheticism

1. Jameson's essay 'Transformations of the Image in Postmodernity' attempts to expound the relationship between populist 'nostalgia films' and the dislocation of the living present from its place in the economic and political history of capitalism. He argues, in a way that is reminiscent of Nietzsche's essay 'On the Utility and Liability of History for Life', that there is a complicity between contemporary culture and the fetishization of the beautiful characteristic of bourgeois art; a complicity which transforms remembrance from a transformative act into a fascination with the spectacle of the recreated past (Jameson, 1998: 131).

4 Capitalism and the Hyperreal

1. In Lyotard's account of the avant garde however the sublime appears as the 'unpresentable event' (of obscenity, distraction, beauty, disorientation) to which art and the artist are ultimately responsible; it is that which outleaps even the operative logic of simulation (Lyotard, 199b1: 210).
2. The term 'lifeworld' is slightly misleading here as it has become associated with Jurgen Habermas's account of communicative rationality. Habermas conceives the lifeworld as the realm of public interaction in which particular interests (religious beliefs, ethnic cultural practices, sexual preference, etc.) are mediated with the universal demands of consensus and solidarity which are essential to the social cohesion of the state. This process of mediation occurs through what he conceives as the universal standards of communicative rationality which have accumulated in the lifeworld – standards which place the state and its citizens under an obligation constantly to refine their democratic practice (recognition of the rights of the other, recognition of the rights of nature, re-negotiation of the 'system necessities' of industrial society, etc.) (Habermas, 1995: 50). For Baudrillard, however, the viral spread of simulation has destroyed every trace of the lifeworld; the temporality of the sign/image and its relationship to the real is such that there is never time for the political question to crystallize into the categories of communicative reason: there is only the immediacy of the sign/image and its labile solicitations.
3. Baudrillard's essay 'The Procession of Simulacra' extends the three stage scheme of simulation which he presented in *Symbolic Exchange* to include a fourth stage in which the sign/image 'has no relation to reality what so ever'. This is done to emphasize the point that with the emergence of new telematic media, the sign/image has become 'its own pure simulacrum', and that nothing antagonistic or transcendent can intervene in the universal exchangeability through which sex, capital, politics and culture are hyperrealized (1999: 6).

5 Ideology and Difference

1. For Derrida, Bataille's account of sovereignty bears directly on the possibility of ethics; for it raises questions about the communicability of transgressive acts, about the possibility of receiving such acts (which are always acts of 'the other'), about what our responsibilities to him or her might be, and about

the relationship of such responsibilities to the formal structures of the law. These questions are treated more fully in the fourth essay of *Writing and Difference*: 'Violence and Metaphysics: An Essay on the Thought of Emmanuel Levinas'.

2. See Ludwig Feuerbach, *The Essence of Christianity* (1841).

3. See 'Marxism Without Marxism', in Sprinker (1999): 83–7.

4. See 'Messianic Ruminations: Derrida, Stirner and Marx', in *Radical Philosophy* 75 (Jan/Feb): 37–41.

5. See 'Reconciling Derrida: "Spectres of Marx" and Deconstructive Politics', in Sprinker (1999): 88–109.

6. Judith Butler, for example, advocates a thoroughgoing critique of the 'correctionist' character of sexual identity. In her article 'Subjects of Sex/Gender/Desire' she argues that the category of sex has always functioned as the point of demarcation between the genders, and that consequently its significance as the essential limit which frames the performativity of gender roles has always been the subject of multiple discourses which seek to establish its pre-social origin (Butler, 1998: 279). The point of this critique of the sex-gender distinction is to expose the fact that the former functions to legitimize certain *a priori* limitations on the concept of sexual difference; both men and women, in other words, have been made subject to the stereotypical ideas of agency, embodiment and community which belong to their respective natural/sex identities. Thus it is only when it is recognized that sex is always already embedded in the social construction of gender, that it is possible to open sexual politics up to a general economy of (unforeseen) effects which put the subject positions of 'masculinity' and 'femininity' in jeopardy.

7. This point is made convincingly in Michael Ryan's *Marxism and Deconstruction: A Critical Articulation*, which argues for a certain deconstructive spirit in Marx's writing that remains open to the general economy of difference provoked by the transformations of capitalism. However, it is clear that there is a certain reserve in Ryan's text; for there are points in his analysis, particularly his comparison between the 'egalitarian' Marx and the 'authoritarian' Lenin, where he appears to claim that *différance* functions to solicit a more comprehensive gathering alterities into the dialectics of class struggle (Ryan, 1986: 164). This is not the argument which Derrida presents in *Spectres of Marx*; rather his position is that class is a structure which belongs to the ontological apparatus which Marx constructed around the disjunctive temporality of capital, and that as such, its 'finality' remains contingent upon the events of difference/alterity which come to disturb the dialectics of historical necessity.

6   Machines and Socialized Production

1. This tendency is presented in volume three of *Capital* as giving rise to certain 'Counteracting Factors' ('more intense exploitation of labour', 'reduction of wages below their value', 'cheapening of the elements of constant capital', 'the relative surplus population', 'foreign trade' and 'the increase in share capital') which ameliorate the effects of overburdening organic labour with a greater and greater volume of fixed capital (Marx, 1991: 339–48). The question which arises from this attempt to dialecticize 'The Law of the Tendential Fall

in the Rate of Profit' therefore, is whether capitalism is capable of techno-
scientific innovations which fundamentally change the nature of the
commodity form, and transform it into an economy of unforeseeable effects
which postpone the final hour of crisis *ad infinitum*.

2. Louis Althusser's account of the 'epistemological break' between the earlier
   and later Marx, of course, maintains that the structuralist science of the commodity form which is expounded in *Capital*, signals a complete departure
   from the Hegelianism of the *Economic and Philosophical Manuscripts* (Althusser,
   1986a: 49–86). This is a highly questionable thesis; for as Derrida has pointed
   out, the attempt to determine 'structure' as a category which is thoroughly
   independent of the ideological forms which it determines, immediately begs
   the question of how the economic base determines its 'presence' in the symbolic order of capital (Derrida in Kaplan and Sprinker, 1993: 208). This question is the one from which *Spectres of Marx* proceeds; for Derrida's reading of
   The German Ideology makes it clear that, for him, the 'structural' powers of capital are always diffused through the unforeseeable economy of effects which
   they produce.

7 The Origins of Technocracy: Heidegger and Marcuse

1. Ulrich Beck's account of risk maintains that the historical complicity between
   capitalism and scientific reason is what eventually precipitates the emergence
   of a 'critical science' which questions the instrumental organization of the
   lifeworld (Beck, 1996: 37–8). His contention is that 'science', considered as an
   instrument of rational inquiry, becomes increasingly self-reflexive, while at
   the same time being forced by the dynamics of the market economy to hold
   on to its public ideology of infallibility. What is important here, according to
   Beck, is that the occurrence of technologically produced 'side effects' whose
   consequences are potentially illimitable (the 'civilization risks' posed by
   nuclear power, genetic engineering, nanotechnologies) is what ultimately
   precipitates a 'scientized' politics of risk. As genetically mutable, biologically
   contaminable beings, in other words, we are all susceptible to the effects of
   radiation and chemical poisoning; and so it is this shared vulnerability which,
   for Beck, becomes the focus of resistance to the power of corporate capital to
   develop and deploy potentially catastrophic forms of technology. Critical science therefore emerges as the counterpart of a 'sub politics' which is formed
   around specific issues of ecological damage, and which, for Beck, configures
   new types of political solidarity which cannot be mapped on to conventional
   models of class struggle.

8 Civilized Capitalist Machines: Deleuze and Negri

1. We should note here that Lyotard's reading of Marx in *Libidinal Economy*
   presents a thoroughgoing critique of this kind of analysis. His argument is
   that the 'polymorphously perverse' body of capitalism is such as to defy comprehensive theorization of the kind which Marx attempted in *Capital*. Indeed
   he claims that Marx, the prosecutor of the case against capitalism and the
   advocate of the suffering body of the proletariat, is simultaneously horrified

and fascinated by the power of capital to transform its economy of exchange, commodification and desire. Conceived as a 'libidinal' rather than a 'dialectical' economy, in other words, capitalism is without immanence; and so Marx's attempt to set out the conditions under which the mode of production would bring forth the organic body of the proletariat, ends up as an infinite multiplication of the theoretical discourse of capital (Lyotard, 1993: 95–103). What is important here is that for Lyotard the libidinal economy of 'theory' and 'capitalism' are related to each other through contingent events of solicitation and conflict, and that, in the absence of a universal theory of the commodity form, we must constantly seek to disclose the complicities that arise between economic powers of appropriation/investment and the discursive constructions which attempt to outplay those powers. This approach to the relationship between theory and capital, as Bennington has pointed out, calls the logic of machinic desire into question; for in so far as *Anti-Oedipus* and *A Thousand Plateaus* give priority to the unexpected flows that arise from civilized capitalist machines, Deleuze and Guattari's attempt to re-establish the ethico-political project of Marxism proceeds on the basis of a pure 'nomadic' contingency which is present in every territorial regime (Bennington, 1988: 34). Thus for Lyotard (and Derrida) such purity is always contaminated by the libidinal regime of capital; and so any hope of remaining faithful to the spirit of Marx depends upon avoiding a clandestine return to the energetical powers of proletarian suffering and resentment, no matter how 'singular' these powers might be.

2. See, for example, Fotopoulos, and Gezerlis (2000) 'Hardt and Negri's *Empire*: A New Communist Manifesto or a Reformist Welcome to Neoliberal Globalization?', http://www.democracynature.org/dn/vol8/alex_takis_negri.htm.

9   The Ethics of Technological Effects: Derrida and Stiegler

1. The *Essay on the Origin of Languages* formed the basis of the more widely read *Discourse on the Origin of Inequality*, and Derrida's exposition of Rousseau's philosophical anthropology alternates between the two texts.

10   Colonialism and Imperialism

1. See *Capital* Volume One. Chapter 3, Part 1.
2. This decrease in value is, of course, usually expressed in the form of *more commodities* whose individual price has been driven down by competition and the technological development of the means of labour.
3. In 'The Contest of the Faculties' Kant argues that the 'guiding thread' of cosmopolitan history is to be found in the implicit moral significance of events, such as the French Revolution, whose immediate form is mired in violence and destructiveness. It is in the general improvement in moral culture which the spectacle of the revolution brought to the onlooking nations of Europe, in other words, that the universal progress of humanity can be discerned (Kant, 1991: 182–90).

11 World Markets and Global Transformations

1. What Held *et al.* refer to as the 'transformationalist thesis' in *Global Transformations* is articulated in a plurality of different discourses. See: Ulrich Beck (1996), *Risk Society: Towards a New Modernity*; Anthony Giddens (1997), *The Consequences of Modernity*; Manuel Castells (2000), *The Rise of the Network Society*; David Harvey (1999), *The Condition of Postmodernity: An Enquiry into the Conditions of Cultural Change*; and David Held (1995), *Democracy and the Global Order: From the Modern State to Cosmopolitan Governance*.

13 Transeconomic Capitalism

1. In chapter 25 of *Capital* Volume Three, Marx sought to expound the relationship between credit and the emergence of what he called 'fictitious capital'. He argued that once the commodity form of production is properly established, 'money now functions only as a means of payment, i.e. commodities are not sold for money, but for a written promise to pay at a certain date' (Marx, 1991: 525). The fact that commodity production expands more quickly if monetary redemption is given the 'fictitious' form of credit, in other words, prompts the emergence of a plurality of different branches of lending at interest which are put at the disposal of capitalist enterprise (*Ibid.*: 529). Marx, we have seen, argues that this mutual expansion of commodity production and finance capital is sustainable only for as long as it is possible for capitalist entrepreneurs to return a viable profit from the sale of their commodities. For once the average rate of return sinks below a certain point, economic rationality dictates that investment in the banking system or stocks and shares is a better option than the production of commodities. Now, for Marx, this migration of capital into the form of loans, securities, bonds and stocks marks a crucial stage in the decline of capitalism; for the shift of investment away from the production of real social goods and use values indicates a terminal crisis of the mode of production. For Baudrillard however it is this 'virtualization' of capital which, in the end, produces the multinational corporations who are able to control the expansion of new markets and the exploitation of new forms of scientific and technological innovation (Baudrillard, 1995b: 27–8).

2. The germ of this idea of the transeconomic is first presented by Baudrillard's in *The Consumer Society*. In the section entitled 'Towards a Theory of Consumption' he argues that the very idea of capital involves the eradication of the needs, and their replacement with pleasures that derive from the expansion of the commodity form. Such pleasure is utterly disconnected from any sense of natural determination; it is produced and re-produced through a system of abstract relations which, as Marx pointed out, has made the abstract and impersonal category of exchange value into the determining factor of social relationships. Thus Baudrillard's account of consumer credit presents a situation in which virtual capital is released into a system of objects (commodities) whose symbolic economy encourages a certain level of affordable/enjoyable wastage (Baudrillard, 1996: 42–4). At the transeconomic level the relationship between virtual capital and the wastage of resources is utterly exorbitant; for once the information technology paradigm becomes the

medium of commodification, the world itself (the diversity of cultures, eth-
nicities, wildlife, etc.) becomes subject to the infinite simulation of desire.
3. This, of course, refers Baudrillard's infamous pronouncement: *La Guerre du
Golfe n'a pas eu lieu* (which has been translated as 'The Gulf war didn't
happen'). It should be noted however that most of the moral outrage which
this statement has provoked is based upon a misunderstanding of what
Baudrillard means by the failure of the Gulf war to determine itself as a real
event. Reflecting on the likely effect of his comment on the first Gulf war,
Baudrillard remarked: 'It was a war without results, but not without aftermath.
Once past the dilemma of the reality/unreality of the war, we are back in the
pure and simple reality of political ignominy. In the most odious *Realpolitik*'
(Baudrillard, 1995b: 63). Thus Baudrillard is not claiming that the violence,
terror and destruction of the American invasion literally 'didn't happen';
rather his argument is that to call the largely unopposed march of the United
States Army into Iraq a 'war' is morally, ethically and politically inappropriate.
For the fact that the technological superiority enjoyed by the United States
meant that Saddam's regime could have been swept away with little more
effort than had been expended in the liberation of Kuwait, should make us
extremely suspicious of the moral rhetoric through which George Bush
senior's administration justified military intervention. In the end Saddam was
left to continue his persecutions for another 12 years; for at least he could be
trusted to bring a certain stability to Iraq and to provide the unacceptable face
of Islamic theocracy. As a supposedly cosmopolitical intervention therefore
the Gulf War was indeed a non-event; for it left the *Realpolitik* of world affairs,
that is, the corrupt order of simulations through which capital asserts its
orbital power, entirely undisturbed (*Ibid.*: 64).

14   The Politics of Hospitality

1. While Derrida's argument is, I think, successful in disclosing the theological
subtext of Levinas' phenomenology, it should be noted that *Totality and
Infinity* provides an account of the relationship between the ontological
organization of justice (totality) and the absolute demand of the other (infinity) which is close to Derrida's own position. Levinas argues that while the
demand of the face-to-face must be considered as illimitable and particularized, this does not mean that it simply transcends the moral, legal, economic
and political obligations which constitute the being of the social. Rather the
ethical commandment refers each of us to the secular bonds of our communal
existence, and so to the more limited, yet necessary, organization of justice in
the law. Thus while we may never realize the transcendent demand inscribed
in the face of the other, we must constantly return to it to redeem the violence
of the state and its institutions (Levinas, 1994: 213). This comes very close to
Derrida's claim that law of hospitality 'appears as a paradoxical law, pervertible and perverting' (Derrida, 2000: 26).
2. See Aijaz Ahmad, 'Reconciling Derrida: "Spectres of Marx" and Deconstructive
Politics', Terry Eagleton, 'Marxism without Marxism', and Tom Lewis, 'The
Politics of "Hauntology" in Derrida's *Spectres of Marx*', all in *Ghostly
Demarcations: A Symposium on Derrida's Spectres of Marx*.

3. My claim is not that Deleuze and Guattari's position simply relapses into a celebration of difference and minority for its own sake, for their account of the nomadic constitution of desire in *A Thousand Plateaus* is clearly an attempt to bring the force of radical alterity to bear upon the established discourse of right and legality. My argument is rather that the ideas of 'minority' and 'becoming other' which they deploy tend to encourage a certain ethico-aesthetics in which 'capital' is understood as the progenitor of lines of flight which, because of their radical difference, exacerbate the crises (of identity, belonging, subjectivity, etc.) produced by globalized commodity production. More chaos, in other words, equals more transgression, and more transgression equals more autonomy (see, for example, Nick Land's essay 'Making It with Death: Remarks on Thanatos and Desiring Production').

4. One of the fundamental aims of *Spectres of Marx* is to uncouple Walter Benjamin's messianic reading of Marx from the theological significance it is given in his later writings (Derrida, 1994: xviii–xix). In both the 'Theses on the philosophy of history' and the 'Work of art in the age of Mechanical Reproduction' Benjamin presents capitalism as a ceaselessly transformative economy whose technological-ideational powers are engaged upon the representation of archaic ideals of truth, beauty and democracy. This mimetic configuration of the 'living present' is what opens the possibility of revolutionary transformation; for the reversion of the state to classical representations of political authority always reopens the irreducible 'now' of the present. Each historical epoch, in other words, constitutes its own particular 'state of emergency'; it is the point at which the unifying force of archaic ideals is risked *once again*, and where the '*weak* messianic power' of each succeeding generation is dealt its fleeting chance of success (Benjamin, 1992: 246). In Benjamin's thought, however, this chance of revolutionary transformation is presented through a Judaic concept of time in which the barbarous repetition of the past becomes a plaintive solicitation of God. Each moment becomes a 'straitgate' through which the messiah might enter historical time and make good what has been smashed in the storm of progress (*Ibid.*: 255). Once again, therefore, the suffering of past and future generations, which is gathered in the living present, assumes a religious significance in which ethical responsibility gives way to the promise of redemption.

5. One of the fundamental aims of *Spectres of Marx* is to uncouple Walter Benjamin's messianic reading of Marx from the theological significance it is given in his later writings (Derrida, 1994: xviii–xix). In both the 'Theses on the philosophy of history' and the 'Work of art in the age of Mechanical Reproduction' Benjamin presents capitalism as a ceaselessly transformative economy whose technological-ideational powers are engaged upon the representation of archaic ideals of truth, beauty and democracy. This mimetic configuration of the 'living present' is what opens the possibility of revolutionary transformation; for the reversion of the state to classical representations of political authority always reopens the irreducible 'now' of the present. Each historical epoch, in other words, constitutes its own particular 'state of emergency'; it is the point at which the unifying force of archaic ideals is risked *once again*, and where the '*weak* messianic power' of each succeeding generation is dealt its fleeting chance of success (Benjamin, 1992: 246). In Benjamin's thought however this chance of revolutionary transformation is

presented through a Judaic concept of time in which the barbarous repetition of the past becomes a plaintive solicitation of God. Each moment becomes a 'straitgate' through which the messiah might enter historical time and make good what has been smashed in the storm of progress (*ibid.*: 255). Once again therefore the suffering of past and future generations which is gathered in the living present, assumes a religious significance in which ethical responsibility gives way to the promise of redemption.

16   A Post-Ontological Marxism?

1. The concept of profane illumination derives from Walter Benjamin's essay on surrealism, and I have used it here to indicate the sense in which Castells traces the new 'technological body' of society and its immediate consequences for the organic relations which had constituted the social bond. The profanity of such an illumination lies in the fact that it is intrinsic to the symbolic economy of the image, and that it marks the point at which 'meta-physical materialism' (in both its Marxist and non-Marxist forms) must give way to a political aesthetics of technological effects (Benjamin, 1997a: 239). For Castells however the transformative power of the aesthetic imagination is now in the balance, for its medium of expression (the internet, cable TV, etc.) is increasingly subject to control by multinational corporations.
2. See David Harvey's *The Condition of Postmodernity: An Inquiry into the Conditions of Cultural Change*, chapter 23.
3. See Max Weber, *The Protestant Ethic and the Spirit of Capitalism*, 182.
4. Scott Lash pursues a rather different line in his *Critique of Information*. His argument follows the same direction as Castells's in so far as he maintains that the information technology paradigm has no 'outside', and that the organic integration of the social bond has been utterly surpassed by the operational powers of new communications networks (Lash, 2002: 210). Lash, however, claims that the operationality of the global information order is not the per-fection of Weber's account of rational disenchantment; rather the velocity with which informatic capital transforms the conditions of its reproduction and recolonizes the new kinds of praxis to which these transformations give rise, opens the possibility of a politics of unforeseen consequences which haunts the informatic paradigm from the beginning. This, of course, is very close to Deleuze and Guattari's conception of the 'minor flows' which arise from the organic differentiations which constitute the symbolic order of the social, although for Lash, the operational speed of the informatic order is now such as to have erased even the traces of the symbolic which are retained in *Anti-Oedipus* and *A Thousand Plateaus*. Ultimately the 'critique of information is in the information itself', for according to Lash, the pure operationality of the informatic order 'excretes' those who it cannot usefully deploy (the pimp, the prostitute, the transsexual, etc.), and constitutes these as the 'accursed share' (*part maudite*) to which the interventions of a pure conceptual art, and the politics of the shocking and the obscene, are responsible (*Ibid.*: 112). This gesture, I would suggest, sits uneasily with the concept of 'aesthetic reflexiv-ity' which Lash presents in his theory of the social self; for it would seem as if the interpretative faculties he has defended in his critique of Derrida are

hardly of a kind which could accommodate the extremity of this Deleuzian provocation (Abbinnett, 2003: 32–3).
5. See particularly the section on 'Prophylaxis and Virulence' in *The Transparency of Evil*.

17 The Protocols of Class Politics

1. What I mean by 'realism' is the kind of analysis which seeks to relate general tendencies and epiphenomenal effects to the ontological structures which underlie them. Thus Keat and Urry's account of Marx's method attempts to show that the economic base functions as a relatively stable set of productive relationships which is the determinant of capitalism's tendency to produce sexist, racist and patriarchal forms of domination (Keat and Urry, 1977: 193). My point is that simply to assume the causal powers of the economic base (an assumption which is shared by Ahmad, Eagleton, Callinicos and Lewis) is to neglect the radical transformations of life, community, value and power which have resulted from the informatic transformation of capitalism.
2. 'Reconciling Derrida: "Spectres of Marx" and deconstructive politics', in *Ghostly Demarcations*, 134–67.
3. 'The politics of "hauntology" in Derrida's *Spectres of Marx*', in *Ghostly Demarcations*, 134–67.
4. These questions are dealt with explicitly in the fourth essay of *Writing and Difference*, 'Violence and Metaphysics: An Essay on the Thought of Immanuel Levinas'.
5. Marx's *Eighteenth Brumaire of Louis Bonaparte* makes it clear that the return of spectres from former epochs is always a process which precipitates unforeseeable consequences. In his attack on the revolution of 1848 he maintained that Louis Bonaparte's attempt to portray himself as the heir to the revolutionary values of 1789 had descended into a farcical walking of ghosts through the revolutionary exigencies of nineteenth-century France (Marx, 1977c: 301). What Derrida takes from this account of the temporality of ghosts is the impossibility of ending the transformative power of their return; for insofar as the question of being is always precipitated by the scientific, media and technological organization of the social (this is the origin of Marx's revolutionary promise), the spectres which arise from the past will always seem to offer the chance of resolving the dilemmas of modernity (Derrida, 1994: 107). Ultimately, therefore, our responses to the return of fascist politics should be informed by an understanding of how technological capitalism has transformed dynamics of geopolitical space, how the emergence of new 'legitimate' forms of right-wing populism (the National Front in France, the National Alliance in Italy, etc.) has impacted upon the ethical constitution of liberal democracy, and how we ought to inherit the *cosmopolitical* demand which is inscribed in Marx's determination to exorcise the ideological power of spectres (*Ibid.*: 109). Such responses precipitate the question of class beyond conventional forms of iterability, and constantly reopen the question of hospitality to who comes from beyond the established constitution of the good (*Sittlichkeit*).
6. This point is developed more fully by Eagleton in *The Illusions of Postmodernism*. He argues that postmodernist theory occupies a fundamentally

ambiguous position with regard to the global technological transformation of capitalism: for while it has produced an acute critique of the transcendental categories through which the state has attempted to recapture the desire and intellect of the masses, postmodernist thought has left the relationship between the global market and the forms of dehistoricized individualism which are deployed in its critiques of totality (events, alterities, genres, differences, performativities, etc.) entirely below the level of analysis. This lack of historical awareness, according to Eagleton, means that postmodernist theory and culture are no more than symptoms of a particular phase in the evolution of capitalism; ideological forms which have the effect of imprisoning the masses in the endless cycle of distracted consumption and lifestyle choices (Eagleton, 1996: 131–5). Perry Anderson makes a similar point in *The Origins of Postmodernity*. His argument is that Fredric Jameson's account of postmodernism has tended to overplay the political significance of cultural innovation, and that consequently his critique obscures the real social antagonisms that are determined by the symbolic economy of global consumerism (Anderson, 1998: 134). I would simply point out here that the theorists I have examined all present sophisticated accounts of the relationship between techno-scientific capitalism and the forms of social and political domination which have arisen from it. Deleuze and Guattari, for example, have set out a complex theory of the forms of capture, overcoding and minoritization which arise from flows of technological capital through the legislative body of the state (Deleuze and Guattari, 2000: 139–273). And Derrida has traced the effects that 'virtual' technologies have had upon the intensification of the commodity form and the public articulation and reception of resistance (Derrida, 1994: 77–94). Might it not be the case then that Eagleton's demand that we should 'return to strong ethical even anthropological foundations' in our approach to the political conflicts of the present, has failed to grasp the concept of 'techno-science' as the horizon of new forms of conflict, liberation and democracy?

Bibliography

Abbinnett, R. (2006) 'Spectres of Class: Marxism, Deconstruction, and the Politics of Affiliation', *Journal for Cultural Research*. 10 (1): 1–22.

Abbinnett, R. (2003) *Culture and Identity: Critical Theories*. London: Sage.

Abbinnett, R. (2000) 'Science, Technology and Modernity: Beck and Derrida on the Politics of Risk', *Cultural Values*. 4 (1): 101–26.

Abbinnett, R. (1998a) *Truth and Social Science: From Hegel to Deconstruction*. London: Sage.

Abbinnett, R. (1998b) 'Postmodernity and the Ethics of Care: Situating Bauman's Social Theory', *Cultural Values*. 2 (1): 87–116.

Abbinnett, R. (1998c) 'Politics and Enlightenment: Kant and Derrida on Cosmopolitan Responsibility', *Citizenship Studies*. 2 (2): 197–220.

Adorno, T.W. (1999) *Aesthetic Theory*. Trans. Robert Hulot-Kentor. London: Athlone Press.

Adorno, T.W. (1996) *Minima Moralia*. Trans. Edward Jephcott. London: Verso.

Adorno, T.W. (1991) *The Culture Industry*. London: Routledge.

Adorno, T.W. (1990) *Negative Dialectics*. Trans. E.B. Ashton. London: Routledge.

Adorno, T.W. (1983) *Prisms*. Trans. Samuel and Shierry Weber. Cambridge, MA: The MIT Press.

Adorno, T.W. and Horkheimer, W. (1986) *Dialectic of Enlightenment*. Trans. John Cumming. New York: Continuum.

Adorno, T.W. *et al*. (1977) *Aesthetics and Politics*. London: Verso.

Althusser, L. (1986a) *For Marx*. Trans. Ben Brewster. London: Verso.

Althusser, L. (1986b) *Reading Capital*. Trans. Ben Brewster. London: Verso.

Anderson, P. (1998) *The Origins of Postmodernity*. London: Verso.

Ansell-Pearson, K. (ed.) (1997) *Deleuze and Philosophy: The Difference Engineer*. London: Routledge.

Avineri, S. (1980) *The Social and Political Thought of Karl Marx*. Cambridge: Cambridge University Press.

Barnet, S. (ed.) *Hegel After Derrida*. London: Routledge.

Bataille, G. (2001) *Eroticism*. Harmondsworth: Penguin.

Baudrillard, J. (2005) *The Intelligence of Evil, or, The Lucidity Pact*. Trans. Chris Turner. Oxford and New York: Berg.

Baudrillard, J. (2004) *Symbolic Exchange and Death*. Trans. Ian Hamilton Grant. London: Sage.

Baudrillard, J. (1999) *Simulacra and Simulation*. Trans. Sheila Faria Glaser. Ann Arbor, MI: University of Michigan Press.

Baudrillard, J. (1996) *Jean Baudrillard: Selected Writings*. ed. Mark Poster. Cambridge: Polity Press.

Baudrillard, J. (1995a) *The Illusion of the End*. Trans. Chris Turner. Cambridge: Polity Press.

Baudrillard, J. (1995b) *The Transparency of Evil: Essays in Extreme Phenomena*. Trans. James Benedict. London: Verso.

Baudrillard, J. (1993) *Baudrillard Live: Selected Interviews*. London: Routledge.

Baudrillard, J. (1983) *In the Shadow of the Silent Majorities*. Trans. Paul Foss, John Johnson and Paul Patton. New York: Semiotex(e).

Baudrillard, J. (1980) 'Forgetting Foucault', *Humanities in Society*. (3) 1.

Baudrillard, J. (1975) *The Mirror of Production*. Trans. Mark Poster. St. Louis, MO: Telos Press.

Bauman, Z. (1998) *Globalization: The Human Consequences*. Trans. James Benedict. London: Verso.

Beardsworth, R. (2003) 'From a Genealogy of Matter to a Politics of Memory: Stiegler's Rethinking of Technics', *http://evansexperientialism.freewebspace.com/beardsworth.htm*

Beardsworth, R. (2000) 'Thinking Technicity', *Cultural Values*. 2 (1): 70–85.

Beardsworth, R. (1996) *Derrida and the Political*. London: Routledge.

Benjamin, W. (1997a) *One Way Street*. Trans. Edward Jephcott. London: Verso.

Benjamin, W. (1997b) *Walter Benjamin: Selected Writings Volume One: 1913–192*. Eds. Marcus Bullock and William W. Jennings, Cambridge, MA: Belknap Press of Harvard University Press.

Benjamin, W. (1992) *Illuminations*. Trans. H. Zohn, London: Fontana.

Bennington, G. (2000) *Interrupting Derrida*. London: Routledge.

Bennington, G. (1994) *Legislations: The Politics of Deconstruction*. London: Verso.

Bennington, G. (1988) *Lyotard: Writing the Event*. Manchester: University of Manchester Press.

Butler, J. (1998) 'Subjects of Sex/Gender/Desire' in A. Phillips (ed.) *Feminism and Politics*. Oxford: Oxford University Press.

Butler, R. (1999) *Jean Baudrillard: The Defence of the Real*. London: Sage.

Callinicos, A. (1996) 'Messianic Ruminations: Derrida, Stirner and Marx', *Radical Philosophy*. 75 (Jan/Feb): 37–41.

Callinicos, A. (1994) 'Crisis and Class Struggle in Europe Today', *International Socialism*. 2 (63) (summer): 3–47.

Callinicos, A. (1993) *Race and Class*. London: Bookmarks.

Callinicos, A. (1990) *Against Postmodernism: A Marxist Critique*. London: Verso.

Callinicos, A. *et al.* (1995) *Marxism and the New Imperialism*. London: Bookmarks.

Castells, M. (2000) *The Information Age: Economy, Society and Culture: The Rise of the Network Society*, Vol. 1. Oxford: Blackwell.

Cohen, T. (ed.) (2001) *Jacques Derrida and the Humanities: A Critical Reader*. Cambridge: Cambridge University Press.

Colletti, L. (1972) *From Rousseau to Lenin: Studies in Ideology and Society*. Trans. John Merrington and Judith White. New York and London: Monthly Review Press.

Critchley, S. (1999) *Ethics of Deconstruction: Derrida and Levinas*. Edinburgh: Edinburgh University Press.

Deleuze, G. (2004) *Difference and Repetition*. Trans. Paul Patton. London and New York: Continuum.

Deleuze, G. (1999) *Foucault*. Trans. Sean Hand, London: Athlone Press.

Deleuze, G. (1995) *Negations: 1972–1990*. New York: Columbia.

Deleuze, G. and Guattari, F. (2004) *A Thousand Plateaus: Capitalism and Schizophrenia*. Trans. Brian Massumi. London and New York: Continuum.

Deleuze, G. and Guattari, F. (2000) *Anti-Oedipus: Capitalism and Schizophrenia*. Trans. Robert Hurley, Mark Seem and Helen R. Lane. London: Athlone Press.

Derrida, J. (2001) *On Cosmopolitanism and Forgiveness*. Trans. Mark Dooley and Michael Hughes. London: Routledge.

Derrida, J. (1997) *Politics of Friendship*. Trans. George Collins. London: Verso.

Derrida, J. (1995) *The Gift of Death*. Trans. David Wills. Chicago, IL: University of Chicago Press.

Derrida, J. (1994) *Spectres of Marx: The State of the Debt, the Work of Mourning and the New International*. Trans. Peggy Kamuf. London: Routledge.

Derrida, J. (1992) *The Other Heading: Reflections on Today's Europe*. Trans. Pascale-Anne Brault and Michael B. Nass. Bloomingdale and Indianapolis, IN: Indiana University Press.

Derrida, J. (1990a) *Of Spirit: Heidegger and the Question*. Trans. Geoffrey Bennington and Rachel Bowlby. Chicago, IL: University of Chicago Press.

Derrida, J. (1990b) *Writing and Difference*. Trans. Alan Bass. London: Routledge.

Derrida, J. (1980) *Positions*. Trans. Alan Bass. Chicago, IL: University of Chicago Press.

Derrida, J. (1976) *Of Grammatology*. Trans. Gayatri Spivak. Baltimore, MD: Johns Hopkins University press.

Derrida J. and Duformantelle, A. (2000) *Of Hospitality*. Trans. Rachel Bowlby. Stanford, CA: Stanford University Press.

Derrida, J. and Tilli, M. (1987) (eds.) *For Nelson Mandela*. New York: Seaver.

Dews, P. (1995) *The Limits of Disenchantment: Essays on Contemporary European Philosophy*. London: Verso.

Dien Winfield, R. (1988) *The Just Economy*. London: Routledge.

Docherty, T. (1993) *Postmodernism: A Reader*. London: Harvester Press.

Durkheim, E. (1992) *Suicide: A Study in Sociology*. Trans. G. Simpson and J.A. Spalding. London: Routledge.

Eagleton, T. (1996) *The Illusions of Postmodernism*. Oxford: Blackwell.

Foster, H. (ed.) (1985) *Postmodern Culture*. London: Pluto Press.

Fotopoulos, T. and Gezerlis, A. (2000) 'Hardt and Negri's *Empire*: A New Communist Manifesto or a Reformist Welcome to Neoliberal Globalization?', *http://www.democracynature.org/dn/vol8/vol8.htm*.

Fukuyama, F. (2000) *The End of History and the Last Man*. New York: Free Press.

Gane, M. (2003) *French Social Theory*. London: Sage.

Giddens, A. (1997a) *The Consequences of Modernity*. Cambridge: Polity Press.

Giddens, A. (1997b) *Modernity and Self-Identity: Self and Society in the Late Modern Age*. Cambridge: Polity Press.

Gramsci, A. (1998) *Selections from the Prison Notebooks*. London: Lawrence and Wishart.

Hardt, M. and Negri, A. (2005) *Multitude: War and Democracy in the Age of Empire*. Harmondsworth: Penguin.

Hardt, M. and Negri, A. (2000a) *Empire*. Cambridge, MA and London: Harvard University Press.

Hardt, M. and Negri, A. (2000b) 'Adventures of the Multitude', *Rethinking Marxism*. 13 (3/4): 167–189.

Harvey, D. (1999) *The Condition of Postmodernity: An Enquiry into the Origins of Cultural Change*. Oxford: Blackwell.

Hegel, G.W.F. (1967a) *Phenomenology of Mind*. Trans. J.B. Baillie. New York: Harper and Row.

Hegel, G.W.F. (1967b) *Philosophy of Right*. Trans. T.M. Knox. Oxford: Oxford University Press.

Heidegger, M. (1983) *Being and Time*. Trans. John Macquarry and Edward Robinson. Oxford: Blackwell.

Heidegger, M. (1996) *Basic Writings*. D. Krell (ed.), London: Routledge.

Heidegger, M. (1987) *An Introduction To Metaphysics*. Trans. Ralph Manheim. New Haven, CT and London: Yale University Press.

Held, D. and McGrew, A. (2004) *The Global Transformations Reader: An Introduction to the Globalization Debate*. Cambridge: Polity Press.

Held, D. *et al.* (2003) *Global Transformations: Politics, Economics and Culture*. Cambridge: Polity.

Horkheimer, M. and Adorno T.W. (1986) *Dialectic of Enlightenment*. Trans. John Cumming. New York: Continuum.

Jameson, F. (2000) *Late Marxism: Adorno, or, The Persistence of Dialectic*. London: Verso.

Jameson, F. (1998) *The Cultural Turn: Selected Writings on the Postmodern, 1993–1998*. London: Verso.

Jameson, F. (1995) *Postmodernism, or, The Cultural Logic of Late Capitalism*. London: Verso.

Jay, M. (1996) *The Dialectical Imagination: A History of the Frankfurt School and the Institute of Social Research, 1923–1950*. Berkeley, LA, and London: University of California Press.

Jay, M. (1984) *Marxism and Totality: The Adventures of a Concept from Lukács to Habermas*. Berkeley, CA: University of California Press.

Kant, I. (1991) *Political Writings*. Hans Reiss (ed.), Cambridge: Cambridge University Press.

Kaplan, A.E. and Sprinker, M. (1993) (eds.) *The Althusserian Legacy*. London: Verso.

Keat, R. and Urry, J. (1975) *Social Theory as Science*. London: Routledge.

Kolakowski, L. (1981) *Main Currents of Marxism Volume Two: The Golden Age*. Oxford: Oxford University Press.

Land, N. (1993) 'Making It with Death: Remarks on Thanatos and Desiring Production', *The British Journal for Phenomenology*. 24 (1): 66–76.

Lash, S. (2002) *Critique of Information*. London: Sage.

Lenin, V.I. (1976) *State and Revolution: The Marxist Teaching on the State and the Tasks of the Proletariat in the Revolution*. Peking: Foreign Languages Press.

Lenin, V.I. (1934) *Imperialism: The Highest Stage of Capitalism*. London: Martin Lawrence Limited.

Levinas, E. (1994) *Totality and Infinity: An Essay on Exteriority*. Trans. Alphonso Lingis. The Hague: Martinus Nijhof.

Lichtheim, R. (1967) *Marxism*. London: Routledge.

Lukács, G. (1971) *History and Class Consciousness*. Trans. Rodney Livingstone. London: Merlin Press.

Luxemburg, R. (1968) *The Accumulation of Capital*. Trans. Agnes Schwazschild. London and New York: Modern Reader Paperbacks.

Luxemburg, R. (1961) *The Russian Revolution* and *Leninism or Marxism*. Ann Arbor, MI: The University of Michigan Press.

Lyotard, J-F. (1993) *Libidinal Economy*. Trans. Ian Hamilton Grant. London: Athlone Press.

Lyotard, J-F. (1991a) *The Postmodern Condition: A Report on Knowledge*. Trans. Geoffrey Bennington and Brain Massumi. Manchester: Manchester University Press.

Lyotard, J-F. (1991b) *The Lyotard Reader*. A. Benjamin (ed.), Oxford: Blackwell.

Lyotard, J-F. (1988) *The Differend: Phrases in Dispute*. Trans. Georges Van Dan Abeele. Manchester: Manchester University Press.

Marcuse, H. (1968) *Reason and Revolution: Hegel and the Rise of Social Theory*. London: Routledge and Kegan Paul.

Marcuse, H. (1964) *One Dimensional Man: Studies in the Ideology of Advanced Industrial Society*. London: Routledge and Kegan Paul.

Marcuse, H. (1962) *Eros and Civilization: A Philosophical Inquiry into Freud*. New York: Vintage Books.

Marx, K. (1998) *The Communist Manifesto*. Oxford: Oxford University Press.

Marx, K. (1993) *Grundrisse*. Trans. Martin Nicolaus. Harmondsworth: Penguin.

Marx, K. (1992) *Capital*, Vol. 2. Trans. David Fernbach. Harmondsworth: Penguin.

Marx, K. (1991) *Capital*, Vol. 3. Trans. David Fernbach. Harmondsworth: Penguin.

Marx, K. (1990) *Capital*, Vol. 1. Trans. Ben Fowkes. Harmondsworth: Penguin.

Marx, K. (1977a) *Economic and Philosophical Manuscripts of 1844*. Moscow: Progress Publishers.

Marx, K. (1977b) *The German Ideology*. C.J. Arthur (ed.), London: Lawrence and Wishart.

Marx, K. (1977c) *Karl Marx: Selected Writings*. D. Mclellan (ed.), Oxford: Oxford University Press.

Nancy, J-L. (2004) *The Inoperative Community*. Trans. Peter Connor, Lisa Garbus, Michael Holland and Simona Sawhney. Minneapolis, IN and London: University of Minnesota Press.

Negri, A. (2003) *Time For Revolution*. Trans. Matteo Mandarini. New York and London: Continuum.

Nietzsche, F. (1995) *Unfashionable Observations*. Trans. Richard T. Gray. Stanford, CA: Stanford University Press.

Nietzsche, F. (1984) *Human, All Too Human*. Trans. Marion Faber and Stephen Lehmann. Harmondsworth: Penguin.

Patton, P. (2000) *Deleuze and the Political*. London: Routledge.

Ryan, M. (1986) *Marxism and Deconstruction: A Critical Articulation*. Baltimore, MD and London: The Jonns Hopkins University Press.

Rose, G. (1981) *Hegel Contra Sociology*. London: Athlone Press.

Rose, G. (1978) *The Melancholy Science: An Introduction to the Thought of Theodor W. Adorno*. London: Macmillan.

Rose, G. (1993) *Judaism and Modernity: Philosophical Essays*. Oxford: Blackwell.

Rousseau, J-J. (1988) *The Social Contract and Discourses*. Trans. G. D. H. Cole. London: J.M. Dent.

Rundell, J. (1987) *Origins of Modernity: The Origins of Modern Social Theory From Kant to Hegel to Marx*. Cambridge: Polity Press.

Smith, A. (1950) *The Wealth of Nations*. Edwin Cannan (ed.), London: Methuen.

Spinoza, B. (1985) *The Collected Works of Spinoza*. Edwin Curley (ed.), volume one, Princeton, NJ: Princeton University Press.

Sprinker, M. (1999) *Ghostly Demarcations: A Symposium on Derrida's Spectres of Marx*. London: Verso.

Stiegler, B. (1998) *Technics and Time, 1*. Trans. Richard Beardsworth and George Collins. Stanford, CA: Stanford University Press.

Weber, M. (1978) *The Protestant Ethic and the Spirit of Capitalism*. Trans. Talcott Parsons. London: George, Allen and Unwin.

Wheen, F. (2000) *Karl Marx*. London: Fourth Estate Limited.

Index

accumulation
  hyper, 35–6, 45
  Marx's theory of, 21–2, 63–8
Accumulation of Capital, The, 122–3
Adorno, T.W., 24–8, 109
aesthetic experience, 29–39
Against Postmodernism, 32–3, 38–9
Ahmad, A., 57–8, 199–203
alienation, 69–73
Althusser, 26–7, 221n
Anderson, P., 208n, 217–18n
Anti-capitalism, 138–9
Anti-Oedipus, 83–9, 184–7
Asiatic society, 120–2
A Thousand Plateaus, 89–94, 112,
  188–91, 216n
authenticity, 75–6, 105, 109
autonomy, 83–4

Bataille. G., 47, 196–7
Baudrillard, J., 3, 40–50, 60, 144–51,
  182–9, 206
the beautiful, 41, 209n
Beck, U., 211n
being
  Heidegger's idea of, 75–7
  Derrida's relationship to, 104–5
Benjamin, W., 7, 18, 59–60, 204,
  208n, 215n
Bennington, G., 212n
biopolitical production, 83–94,
  133–43
body without organs, 190
bourgeois economics (see classical
  economics)
bourgeoisie, 13–17
Butler, J., 210n

Callinicos, A., 3, 126, 160, 195, 200–3,
  216n
Capital
  Volume One, 14, 20–3, 63–73

  Volume Two, 66–7
  Volume Three, 117–20
capital
  fictitious, 145, 213n
  fixed, 65–73
  organic, 69–72, 93, 108
capitalist mode of production
  historical tendency of, 21–2, 208n
  contradictions of, 63–73, 117–23,
    175–6
Castells, M., 178–84, 192
civil society, 9–17, 28, 57–8, 154–5
civilized capitalist machine, 87–90
class
  consciousness, 12–16, 23, 69–73, 81
  politics, 57–8, 120–5, 195–207
colonialism, 117–25
commodification
  of culture, 18–28
  of the image, 33–9
commodities
  Marx's theory of, 63–8, 117–20
communism, 43, 56–9, 141–3,
  175–6
Communist Manifesto, The, 2, 55,
  102–3, 152, 201
Condition of Postmodernity, The, 30–1,
  213n, 216n
Consequences of Modernity, The, 127–8,
  213n
Consumer Society, The, 213n
Contest of the Faculties, The, 212n
Contradiction and
  Overdetermination, 26–7
cosmopolitanism, 120–1, 126–31,
  150–7
credit (see fictitious capital)
critical theory, 5, 18–22, 77
Critique of Hegel's Philosophy of Right,
  9–16
Critique of Information, 216n
cubism, 59

culture industry thesis, 22–8
cybernetics, 103, 105–6, 187

dadaism, 59
death instinct (see Thanatos)
Deleuze, G. and Guattari, F., 83–94,
    95–100, 112–14, 160–2, 184–91,
    215n, 216n
Derrida, J., 3, 51–9, 101–8, 252–66,
    190–4, 198–207, 211n, 217n
despotic social machine, 85–7
dialectics
    materialist, 9–13, 63–73
    idealist, 195–7
Dialectic of Enlightenment, 5, 18–24
différance, 109–10, 202–3
Difference and Repetition, 98–9
Discourse on the Origin of Inequality, 212n
distraction, 30, 37–8, 179–80, 200–1
Durkheim, E., 186

Eagleton, T., 3, 194, 203, 217–18n
Economics
    classical, 41–2, 69
    Marxist, 63–73
*Economic and Philosophical Manuscripts
    of 1844, The*, 9, 16, 42–3, 69–72
*Eighteenth Brumaire of Louis Bonaparte,
    The*, 191, 217n
Empire, 94–100, 134, 161–2, 186–7
enframing (*Gestell*), 76–7, 109
Enlightenment, 1, 83–9, 97, 121–2
equality
    Marx's concept of, 12–14
Eros, 46
Eros and Civilization, 81–2
Eroticism, 47
Essay on the Origin of Languages, 102,
    112n
ethical life (*Sittlichkeit*)
    Hegel's concept of, 9–11
    Marx's critique of, 12–14
ethics
    of cosmopolitanism, 126–32
    of hospitality, 152–66
exchange value, 63–4, 70–1, 79
expropriation
    Marx's theory of, 69–70

fascism, 77, 182, 190, 200–1
the feminine, 155–7
fetishism of commodities, 23, 48
feudalism, 13–14, 86–7, 134–5
Feurbach, L., 54–5, 210n
film, 17, 24–5, 38, 56, 40, 209n
For Marx, 26–7, 221n
the fold, 188–9
Frankfurt School (see critical
    theory)
Freud, S., 46–7, 80, 90
Freedom
    Marx's theory of, 12–17
French Revolution, 97, 212n
Fukuyama. F., 126, 132

genetic technologies, 183
The German Ideology, 9, 13–17, 54–5,
    197–8
Giddens, A., 127–8, 213n
globalization
    hyperglobalist thesis, 126, 128, 132,
        136, 144
    sceptical thesis, 126, 128–9
    transformationalist thesis, 126–8,
        213n
Gramsci, A., 149
Grundrisse, The, 65–6, 70–3, 78, 94,
    140, 142, 152, 160
Gulf War, 214n

Habermas, J., 129, 165, 209n
Hardt, M. and Negri, A., 94–100,
    133–43
Harvey, D., 3, 30–2, 50, 181, 213n,
    216n
Hegel, G.W.F., 2, 9–11, 172, 196–8,
    208n
hegemony, 120–1, 127, 134–5,
    194–50
Heigegger, M., 108–12, 150,
    155–6
Held, D., 126–32, 165
History and Class Consciousness, 23
Holy Family, The, 9
hominization
    neanthropian, 110
    zinjanthropian, 110

Horkheimer, M. and Adorno, T.W, 5, 18–24
Husserl, E.,78–9.
hyperconformity of the masses, 41–2
the hyperreal, 34, 40, 145–50, 182–3, 188

idealist philosophy, 9–12
Idea for a Universal History with a Cosmopolitan Purpose, 128
ideology
    Marx's concept of, 9–17
    Jameson's theory of, 33–9
Illusions of Postmodernism, The, 217–18n
image technologies, 27–8, 29–33
imagination
    protentive, 110
    reification of, 80–1
imperialism,
    Marx's theory of, 117–22
Imperialism: The Highest Stage of Capitalism, 123–4
In the Shadow of the Silent Majorities, 48–9,
industrial revolution, 66
information technology paradigm, 178–9
Inoperative Community, The, 163–4
international law, 128–32, 165–6, 192, 202–3

Jameson, F., 33–9, 204–5, 217n
Jay, M., 3, 75
justice
    Derrida's concept of, 104, 109–10, 113–14, 152–66, 191–4, 205
    Marx's concept of, 16–17, 72, 175–6

Kant, I., 20, 128, 212n
Keat, R. and Urry, J., 216n
Kolakowski, L., 125

labour
    abstract, 14–15, 70–3
    immaterial, 95–6, 133, 137–8, 150
    theory of value, 63–9, 117–20
Land, N., 112
language
    Derrida's theory of, 152–6, 16
    operational regimes of, 135,137–9

Lash, S., 216n
Late capitalism
    Jameson's theory of, 35–9
Late Marxism, 34–5
Lenin, V.I., 123–6, 141–2
Levinas, E., 153–5
Lewis, T., 28–203
Libidinal Economy, 211–12n
lifeworld (*Lebenswelt*), 35–9, 78–9, 165n, 129–32, 164–5, 205
love (see Eros)
ludic aestheticism, 29–39
Lukács, G., 23–4
Luxemberg, R., 122–5, 136, 165
Lyotard, J-F., 209n, 211–12n

machinery
    and relative surplus value, 63–8
    and social production, 71–3
machinic desire, 83–94
Marcuse, H., 77–81, 89–90, 93, 109
Marx, K., 9–17, 63–73, 117–22, 169–74, 206
Marxism
    and ontology, 177–94
    and politics, 195–203
mass culture, 23–8
Master-Slave relation, 196
materialism, 9–13, 63–73
messianic time, 59–60, 200–2, 204, 210n
metaphysics (see philosophy)
Mirror of Production, The, 41–4
modernity, 1, 83–4, 89–90, 97, 121–2
M-C-M relation, 63–8
the multitude, 94–100, 133–42, 150, 160–2
Multitude, 133–42, 160–2, 186–90

Nancy, J-L., 163–4
nation state, 126–31, 136–7, 148–9
nature
    inorganic body of, 85
    and technology, 76–81
Nazism (see fascism)
Negations, 189–90
Negative Dialectics, 27–8

neo-liberalism, 3, 126, 128, 135, 144, 159, 177, 194, 202
New International, 151, 163–6, 202–3, 204–7
Nietzsche, F., 209n
nomadism, 90–4

Of Grammatology, 101, 154–5
Of Spirit, 105–6
On the Utility and Liability of History for Life, 209n
One Dimensional Man, 78–81, 89
One Way Street, 59, 215n
ontology
    Marxism and, 68–72, 174–5
    postmodernist critiques of, 177–94
Orientalism, 121–2
originary technicity, 108–14
Origins of Postmodernity, The, 208n, 217–18n
the other
    Derrida's concept of, 104–8, 156–9, 163–4
    Levinas's concept of, 153–5

patriarchy
    metaphysical foundations of, 156–7, 210n
Patton, P., 112–14
Phenomenology of Mind, 2, 9, 196, 208n
Philosophy of Right, 2, 9, 172, 197
philosophy
    Derrida's relation to, 154–7, 196–7, 201–2
    Marx's critique of, 9–12
Politics of Friendship, 131, 156–7
Positions, 152
post-auratic art, 59–60
Postmodernism, or, The Cultural Logic of Late Capitalism, 33–9
postmodernism
    and Marxism, 1–6, 29–39
    and politics, 195–203, 204–7
Poverty of Philosophy, The, 79
primitive social machine, 84–6
Procession of Simulacra, The, 147–8
proletariat (see working class)
prosthetics, 106–8, 113–14

Protestant Ethic and the Spirit of Capitalism, The, 216n
public space,
    technological transformation of, 183, 200–1, 202–3

Question Concerning Technology, The, 75–7, 104–5, 108–9

rationalization, 1, 5, 78–9, 187–9
real subsumption of labour, 70–2, 94–5, 160
reality
    and aesthetic experience, 29–39
    and simulation, 43–50, 147–51
Reason and Revolution, 78
reification, 18–28
religion, 12, 15, 19
responsibility (see ethics)
revolutionary promise, 55–6, 217n,
Rise of the Network Society, The, 178–84, 192
Risk Society, 211n
Rose, G., 27–8, 208n
Rousseau, J-J., 101–2, 212n
ruling ideas (see ideology)
Ryan, M., 210n

Said, E., 121–2
Science of Logic, 2
scientific knowledge, 65–6, 77–9
Second International, 3, 16, 120, 122–3
self-consciousness
    Hegel's concept of, 9–13, 52
simulation
    fourth order, 49–50
    third order, 48
Sittlichkeit (see ethical life)
slavery (see colonialism)
Smith, A., 42, 69
socialized production, 73, 80, 84–5, 93, 97–8, 109, 113–14
sovereignty
    of the multitude, 138–43
    transcendental categories of, 133–8
space-time compression
    Harvey's theory of, 30–2, 181

spectralization
    Derrida's concept of, 103–8,
        200–1, 206
Spectres of Marx, 54–8, 103–8, 157–66,
        190–5, 198–203, 211n
spirit (*Geist*)
    Hegel's concept of, 9–13, 52
State and Revolution, 141–2
Steigler, B., 108–14
Stirner, G., 54–5
the sublime, 43, 209n
surrealism, 59
Symbolic Exchange and Death, 44–8,
        145–47

Technics and Time, 1, 108–14
technocratic control, 74–81
technology
    and the human, 88–93, 94–7, 108–14
Thanatos, 46
Theses on the Philosophy of History,
        204
Third World economies, 147–8,
        150–1, 164–5, 192–3

Totality and Infinity, 153–5
transeconomic capitalism, 144–51
Transparency of Evil, The, 48–9, 183
truth
    Heidegger's concept of, 75–7, 81

use value, 41–4, 71, 101

Violence and Metaphysics,
        153–4
viral racism, 49

war
    Hardt and Negri on, 135–6
Wealth of Nations, The, 69
Weber, M., 181
wildstyle
    Deleuze and Guattari on, 113–14
working class
    as a revolutionary subject, 72–3,
        122–5, 195–203
Work of Art in the Age of Mechanical
        Reproduction, The, 59–60
Writing and Difference, 196–7, 217n